Adult Education in Uganda
Growth, Development, Prospects and Challenges

Editor
Anthony Okech

Fountain Publishers

Fountain Publishers
Plot 55 Nkrumah Road
Kampala, Uganda
Email: fountain@starcom.co.ug
Website: www.fountainpublishers.co.ug

© Fountain Publishers 2004
First published 2004

All rights reserved. No part of this publication may be reproduced or transmitted, in any form or by any means, electronic, mechanical, photocopying, recording or otherwise or stored in any retrieval system of any nature without the written permission of the publisher.

ISBN 9970 02 439 6

Contents

Contributors   v
Acronymns   vii
Preface   xii

1: Introduction: an Overview of the Field   1
Anthony Okech

2: The Evolution of Adult Education in Uganda   15
David Atim and Willy Ngaka

3: The Political Economy of Adult Education in Uganda   35
Daniel Babikwa

4: Government Policy and Strategies for Adult Education in Uganda   51
Demetrius K. Obbo

5: The Role of Civil Society in Shaping Adult Education Practices in Uganda   67
George L. Openjuru

6: University Adult Education in Uganda   88
Yolamu N. Nsamba

7: Challenges of Developing Professional Adult Educators in Uganda   110
Patrick K. Kagoda and Anne R. Katahoire

8: Economics and Financing of Adult Education in Uganda   124
Anthony Okech

9: Distance Education and Open Learning   146
Jessica N. Aguti

10: Adult Literacy Efforts 178
Anthony Okech

11: Meeting the Needs of the Marginalised in Uganda
Alice N. Ndidde 210

12: The Afrikan University Adult Educator and the Challenge of Language, Education, Development and Empowerment 225
Paulo Wangoola

13: International Partnership and Co-operation in Adult Education 247
Anthony Okech

14: Challenges and Prospects of Adult Education in Uganda
David K. Atim and Anthony Okech 267

15: Epilogue: Why Andragogy? 290
Charles Kabuga

Bibliography *298*
Index *318*

Contributors

Jessica N. Aguti (Ph.D, MA, M.Ed, B.A., Dip.Ed.) Senior Lecturer, Department of Distance Education, former Director African Virtual University centre, Makerere University.

David Atim (B.A.Soc.Sc., M.Ed. Admin, PGDip. Tert Educ., PGDip Dev. Studies, Cert. RRP, Cert. Prof. Deve. in Systematic Design and Mgmt of Training)) Senior Lecturer, Department of Community Education and Extra-Mural Studies, Makerere University

Daniel Babikwa (B.Ed, M.A, Ph.D.) Lecturer, Department of Adult Education and Communication Studies

Charles Kabuga (B.A., M.A.) Consultant in Cooperative Development and Education, former Lecturer in Adult Education, Makerere University, former Secretary General Uganda Cooperative Alliance, former Head, Developing Countries Activities, International Federation of Agricultural Producers

Patrick K. Kagoda (B.A., M.A.) Lecturer, Department of Adult Education and Communication Studies, Makerere University

Anne R. Katahoire (B.A., M.Ed., Ph.D., Cert. Eval.) Senior Lecturer, Department of Adult Education and Communication Studies, Associate Director, Institute of Adult and Continuing Education, Makerere University

Alice N. Ndidde (B.A., M.Ed.) Lecturer, Department of Adult Education and Communication Studies, Makerere University.

Willy Ngaka (B.A., M.Ed.) Lecturer, Department of community Education and Extra-Mural Studies, Makerere University

Yolamu N. Nsamba (Dip. Ed., B.A., M.A., M.Ed.) Principal Private Secretary to the Omukama, Bunyoro-Kitara Kingdom, former Extra-Mural Resident Lecturer, Makerere University.

Demetrius K. Obbo (B.A, M.A.) Principal, Nsamizi Training Institute of Social Development, Uganda

Anthony Okech (STL, B.A., L&M es Lettres, Cert. Adult Educ., Cert. Eval.) Senior Lecturer (former Head), Department of Adult Education and Communication Studies, former Director Institute of Adult and Continuing Education, Makerere University.

George L. Openjuru (B.A., M.Ed.) Lecturer and Ag. Head, Department of Community Education and Extra-Mural Studies, Makerere University

Paulo Wangoola (B.A.) Founder and Nabyama, Mpambo, the Afrikan Multiversity and special adviser to the Clans Council of Busoga Kingdom, former Extra-Mural Resident Lecturer, Makerere University, former Secretary General African Association for Literacy and Adult Education.

Acronymns

AALAE	African Association for Literacy and Adult Education
AAU	Action Aid Uganda
AAUK	Action Aid UK
ABEK	Alternative Basic Education for Karamoja
ACDI	Agricultural Cooperative Development International
ACFODE	Action for Development
ACORD	Agency for Cooperation and Research in Development
ADRA	Adventist Development and Relief Agency
Afrolit	African Society for Literacy
AIDS	Acquired Immunodeficiency Syndrome
ALBEC	Adult Literacy and Basic Education Centre
AMREF	African Medical Research Foundation
APAL	African Perspectives in Adult Learning
AVU	African Virtual University
B.Com.	Bachelor of Commerce
B.Ed.	Bachelor of Education
BACE	Bachelor of Adult and Community Education
BEIRD	Basic Education Integrated in Rural Development
BREDA (UNESCO	Bureau Regional pour l'Education en Afrique Regional Office for Education in Africa)
B.Sc.	Bachelor of Science
CAS	Certificate in Adult Studies
CBO	Community Based Organisation
CCE	Centre for Continuing Education
CDA	Community Development Assistant
CDD	Control of Diarrhoeal Diseases
CDO	Community Development Officer
CDRN	Community Development Resource Network
CEFORD	Community Empowerment for Rural Development

CHDC	Child Health and Development Centre
CIDA	Canadian International Development Agency
CMS	Church Missionary Society
CONFINTEA V	Fifth International Conference on Adult Education
CRS	Catholic Relief Services
CSDR	Child survival and Development Revolution
CSO	Civil Society Organisation
CUAMM	Collegio Universitario Aspiranti e Medici Missionari (International College for Health Cooperation in Developing Countries)
DANIDA	Danish International Development Agency
DENIVA	Development Network of Indigenous Voluntary Associations
DEP	Diploma in Education (Primary)
DFI	District Farm Institute
EDP	External Degree Programme
EPI	Expanded Programme of Immunisation
EPRC	Economic Policy Research Centre
ERIC	Education Resources Information Centre
EU	European Union
FAL	Functional Adult Literacy
FALP	Functional Adult Literacy Programme
FM	Frequency Modulation
FY	Financial Year
GAD	Gender and Development
GOU	Government of Uganda
HIV	Human Immunodeficiency Virus
IACE	Institute of Adult and Continuing Education
ICEIDA	Icelandic International Development Agency
ICT	Information and Communication Technology
INFOBEPP	Integrated Non-Formal Basic Education Pilot Project

Acronymns

IIZ/DVV	Institut fur Internationale Zusammenarbeit des Deutschen Volkshochschul-Verbandes (Institute for International Development of the German Adult Education Association)
ITEK	Institute of Teacher Education Kyambogo
KDDO	Karamoja Diocese Development Organisation
LABE	Literacy and Adult Basic Education
LERN	Learning Resources Network
LitNet	Literacy Network for Uganda
MAAIF	Ministry of Agriculture Animal Industry and Fisheries
MFPED	Ministry of Finance, Planning and Economic Development
MGLSD	Ministry of Gender, Labour and Social Development
MITEP	Mubende Integrated Teacher Education Project
MOES	Ministry of Education and Sports
MOH	Ministry of Health
MTAC	Management Training and Advisory Centre
NAADS	National Agricultural Advisory Services
NABCE	Non-Award Bearing Continuing Education
NABOTU	National Book Trust of Uganda
NAEA	National Adult Education Association
NALSIP	National Adult Literacy Strategic Investment Plan
NAWOU	National Association of Women Organisations of Uganda
NEMA	National Environment Management Authority
NGO	Non-Government Organisation
NIACE	National Institute of Adult Continuing Education (England and Wales)
NITEP	Northern Integrated Teacher Education Project
NOTU	National Organisation of Trade Unions
NRM	National Resistance Movement

NUDIPU	National Union of Disabled Persons of Uganda
NWASEA	National Women's Association for Social and Economic Development
ODA	Overseas Development Agency (UK)
OECD	Organisation for Economic Cooperation and Development
PAF	Poverty Action Fund
PEAP	Poverty Eradication Action Plan
PLE	Primary Leaving Examination
PMA	Programme for Modernisation of Agriculture
PTC	Primary Teachers College
RDDA	Research, Develop, Disseminate and Adopt
REFLECT	Regenerated Freirean Literacy through Empowering Community Techniques
RITEP	Rakai Integrated Teacher Education Project
RTC	Rural Training Centre
SNV	Stichting Nederlandse Vrijwilligers (SNV Netherlands Development Organisation)
SOCADIDO	Soroti Catholic Diocese Development Organisation
TASO	The Aids Support Organisation
TDMS	Teacher Development and Management Services
TOCIDA	Tororo Community Initiated Development Association
UACE	Uganda Advanced Certificate of Education
UCA	Uganda Cooperative Alliance
UFPP	Uganda Food and Peace Project
UGAADEN	Uganda Adult Education Network
UJAFAE	Uganda Joint Action for Adult Education
UK	United Kingdom (Britain)
ULALA	Uganda Literacy and Adult Learners Association
UNEB	Uganda National Examination Board

UNESCO	United Nations Education Scientific and Cultural Organisation
UNICEF	United Nations International Children's Fund
URDT	Uganda Rural Development Training Programme
UWFT	Uganda Women's Finance Trust
VEDCO	Volunteer Efforts for Development Concerns
WEP	Women's Empowerment Programme
WID	Women in Development
WUS	World University Service
YMCA	Young Men's Christian Association
YWCA	Young Women's Christian Association

Preface

Adult education has been practised in Uganda in various forms perhaps since human beings first inhabited this land, but rather little has been written about it. As a result, it has been difficult to find relevant materials to use for the study of adult education in Uganda. Makerere University has, in particular, been engaged in adult education especially through its Institute of Adult and Continuing Education. This institute started as the Department of Extra-Mural studies in 1953 and so celebrated 50 years of existence and service in 2003.

The institute took advantage of its 50th anniversary to reflect on its own work and on adult education work in Uganda in general. To assist this process of reflection and to lay a foundation for further reflection, the institute decided that one of the activities of the Golden Jubilee celebrations would be the production of a book on adult education in Uganda.

A long-time partner in the development of adult education in Uganda, the German Adult Education Association (DVV), agreed to cooperate with the institute in the project. Indeed, without the financial support from the DVV, the project may not have been possible, because most of the work towards the realisation of the book has depended on DVV funding. Makerere University, and Uganda as a whole are grateful for the support. The book marks an important milestone in the professional development of Adult Education in the country.

The book will be a reference for those who want to know more about adult education in Uganda. It will also be a base for further specialised study on adult education in Uganda and a useful teaching resource. Its objectives are to: document the development of adult education in Uganda; provide insight into pertinent current issues in adult education in Uganda; establish a base for further specialised study on adult education in Uganda; provide a teaching resource for the study of adult and community education; and raise signals for future adult education work in Uganda.

Preface

The Makerere University Department of Adult Education and Communication Studies coordinated the development of the idea, the preparation of the manuscript and the management of the whole project. Special mention should be made of the former Head of Department, Dr. Anne Katahoire, who initiated the idea. The Department acknowledges with thanks the support received from the rest of the institute in this task. Special thanks are due to the authors and those who gave advice in various ways. May the fruit of their contribution be seen in the rapid growth of the body of knowledge on adult education in Uganda.

Anthony Okech
Editor

1
Introduction: an Overview of the Field

Anthony Okech

This book, published to commemorate fifty years of the work of the Makerere University Institute of Adult and Continuing Education in Uganda, is a critical review of aspects of adult education in Uganda. It does not set out to be either a comprehensive or even a systematic history of adult education in Uganda. It merely reviews and reflects on some aspects of adult education that a group of adult educators consider most useful to include in a book – the first such publication on adult education in the country. The group hope that the topics selected will serve as a useful starting point for critical reflection on adult education in Uganda and will stimulate further studies and reflections in the field.

As can be seen from the various chapters of the book, there is no commonly accepted definition of adult education in Uganda, either in theory or in practice. It has therefore been difficult for the different authors to know what to include under adult education and what to leave out. There was originally a tendency by some authors to differentiate between adult education and education of adults, a distinction sometimes used by writers in this field from various countries. To avoid confusion, this distinction has been almost completely eliminated at the editorial stage and preference has been given to using the common term *adult education*.

In the absence of a commonly expressed Ugandan definition, the authors of the different chapters have tended to use the definitions adopted by international forums and institutions, especially those from UNESCO and its forums. Some of the authors have used the 1976 Nairobi definition, which restricts adult education to 'organised educational processes' in which adults participate; others have adopted the 1997 Hamburg definition, which opens the field up to 'the entire body of learning processes' by adults. Rather than worrying about definitions, however, it is perhaps more important to see what the authors include under their treatment of adult education. This is presented below with a brief explanation of each, indicating its status in Uganda.

This first chapter benefits from the work of Merriam and Muhammad who examined the concepts, purposes, organisation and delivery and challenges of adult education in Malaysia (Merriam and Muhammad, 2001). In their book they look first at these aspects from a global perspective, then focus on its application to Malaysia. Here we reverse the order of focus, looking first at adult education in Uganda and then reflecting on it in the light of the global context.

Concepts

The different chapters of the book cover a wide variety of practices included within the framework of adult education. Here we try to organise that variety by categorising the different practices using three parameters: level of learning, focus or content of learning and mode of provision or delivery system. This is not a totally new organising scheme and has to some extent benefited from schemes proposed by various authors (Knowles 1964; Coombs, Prosser and Ahmad 1973; Darkenwald and Merriam 1982; Coombs 1989).

Categorisation by level of learning

When they are categorised according to levels of learning, adult education practices can be divided into *adult basic education* and *continuing* or *further education*.

Adult basic education covers what the Nairobi recommendation on adult education describes as 'learning to replace initial education in schools' (UNESCO 1976). In Uganda, adult basic education is usually referred to in the same breath as *adult literacy education*. There are two main reasons for this. First, many people consider the two to be one and the same. Secondly, others see them as different but usually provided together as *functional adult literacy*.

Uganda's official education policy document, the Government White Paper 1992, defined basic education as 'the minimum package of learning which should be made available to every individual to enable him/her live as a good and useful citizen in society', and pledges to provide every Ugandan with adequate basic education in a phased manner through 'formal primary education as well as the non-formal education system' (Republic of Uganda 1992: 37). The document lists ten aims and objectives of basic education but does not define the levels to be attained to constitute that minimum package. The upper limit of basic education is accordingly not clear, whether for formal school education or adult education.

The terms *continuing* and *further education* are used in various chapters of this book to refer to adult education at a level beyond the basic. The government education policy provides that 'Government, with the support of the private sector, should assume full responsibility for the development of continuing or further education in Uganda' (Republic of Uganda, 1992: 183). It is clear from the chapters of this book that this provision has been left as a recommendation without putting in place legislation or other mechanisms to bind anyone to implement it. However, as explained in Chapter 8, the public demand for such education has in recent years led to increased provision of opportunities, at a fee, by both government and the private sector.

Some of the authors have made a distinction between the two concepts, restricting *continuing education* to learning activities outside the formal education system and using *further education* to refer to the more structured programmes leading to accreditation within the formal education system. However, this distinction is not universally made in Uganda and to avoid trying to figure out the exact difference, the two terms are often used together as 'continuing *and* further education' or, in some cases, as 'continuing *or* further education'. The education policy White Paper uses also 'continuing and lifelong education' in a manner that seems interchangeable with continuing and further education (Republic of Uganda 1992: 183).

Categorisation by focus of learning

Adult education, as has been mentioned, covers a wide area of learning. Some of the areas of learning mentioned in this book are: functional adult literacy, extension education, health education, civic education, environmental education, co-operative education, vocational education and workers' or trade union education. Many of these are currently provided in programmes for adults, mainly at the basic level. Some, however, go further. For example, adults who have completed their basic education often enrol for vocational education to acquire skills that can gain them employment.

Functional adult literacy is perhaps the most outstanding programme area of adult education in Uganda. As we saw above, in common perception, many Ugandans tend to equate adult education with adult literacy. The government ministry with the mandate to provide adult education has perhaps played a part in reinforcing this perception. The ministry is engaged in a wide range of activities, each handled by a separate department. It does not, however, have any department or section specifically charged with adult education. Currently, it has only a small functional adult literacy unit in the Department of Disabilities and Elderly.

Government gives the following objectives for functional adult literacy:
1. To encourage the acquisition of knowledge, skills and attitudes in reading and writing and numeracy based on the needs and problems of the learners and their community
2. To create awareness among learners concerning the causes, and possible solutions of their problems
3. To enable learners to actively participate in their personal development and that of their communities and to improve the quality of life
4. To provide integrated, functional non-formal basic education to learners through a problem-solving approach
5. To promote the appreciation and enjoyment of the benefits and opportunities acquired through the mastery of the skills of reading, writing and numeracy.

Reflecting the above objectives, the government programme and practically all functional adult literacy programmes in Uganda cover a number of other programme areas in addition to reading, writing and numeracy. These commonly include agriculture, health, skills for income-generating activities, marketing and trade, gender, culture and civic consciousness, environmental education and co-operative education. While functional adult literacy programmes cover these programme areas in an integrated manner, the different topics are also offered separately by different programmes and agencies.

It is because these additional subject areas are covered in literacy programmes that many people in Uganda refer to the programmes as *functional*. (A number of authors from other parts of the world have also referred to these programme areas as 'functionality' components (e.g. Bhola 1994).) In associating functionality with learning subjects other than reading, writing and numeracy, people have sometimes tended to lose the original understanding of functional literacy as literacy acquired to a level of proficiency at which one can use it to function effectively in a given setting where reading and writing are required. At times, the term functional literacy has even been applied to programme areas which exclude reading and writing skills. Thus, training programmes in horticulture or beekeeping, without any training in or use of reading and writing, have been referred to as functional literacy. Some politicians and other public figures have even advocated for 'functional literacy' as opposed to reading and writing.

Another development in Uganda has been the close association of functional adult literacy, under the acronym FAL, with the government-run programme as opposed to adult literacy programmes provided by other agencies. The introduction in 1993 of ActionAid's REFLECT programmes – using a community development approach that includes functional adult literacy – further sharpened the dichotomy, since it was considered important to make a clear distinction between the approaches used by the government FAL programme and by REFLECT.

Extension education is a relatively new term, generally used in Uganda to refer to agricultural education provided to farmers in the communities. The more common term has, in fact, been *agricultural extension*. In the past, agricultural extension tended to lay more emphasis on the technical aspects of scientific agriculture than on education. Today, a growing recognition of the educational aspects of extension work has led not only to the adoption of the new terminology but also to the introduction of training in adult education in courses for teachers of extension education.

Health education is the most significant strategy that the Ministry of Health and other health service providers in Uganda use for disease prevention and health maintenance. The mainstream health education provision is supplemented by other awareness or educational strategies focusing on specific health concerns. One of these has been the promotion of immunisation of children against what are referred to as the six killer diseases. Other educational campaigns have focused on epidemics such as cholera and ebola. In recent years HIV/AIDS awareness programmes have been at the forefront.

Civic education is education designed to develop the citizens' awareness and knowledge of their duties and rights. The areas usually covered in Uganda include human rights and basic essential laws; basic facts about the country, its governance, social structure and economics; participation in elections for representatives at various levels; and taxation and its benefits. Various government ministries carry out civic education on laws, policies and other provisions. There are also special institutions such as the Electoral Commission, the Human Rights Commission, the Inspector General of Government and the Uganda Revenue Authority, which carry out civic education relevant to their areas of competence. In recent years a number of non-governmental organisations have also provided various types of civic education.

Environmental education has of late become an increasingly significant component of adult education, because of the growing concern for the environment. A number of government ministries have a mandate that covers some aspect or other of the environment: land, forestry, water, wildlife, mining, industry and so on. The ministries carry out specifically organised educational activities as well as public awareness programmes on their particular aspect of the environment. The National Environment Management Authority (NEMA) is charged with monitoring and co-ordinating environment management activities in Uganda. One of its important functions is the promotion of environmental education, carried out by working with the relevant government ministries and agencies, local governments and non-governmental organisations (NGOs). There are indeed a large number of NGOs that claim to be doing some environmental education, many of them among adults.

Co-operative education has been an important component of adult education provision because of its close link to agriculture, in which the majority of the participants in adult education activities are involved. Co-operative education is provided through the Government Co-operative Department and the co-operative unions and societies. Most of the co-operative societies in Uganda are agricultural growers and marketing societies. The education that is provided covers co-operative laws, rules and procedures, co-operative management, improved agricultural practices and marketing of agricultural produce.

Vocational education is used in Uganda to refer to various forms of education through which adults acquire practical and employable skills. It, however, excludes the basic agricultural improvement education that adults receive through functional adult literacy programmes and agricultural extension education. The tendency has been to restrict the use of the term to education provided in formal institutions, generally leading to formal qualifications. Vocational education thus tends to refer to training at the post-basic level.

Workers' education or *trade union education* is provided mainly by the trade union movement. One of the objectives of the trade unions is to provide education to their members. The distinction between workers' education and trade union education is sometimes made by restricting the latter to refer to education on trade union issues, while workers' education covers education provided to workers on other topics. The government ministry mandated to look after employment and labour hosts the Directorate of Labour. Among other things, this directorate caters for occupational health, which is promoted partly through workers' education.

Categorisation by mode of provision

A third method of categorising adult education is by the way in which it is provided. The classification of education into formal, non-formal and informal is accepted at all levels of education in Uganda. In earlier references to adult education in Uganda there was a tendency to exclude any form of formal education from the concept of adult education (Okech 1984). Today, as can be seen in several chapters of this book, education in the formal setting is readily accepted as part of adult education. From the point of view of the mode of delivery, a distinction is made between face-to-face and distance education. The use of these concepts and the practices they cover in Uganda are briefly explained below.

Formal adult education, referring to education provided in a hierarchically structured and accredited setting, is currently found mainly at the continuing and further education level. There has of late been a rapid opening up of higher-level formal educational institutions to adult entrants. The response has been a very significant re-entry of adults into the formal system. Adults, some of a relatively advanced age, are enrolling in large numbers for programmes that have a ready market value. Recently, programmes on business management and information and communication technology have had a particularly high appeal to adults. Many adults have also realised that continued job security in almost any employment area will increasingly depend on competitive advantage, which is to a great extent provided by appropriate academic advantage. Adults without university degrees in their field of work have therefore rejoined formal higher education to obtain one. This has been made more possible by the growing provision of distance and open learning at that level (see Chapter 9).

One Ugandan author has categorised some forms of indigenous education as formal (Ocitti 1994). He explains that prolonged formal learning took place in organised learning groups under the guidance of recognised and acceptable instructors, in fixed places that were usually secluded. Since some of the forms of learning that he cites were for adults, one could say that in his categorisation indigenous education includes some formal adult education. However, indigenous education is not included in the review covered by this book.

Non-formal adult education is the most commonly recognised mode of adult education in Uganda. It refers to organised educational opportunities provided outside the formal education system. It is not hierarchically structured and is meant to be more flexible, responding to specific learning needs. Adult education has been so closely linked in people's minds to non-formal education that the two terms are sometimes used synonymously. According to Merriam and Mazanah (2001) non-formal education programmes are typically non-government sponsored. Whereas this may be true in Malaysia and other countries, many non-formal adult education programmes in Uganda are government sponsored. The functional adult literacy programme and many of the other educational programmes described above are offered on a non-formal basis.

Informal adult education is learning that takes place without the learner deliberately taking part in an organised educational activity and is probably the most prevalent mode of adult learning in Uganda, as it may also be elsewhere (Coombs 1985). It is often a by-product of some other activity. However, it is also often the result of an education provision deliberately planned to reach either the public in general or certain categories of the public. Many educational programmes and short educational messages are organised over the mass media to reach an audience that is fairly well defined. Uganda has carried out a number of awareness and educational campaigns in this way. The most notable in recent years has been education on HIV/AIDS, which has had quite a significant impact.

Distance education and open learning is a new term that is gaining popularity in Uganda, which has in fact provided some form of distance education for about fifty years. It was first known as correspondence studies, supplemented by mass media programmes. The term distance education came into use late, especially with the arrival of computer technology. More recently, the compound term *distance education and open learning* has been adopted, following a trend in other parts of the world. This mode of provision is gaining prevalence especially at the higher levels of education, particularly at university level.

A preview of the chapters

Chapter 2 traces the evolution of adult education in Uganda. This is also the chapter that lays the foundation for the rest of the book by examining the concept of 'modern' adult education. The authors, David Atim and Willy Ngaka, use 'modern' to describe the kind of adult education conducted by organised specialised agencies through planned programmes operating on a large scale as defined by Odurkene and Okello (1985).

The chapter begins with an outline of the scope and purpose of adult education. It then discusses the global context and trends and the ideological perspective of adult education. In tracing the evolution of adult education in Uganda, it looks at the chronological development from 1876 to 2002 and analyses its provision, trends and problems at the different periods.

In Chapter 3, Daniel Babikwa discusses the political economy of adult education in Uganda. He analyses the theoretical underpinnings, meaning, application and relevance of political economy to the field of adult education. The chapter is an attempt to clarify some of the important theoretical issues underlying education practice in general and in Uganda in particular. The author analyses the key theoretical assumptions informing educational practice. He then analyses adult education practice in Uganda and assesses that it tends, in general, to be instrumentalist, rather than empowering and liberating.

Chapter 4 examines government policies and strategies for adult education. D.K. Obbo starts by defining the concepts of policy and strategies, pointing out that the concepts are sometimes used interchangeably, whereas it is important that they should be distinguished. He then explains some policies that directly address adult education and others that address issues that have close bearing on it. In his assessment, adult education is accorded a low profile in comparison to formal or school education and he concludes that the position of government policy and strategy for adult education shows that much remains to be done.

In Chapter 5, George Openjuru examines the role played by civil society organisations in shaping adult education practices in Uganda. He explains his use of the concepts of civil society organisation and adult education and then looks at the contribution civil society organisations have made by selecting examples of organisations involved in different aspects of adult education. In his assessment, without the activities of these organisations, adult education would have no significant claim in this country. However, he also points out that adult educators still need to do a lot to enlighten the civil society organisations about the benefit of gaining professional skills in doing community development work through community education.

In Chapter 6 Yolamu Nsamba reviews university adult education in Uganda with great emphasis on assessing it against its roots in adult liberal education offered in Britain. He explains how university adult education in Uganda failed to live up to British ideals and objectives of liberal adult education and condemns the very inadequate staffing and lack of professional capacity in the department, especially during the 1970s. Although he seems to ignore the impact of Idi Amin's destructive dictatorship, and the changing needs of adult education in Uganda, his candid criticism of the work of the Department of Adult Education and later the Centre for Continuing Education, is a good reminder of weaknesses and errors to be avoided or rectified.

Chapter 7 explores the challenges of the professional development of adult education in Uganda. The authors, P.K. Kagoda and A.R. Katahoire start by referring to the debate on whether adult education is a profession. They then trace the development of professional training in adult education in Uganda and highlight the challenges. They explain that while adult education as a profession continues to develop in Uganda, it also continues to face major challenges. The fact that the majority of educators of adults are untrained compromises the quality of their work and in the long run the overall development of the communities they seek to serve.

In Chapter 8 Anthony Okech discusses the economics and financing of adult education in Uganda. The chapter first looks at the challenges of discussing the financing of adult education, because of its multiple forms and the difficulty of obtaining information on finances. It then outlines the different types of financing, trying to establish the level of funding priority adult education has enjoyed among the different financing agencies in Uganda and the different levels of provision. The chapter also assesses the impact of national economic and financial policies and strategies and presents some ideas on the cost-benefit analysis of adult education. Finally, the chapter examines the implications of the financing for the practice and development of adult education in Uganda.

Jessica Aguti looks at distance education and open learning in Chapter 9. She first discusses the different generations of distance education and the terminologies used to refer to it. She then discusses the reasons for the growth of open and distance learning in Uganda and analyses the different programmes available and their features. She ends by looking at the challenges to distance education and open learning in Uganda.

In Chapter 10, Anthony Okech looks at efforts to promote adult literacy in Uganda, assessing the extent to which these efforts have enabled adults to acquire and make use of literacy and what factors have been favourable or constraining in the process. To start with, the chapter explains the way literacy is understood in this review and highlights some of the recent and current debates on literacy. A historical overview then traces the development of literacy in Uganda, with particular emphasis on adult literacy efforts. Based on the view that literacy can only be meaningfully conceived of and discussed in its social context, the chapter also examines the context of literacy practices in Uganda to bring out the factors that affect the potential of literacy efforts to result in the beneficial use of literacy and the creation of a literate society.

In Chaper 11, Alice Ndidde examines the extent to which adult education has contributed to the empowerment of marginalised groups in Uganda. She explains that adult education includes imparting knowledge and skills to adult men and women for their day-to-day survival, but goes beyond this to include a transformative process that enables the marginalised to understand, analyse and respond to their environment in a proactive manner. It also refers to a process that can lead to changes in social and power relations and is therefore vital in bringing about empowerment. The author argues that alleviation of the conditions of the marginalised groups in Uganda is reflected in both constitutional and policy provisions and that the aims and objectives of adult education also reflect an inclination toward the social, economic and political empowerment of the marginalised. However, she argues, due to inherent weaknesses in the adult education policy and the implementation process, most attention is paid to meeting practical needs while the transformative educational needs of the marginalised groups are not yet adequately met.

In Chapter 12, Paulo Wangoola raises the issue of language in education in the neo-colonial setting of a country like Uganda. He argues that, as a product of an education system which outlaws the use of the mother tongue, the African university adult educator, intellectual and scholar cannot be an empowered adult educator. Consequently she/he cannot empower others in a systematic and sustainable manner. The chapter identifies three other important knowledge sites – sources of knowledge – which are disempowered: the Western-trained intellectual and scholar; the NGOs, CBOs and CSO sector; and mother-tongue intellectuals and scholars, who are also custodians of indigenous knowledge. He argues that as these three are disadvantaged together, only united and co-ordinated action can empower them, severally and collectively. The chapter challenges the university adult educator to spearhead a collaborative partnership for the three potential sources of knowledge, to articulate a new knowledge paradigm rooted in African indigenous knowledge, ways of knowing and language.

Chapter 13 reviews international co-operation, seeking to assess, on the one hand, the extent to which adult education in Uganda has benefited from international co-operation and, on the other, to what extent adult education in Uganda has contributed to international co-operation. The chapter is not a detailed record of all the co-operation activities that have taken place. Anthony Okech just reviews examples of co-operation that addressed the various aspects of adult education as: professional development; infrastructure and equipment; curriculum and materials; research and publications; and the development of an enabling environment for adult education.

In Chapter 14, David Atim and Anthony Okech summarise the key challenges and prospects of adult education in Uganda, drawing mainly from what is presented in the previous thirteen chapters of the book. They summarise the challenges as: developing a common understanding of adult education; the demand for adult education; policy, legislation and national commitment; planning, networking and co-ordination; resources and financing; language; research and professional development; and external relationship. They conclude the chapter on a hopeful note by stating that, if the current impetus continues, Uganda will in the near future benefit from improvements in provision and participation in adult education by all stakeholders, both from the supply and the demand side. The many more beneficial results and impacts can contribute significantly to poverty eradication, development and prosperity in all aspects of life. The precondition they give is, however, that government, various agencies and the civil society all work together to address the gaps and weaknesses that have been highlighted through this review.

Chapter 15 is a kind of epilogue in which Charles Kabuga's case for the adoption of andragogy – the art and science of helping adults learn (Knowles 1980) – first published more than twenty years ago, is reproduced because of the criticism of the methods currently used in Uganda, found in this book. This epilogue could serve as a point of reference in assessing the appropriateness of the methodology in use. As argued in the chapter on professional development of adult educators, the quality of the work of the educators shows gaps that could affect the impact of their work on the overall development of the communities they seek to serve. Reflection on improving methodology is, therefore, one of the challenges, which, if addressed, could brighten the prospects of adult education in Uganda.

2
The Evolution of Adult Education in Uganda

David Atim and Willy Ngaka

Introduction

In African societies, adult education has been practised traditionally and informally since time immemorial as an integral part of life within a community. The adult education process in the African context is incidental and lifelong. It is conceived broadly as a concomitant of life, a socialisation process through which relevant knowledge, skills and the values of society are transmitted from one generation to another. Every adult received appropriate exposure to indigenous education, depending on his or her role in the community. However, the advent of formal (school) education in Uganda in the nineteenth century brought with it the assumption that childhood is uniquely the time of learning. This widespread assumption led to inadequate attention being given to the educational needs of adults in particular and of the community in general. It eroded beliefs in African indigenous education and culture.

This chapter is concerned with what is known as 'modern' adult education, by which we mean here the kind of adult education conducted by organised and specialised agencies through planned programmes operating on a large scale (Odurkene and Okello 1985).

It traces the evolution of adult education in Uganda over about twelve and half decades (1876-2002), considering its provision, trends and problems, the global context in which it operates and its ideological perspective.

The scope and purpose of adult education

The term adult education means different things in different regions (Lowe 1975; Darkenwald and Merriam 1982). Even in one country, different writers use the term so differently that no uniform or precise definition can be arrived at (Alan 1992 and Brookfield 1987). These differences in perception and the use of the term arise from the fact that adult education is closely related to the social, political and cultural conditions of each country (Darkenwald and Merriam 1982). It is important to consider this in defining the scope and purpose of adult education.

However, notwithstanding the variations in the perceptions and use of the term 'adult education', the definition adopted by UNESCO in 1976 and modified by the Fifth International Conference on Adult Education (CONFINTEA V) in 1997 is broad enough to take care of variations in socio-political and cultural conditions in different countries. The 1976 definition was:

> Adult education denotes the entire body of organised educational processes, whatever the content, level and method, whether formal or otherwise, whether they prolong or replace the initial schools, colleges, and universities, as well as an apprenticeship, whereby persons regarded as adults by the societies to which they belong develop their abilities, enrich their knowledge, improve their technical or professional qualifications or turn them in a new direction and bring about improved changes in their attitudes or behaviour in the twofold perspective of full personal development and participation in balanced and independent social, economic and cultural development (UNESCO 1976 in Townsend Coles 1977: 4-5).

The definition adopted in Hamburg in 1997 changes the phrase in the first line from 'organised educational processes' to 'learning processes', thus broadening the scope of adult education even further. According to these definitions adult education would include all those activities or programmes intended to meet the needs of various individuals considered by the society as adults, including out-of-school youths forced by circumstances to play the roles normally played by adults.

The purpose of adult education in Uganda is close to that given by Darkenwald and Merriam (1982) which generally aims at providing:
1. Basic or fundamental education so as to make good the deficiencies many people experience because of curtailed education or non-existent period of formal schooling.

2. Opportunities for further or continuing education in order to update professional competencies required by the world of work.
3. Vocational and technical education necessary for the acquisition of certain specific skills needed for improvement of job performance.
4. Education for building social, political and civic competencies, including instructions on national and international issues.
5. Education for leisure and relaxation.
6. Education on health, welfare and family life including guidance on physical and mental health, family problems, parenthood, etc.
7. Extra-curricular activities for out-of-school youths.

These aims reflect the high degree of flexibility that characterises adult education and which, in turn, reflects the varied nature of the needs of the target groups in the prevailing social, political and cultural conditions. Uganda today requires the same kind of diversity of adult education programmes: adult education should not be considered, as it has sometimes been in Uganda, as teaching only literacy.

The global context and trends in adult education

Clarke (1967) traces the roots of adult education as a movement to the ancient Greeks and the people of other early civilisations where education was considered as a continuous process that goes on throughout a person's life. Unfortunately, the introduction of schools and colleges in Western Europe and other parts of the world swept aside this wonderful idea of education being a lifelong process. Education came to be seen as an activity that takes place in schools and colleges only. Some people in many parts of the world still hold this view as can be seen in the peripheral and unco-ordinated way in which adult education is managed in different countries.

It is not clear when the global modern adult education movement exactly began. Clarke traces it to the last years of the eighteenth century when countries like Britain were experiencing the industrial revolution. The need for the adult education movement in different parts of the world also seems to have been precipitated by socio-economic and political conditions of the period that arose out of demands for new skills, competencies and attitudes.The adult education movement evolved steadily in Britain and influenced the development of adult education in other regions like North America, where great strides were made in adult education, and the British Commonwealth countries. Scandinavian countries, too, have a long history of adult education, dating from about the same time. During the twentieth century the Soviet Union implemented a programme of adult education with great commitment to eradicate illiteracy almost completely. Cuba, which adopted the Soviet communist system, undertook a similar campaign. Everywhere, the desirability of maintaining a close relationship between education and work, and the challenges brought about by the social and economic conditions of modern life gave impetus to modern adult education.

Some African leaders after independence, such as Julius Nyerere of Tanzania, Kwameh Nkruma of Ghana and Kenneth Kaunda of Zambia, emphasised the need to promote adult education. However, adult education work in most developing countries was conducted at different levels by different agencies, governmental and non-governmental, leading to duplication of efforts, resources and services. Attempts were in some cases made to bring together people's efforts by putting in place national adult education associations (Clarke 1967). These were similar to the Workers' Educational Association (WEA) of Britain, formed in 1903. The People's Education Association of Ghana was formed just before the country attained Independence; the Uganda National Adult Education Association was formed in 1980 in an attempt to strengthen the growth of adult education. The intention of these associations was to complement the work of university extra-mural departments and government departments in charge of adult education and to enable them to give people further education opportunities.

The struggle to enable adult education to gain its position among other disciplines has been global in nature and has required a concerted effort from individuals, groups, associations and governments. A focal point for this struggle was the international discussions and conferences on adult education spearheaded by UNESCO and involving other organisations. The first conference of this kind took place at Elsinore, Denmark, in 1949 and the most recent in 1997 at Hamburg in Germany. Through these international conferences, the challenges faced in promoting adult education at global level have been addressed and the resolutions that were arrived at have continued to guide efforts to develop and promote adult education in the various countries.

Ideological perspectives on adult education

A discussion on the growth, development, prospects and challenges of adult education in a country cannot be done without taking account of the ideological framework in which these take place and which influences the country's development. This is probably why it has been said that the study and practice of adult education in the countries of the South are framed by the context of development, the idea of the necessity and possibility of progress towards a 'more desirable kind of society' (Youngman 2000 quoting Bernstein 1983: 48). As efforts to build and strengthen the adult education movement in various parts of the world started to gain momentum, the movement began to be used to support each country's strongly held ideological principles. This has been evident in the ideas propounded by Lindeman, Paulo Freire, and Julius Nyerere. Hence, adult education embodies deliberate actions to change society in chosen directions (Youngman 2000).

The ideological perspective of adult education can be seen in the attempt to use it in seeking solutions to the global economic depression of the nineteen forties and fifties and the emergence of the concept of 'economically backward' areas of the world. Adult education involves different bodies including the state and civil society organisations that are seeking to respond to the needs, interests and values of different groups. As a form of social policy, the product of deliberate action by organisations to influence society, it was a useful tool.

Quite often, the different kinds of social interventions in the South have been articulated in terms of ideas and values underpinned by theories of development, which have in turn influenced the nature of adult education. The development theories include theories of modernisation, dependence, liberalism and neo-liberalism. The underlying values informing these are the powerful ideologies of capitalism, socialism or communism, which have tended to emphasise different styles of economy, free market under capitalism, command economies under socialism or communism. In Uganda, adult education, especially that provided by the university, has mainly been influenced by liberalism with the main aim, as noted by Boshier, of complete fulfilment of a man (sic) in the richness of his forms and expression (Boshier in Halford and Jarvis 1998).

The twenty-first century has ushered in globalisation where the driving force is free competition in the global market. Inevitably, this has an impact on the education 'market'. The current trend throughout the world is that education should now be seen as a lifelong process, hence the neo-liberal concept of lifelong learning, based on the notion of an autonomous free floating individual learner who must choose what to learn, why, when and how. In this case, learning is put on the open market for those who can afford it. The implications of neo-liberal thinking are that the state will abandon its responsibilities to those of the free market. In the words of the OECD:

> Hence, governments will seek to establish an environment that encourages individuals to take greater responsibility for their own and their children's learning, and where appropriate permit a choice as to where they acquire the learning they need (Halford and Jarvis 1998: 15).

This kind of tendency now cuts across all sectors of Uganda's economy, and adult education is no exception. It can therefore be said that neo-liberalism has a considerable influence on the development of adult education in Uganda today.

Adult education in Uganda

This section traces the growth of modern adult education in Uganda starting from the pre-colonial time up to the present. An attempt is made to critically assess the provision, trends and problems associated with adult education activities in the country during this period.

The beginning of modern adult education in Uganda, 1876-1945

Modern adult education in Uganda dates from the late nineteenth century when contact with the wider world began with the coming of Arab traders, followed by European explorers, missionaries and colonial officials. The first Christian missionaries in Uganda were Smith and Wilson of the Church Missionary Society (CMS) (Protestants) who arrived in Buganda in 1876 following the visits by explorers Speke in 1862 and Stanley in 1875 at the court of Mutesa I (Wandira 1972). The first group of White Fathers (Catholics) arrived in 1878. The CMS and White Fathers dominated the early years of missionary involvement in Uganda. They identified themselves as agents of civilisation and their activities extended over almost every field in which they saw the need for assistance. Mackay's engineering and technical expertise in building brick-houses, sanitation, digging wells and curing diseases had great influence on the indigenous population. (Wandira 1972).

The missions became particularly conscious of the needs for technical, or 'manual' skills. The CMS strongly believed that 'no training which only imparts book knowledge is complete' but that 'Eye, ear and hand must be trained, the educational value of labour must be taught...' (Wandira 1972). The CMS apparently had a correct view at the inception of modern education in Uganda. They proceeded to train the converted and lay-brothers in various skills such as blacksmith work, carpentry, shoe-making, moulding roof and floor tiles, brick-making, masonry, printing, book-binding, drawing, etc. Paradoxically, the beginnings of technical instruction in Uganda were limited to the internal needs of the individual missions. During the course of conducting their religious mission, the churches also taught adult converts literacy, numeracy and agriculture. To support their teaching programmes, they produced limited reading materials in some vernacular languages. The CMS produced newspapers such as Mengo Notes in 1900 and *Ebiffa mu Buganda* in 1907, and the White Fathers began publishing *Munno* in 1911. Church activities started in Kampala and, in due course, spread throughout the country.

The first relevant efforts in education by the colonial government were aimed at conditioning Ugandans to serve, accept and sustain the colonial administration. In a bid to introduce a modern economy, adults were taught to grow a few cash crops such as cotton in 1903, coffee in the 1920s and tea. The colonial state, European firms or Indian entrepreneurs introduced processing industries based on the cash crops. No government institution was started, during this period, specifically to initiate and develop adult education programmes. There was neither conscious educational planning to extend technical skills to Ugandans nor formal declaration of educational policies.

Overall, during the first period of colonial rule and missionary work, very little was done to develop adult education: the various missions conducted the real pioneering work. Efforts to expand adult education in the country were constrained by lack of planning and policy and lack of agreement and co-operation between the state and the churches. Other voluntary agencies that contributed to early adult education in Uganda were the Islamic organisations, the Uganda Scouts Association, started in 1915, the Uganda Girl Guides Association (1922), St John's Ambulance Brigade (1930) and the Uganda Red Cross Society (1942).

Adult education in Uganda after World War II, 1945-1962

In the period 1945-1962, many adult education institutions and programmes were initiated and developed (Odurkene and Okello 1985). The creation of the Public Relations and Social Welfare Department in 1946 marked the beginning of government involvement in the development of adult education programmes in a systematic way. The department, staffed by resettled ex-servicemen, was divided into two sections, the Information and Broadcasting Section and the Community Development Section (rural and urban). It supported community leaders and local government workers by providing cinema vans and demonstration teams, which toured the whole country and taught the public social welfare and self-help matters. It organised activities for women and trained ex-soldiers in skills such as brick-making, musical instrument playing and extension work techniques.

Important adult education and information institutions created under the Department of Public Relations and Social Welfare included:

Uganda Council for Women in 1947, Radio Uganda in 1954, and the Local Government and Community Development Training Centre at Nsamizi in 1954, which was set up to train administrative personnel in social, economic and political fields. In 1952, there was a review of community development policy following the Governor's Despatch No. 490/52 of 22nd July 1952 to the Secretary of State. A separate Department of Community Development was created from the former combined Department of Public Relations and Social Welfare. The new Department was able to concentrate more on the provision of adult education.

The establishment of District Farm Institutes (DFIs) between 1957 and 1962 at Ngetta, Ikulwe, Mukono, Tororo and Kyambogo was another important development in favour of adult education in Uganda. DFIs were established under the Ministry of Agriculture to train local government staff and to provide short courses for chiefs and progressive small-scale farmers. They were used for in-service training and other courses for government and field staff. They also offered facilities for residential and non-residential courses, conferences, seminars and similar learning experiences. Attached to the DFIs and sharing facilities with them were the Rural Training Centres (RTCs) whose aims were to provide a practical demonstration of a new and improved way of life for those who passed through them, and a forum for discussion of local affairs. The RTCs were multi-purpose and ran multi-disciplinary courses, which included civic education, home economics, handicrafts and agriculture.

The Ministry of Health's adult education activities also increased after 1945 when returning ex-soldiers, trained as hygiene orderlies, demonstrated a hygienic way of life in most parts of Uganda. A number of parastatal and semi-autonomous national institutions began to run adult education programmes. These included the Department of Extra-Mural Studies at Makerere College, now Makerere University, and co-operative unions. In 1950, Dr Hakin organised a series of 'health week' activities throughout Uganda using diverse techniques such as lectures, posters, films and demonstrations to give information on health and hygiene.

In October 1953, a Department of Extra-Mural Studies was

established at Makerere College, then affiliated to the University of London. This department was charged with the responsibility of 'taking the University to the people'. Its mission was to spread the principles and quality of university adult study and thought to the great majority of people who were unable to attend its internal courses (Atim 1984). It mainly encouraged the formation of 'extra-mural groups' or classes, made up of English speakers interested in education and self-education. They attended university classes taught by graduates qualified in the subjects that they taught. Besides evening classes, there were a series of public lectures and some short residential courses. Other programmes were organised in collaboration with government departments, which included the new Radio Uganda (created in 1953) the Community Development Department, the Commerce Department, the Co-operative Movement, the Uganda Police as well as membership organisations such as the Uganda Club.

In 1955, an education section was created in the Ministry of Health to spearhead the production of health education materials. In the Ministry of Internal Affairs, the Prisons Department offered opportunities to prisoners and warders in each district to learn various skills and crafts, including modern agriculture, brick-laying, carpentry, weaving, retail trade and other skills.

Voluntary agencies connected with the Churches and Islamic organisations continued to be active during this period, together with the St John's Ambulance Brigade and the Uganda Red Cross Society. The Family Planning Association of Uganda started in 1957.

Co-operative unions were initiated in Uganda in the 1950s, primarily to reduce the exploitative activities of intermediaries, who cheated farmers in the marketing of coffee, cotton and other commodities. The unions not only bought coffee, cotton, tobacco and other produce from the farmers and peasants, but they also acquired cotton ginneries and coffee processing plants. These union assets and facilities enabled many adults to acquire skills and get employment in new jobs. Among other educational initiatives, the unions encouraged better farming and the spirit and practice of thrift and corporate self-help.

Mention must also be made of trade unions, and multi-national and national companies, which conducted adult education and training during this period. Trade union activities became firmly established in the 1950s. From 1955-1964, union activities were co-ordinated by the Uganda Trade Union Congress. Education for trade unionists was provided by the Labour College, which was established in Kampala in 1958. Squabbles among the union leaders, however, prevented effective work from being developed in the fields of Trade Union and Workers' Education.

Multi-national and national companies also conducted some training for their workers. These companies included Shell, BP, Esso, Singer, Gailey & Roberts, British American Tobacco, Bata Shoe Company, Madhvani Sugar, commercial banks and the insurance companies.

English was not the only medium used for adult education: local languages were promoted by the local press. Newspapers written in Luganda included *Ebiffa Mu Buganda, Munno, Munyonyozi, Njuba Ebirese, Sekanyolya* and *Mutalasi*. Newspapers produced in other languages included *Apupeta, Amut, Musisi, Taifa Empya* and *Taifa Uganda Empya*. These newspapers supplied their readers with a lot of information about important current events in Uganda and about local activities.

To promote the availability of reading materials in vernacular languages, the government formed the Uganda African Literature Committee. It had various sub-committees that translated and supplied reading materials in five officially recognised vernacular languages of instruction in schools, namely, Luganda, Runyoro-Rutoro, Luo, Ateso and Lugbara. The East African Literature Bureau and the Uganda Bookshop published the material. By 1950, over 170 books had been translated into various vernacular languages by teachers, civil servants, private individuals, and Makerere University College students. Charts were also produced in many other vernacular languages.

During the period 1945-62 adult education activities in Uganda picked up impressively. Many institutions were founded to carry out some kind of adult education programmes. A lot of work was done but much of it was scattered and unco-ordinated. Neither money nor labour were used to the best effect (Odurkene and Okello 1985).

There were also gaps in the organisational structures and thousands of people were not reached by any of the organised adult education activities. The curricula were not based on proper needs assessment. Educational materials were of foreign origin and were in short supply. 'The attitude of the colonial government was half-hearted towards adult education' (Clarke 1967). This half-hearted attitude is apparent in the failure of the colonial government to implement many of the recommendations of the conference on 'Adult education in the colonies' which took place in 1951.

The development of adult education, 1962-1971

This period marks the attainment of national independence in 1962 and effectively ends with the establishment of military rule by Amin in 1971. In Uganda, the period 1962-71 was a period of real growth in the development of adult education. Institutions created during colonial rule continued to expand and the number of adult education institutions, programmes, personnel and learners increased. The institutions that continued evolving and expanding were the District Farm Institutes, Nsamizi Training Centre and the Department of Extra-Mural Studies. By 1971, DFIs and RTCs had also spread from five districts to 15 of the 18 districts in Uganda at that time.

Nsamizi Training Centre evolved from being a multi-purpose centre to specialising in running courses in community development and welfare. In the early 1960s the objectives of the centre were:
1. To develop the centre as the main adult education centre in Uganda closely tied to the RTCs.
2. To cater for needs connected with the achievement of independence such as training suitable personnel to take over posts from the whites.

To achieve these objectives, the courses offered at the centre were Leadership, Law, Citizenship and Community Development. Several seminars, conferences and refresher courses were also offered to meet the needs of various government departments. In 1969, Dr A.H. Shawky, a United Nations regional adviser and social welfare policy and training expert evaluated the Centre, made recommendations on staffing, curricula, teaching methodology,

teaching materials, and related activities. His recommendations resulted in the creation of two long courses that were initiated at the Centre in October 1970. They were:
1. The Certificate in Social Development Course (1 year)
2. The Diploma in Social Development Course (2 years)

The main objective of these courses was to offer professional training to already serving community development workers and to prepare recent recruits for professional training.

In 1967, the Department of Extra-Mural Studies was renamed the Centre for Continuing Education (CCE) following the recommendation of the Kironde Report of 1966. Seven regional centres were established to continue with the traditional extra-mural work. The Centre for Continuing Education became preoccupied in this period with the provision of further and continuing education programmes of various types, offered through correspondence and residential studies.

The other government departments which continued to make considerable contributions to the development of adult education in this period were: Agriculture, Health, Community Development, Co-operatives, Local Government, Veterinary, Labour and Information and Education.

A number of new Government Institutions were founded during the first decade of independence. They included the Institute of Public Administration (now re-named the Uganda Management Institute). Then there was the Law Development Centre, the Fisheries Training Institute and the Reformatory School of Young Offenders. Others were the Management Training and Advisory Centre, the Mwana-Mugimu Nutrition Rehabilitation Unit at Mulago Hospital, Kampala, the Public Libraries Board, Uganda Television and numerous community centres all over the country to serve mainly as venues for adult education. The government also established or sponsored a number of organisations and associations including the Milton Obote Foundation Adult Education Centre, the National Union of Youth Organisation, the Young Farmers' Association and the Uganda Association of Women's Organisations formed in 1965 by voluntary women's organisations. This association promoted women's activities until Amin, who wanted all women's organisations represented by a single body, ended it.

Adult education programmes and projects initiated in this period included the mass Literacy Campaign in 1964, the Ministry of Health's Home and Environment Competition, the Ministry of Education's Namutamba Project and the promotion of newspapers, periodicals and journals. Voluntary organisations that had started earlier continued to expand their activities. This was clearly the case regarding Church activities.

It can be seen from the above survey that the period 1962-72 was, from the perspective of government, the peak period in the development of adult education in Uganda. New and old institutions expanded their programmes. Adult educators reached thousands of Ugandans. 'Fringe' activities included film shows, informal talks, debates, concerts, festivals and exhibitions. The staff of Nsamizi Training Centre, Centre for Continuing Education and the Churches, as well as those sponsored by the East African Literature Bureau, produced many books and charts. A lot was done. However, the impact of all these efforts still has to be properly evaluated.

The impact of the military regime on the evolution of adult education, 1971-1980

The period 1971-1980 was a period of military rule in Uganda. For most Ugandans it was a very sad time. Every aspect of life was affected badly. All institutions suffered in varying degrees. Education was one of the national services worst hit. The impressive trend in the growth of adult education programmes was interrupted by the pervasive, inconsiderate and arbitrary conduct of the military regime. The following statements describe the situation that prevailed with regard to adult education during that regime. Professor Ojok, then Minister of Education, stated in 1983:

> When a vicious military dictatorship took root in the country in 1971, education, together with other social services and the economy, suffered from neglect, abuse and degeneration, thereby causing, in its wake, a huge backlog of illiteracy,

aspirants of further education and training, and wasted manpower. Most of the country's best brains were killed or fled into exile (Odurkene and Okello 1985).

Daniel Okunga, the Director of the Centre for Continuing Education 1969-1977, describing the effect of the military regime on University adult education.

> Seminars and short weekend courses used to be very popular and useful pass time. Now they are a never thought of luxury. No one can afford either the fee or the time...Public lectures have, for different reasons, suffered a similar fate (Okunga 1980).

Okunga explained that the main trouble in respect of public lectures was that no one was prepared to give a public talk. There was no safe topic to talk about because intelligence reporters would be among the audience and their understanding of issues was minimal. So, their reporting was deadly.

The government, through the Ministry of Culture and Community Development, did plan and conduct a national literacy campaign in 1975, but it was planned and conducted in a hurry. A great deal was initiated and done but not sustained. The campaign was short lived.

Despite hardships and unfavourable circumstances during the military regime, all the adult education institutions founded earlier at first expanded or, until 1976, maintained their activities. Community Development clubs organised classes on subjects such as nutrition, child-care and home gardening. These continued to expand throughout Uganda and, in addition to organised classes, provided a basis for dialogue on information that was broadcast by radio. Men were also encouraged to form clubs for literacy and training in vocational skills. The voluntary organisations such as YMCA, YWCA and the Churches continued their activities. In 1976, the Church of Uganda bought Lweza Mission Station and turned it into a conference centre, which served many adult education activities. In the same year the Kiira Adult Education Association was started in a village in Iganga to spearhead functional literacy programmes and promote agricultural, civic, and nutrition education in the local community.

However, the increasingly arbitrary and murderous rule by the military regime forced most adult education institutions and activities to decline and collapse. Many churchmen fled the country in 1977. Economic hardships worsened the already bad situation. It is lamentable that such an impressive start in the evolution of adult education in Uganda was almost ruined by a regime of illiterates. That such a regime can still do harm on such an extensive scale and for so long in the modern world should surely be a lesson to all people. It should strengthen the resolve to eliminate illiteracy and inculcate positive attitudes in all people wherever they may be and whatever their occupation.

The revival of adult education, 1980-1985

After the end of Idi Amin's rule in 1979, an elected government led by Uganda People's Congress produced a recovery programme with provisions for rectifying the damage done to Uganda's economy, institutions and services by the military regime. Government adult education institutions, including the Centre for Continuing Education of Makerere University were revived with funds from the government and donor aid from various international organisations and foreign governments. Organisations affiliated to overseas parent organisations, such as YMCA, YWCA and the churches, were once more able to receive substantial support from overseas.

Associated with this revival was an increase in systematic and comprehensive plans for programmes. Major programmes planned and executed were National Expanded Programmes of Immunisation (EPI) launched in 1983, Control of Diarrhoeal Disease (CDD) launched at a National Conference on Oral Dehydration Therapy in March 1984 and integrated with the EPI Programmes in April 1984, and Child Survival and Development Revolution (CSDR) initiated by UNICEF in 1982. All of these were under the Ministry of Health, Primary Health Care Programmes. They were implemented in partnership with the government and other agencies such as the Red Cross Society and YWCA. Other programmes and projects introduced during this period included programmes for crop producers, appropriate technology in DFIs and vocational training. The Ministry of Labour organised basic craft courses and apprenticeship programmes for school leavers to enable them to enter the employment market with basic technical skills. Successful apprentices were awarded trade certificates. The Management Training and Advisory Centre (MTAC) offered entrepreneurial courses for trainees from rural areas.

Under the Ministry of Education's Basic Education Integrated into Rural Development (BEIRD) Programme, the National Curriculum Development Centre formed an Adult Education panel in 1983. The panel had the responsibility of developing curricula for skill training in crop and animal husbandry, carpentry, shoe-making, basic mechanics, brick-making as well as the teaching of reading, writing and numeracy. Non-formal education techniques were also incorporated into the curricula of teacher training colleges. Among the topics included were psychology of adult learning, the integrated approach in environmental activities, communication skills and assessment of community needs.

A number of new adult education institutions and organisations were formed during this period. The Uganda National Adult Education Association (NAEA) was inaugurated in November 1980 with the aim 'to promote adult education throughout Uganda according to modern concepts and practices of comprehensive adult education with special emphasis on functional literacy and rural development' (Odurkene and Okello 1985). The Uganda Food and Peace Project (UFPP) was started in 1981 in five villages in Kabarole District, Western Uganda. Its aim was 'to bring about an attitude that can create and bring about irreversible conditions for development centering on the people and their resources' (op. cit.). What is today known as the Uganda Rural Development Training Programme based in Kagadi, Kibale District originated from UFPP. Other professional associations, societies and self-help groups were also formed.

In summary, during 1980-1985 all the adult education institutions formed during the pre-Amin days revived their activities almost fully. Some even extended their scope of activities. A few new adult education agencies were founded. It was clear, therefore, that adult education activities were establishing strong roots throughout Uganda, and that, though clear government directives did not guide these activities, adult education in Uganda was evolving impressively.

This impressive evolution of adult education notwithstanding, a number of constraints were not dealt with. These included lack of:
- Clear and comprehensive government policy and directives
- Effective co-ordination of existing adult education activities
- Funds for programmes
- Provision of educational equipment and materials
- Suitable personnel trained for and committed to adult education work
- Appreciation of the role of adult education and social and economic development, and
- Effective mobilisation of the people for participation in adult education programmes.

In addition to these, Uganda was not at total peace at this time. The protracted bush war waged by the National Resistance Army (NRA) paralysed many parts of Uganda and turned away the attention of government from the business of recovery and reconstruction. Misunderstandings within the Uganda National Liberation Army (UNLA) led to another coup in May 1985, which gave power to a new military junta. The military regime led by Okello Lutwa was soon removed by Yoweri Museveni's National Resistance Army, which took power in Uganda in January 1986.

The development of adult education, 1986-2002

When the Government of the National Resistance Movement (NRM) took over government in 1986, it emphasised the need to transform Uganda from a 'backward' to a modern society (NRM's Ten Point Programme, 1986). Its efforts at improving the literacy and educational levels of the population produced policies based on the Education Policy Review Commission (EPRC, 1989) and the subsequent White Paper on Education of 1992. In 1988, a National Inter-Sectoral Committee for Eradication of Illiteracy was formed. A plan for an Integrated Non-Formal Basic Education Pilot Project (INFOBEPP) was completed in 1991 and the project executed in eight districts of Apac, Hoima, Kabarole, Mbarara, Mpigi, Mukono, Kamuli and Iganga. A process review was conducted in 1995 and a new plan to consolidate the programme in the pilot districts and expand to new ones was developed (Okech et al 1999).

Overall, the Functional Adult Literacy Programme has scored success and recognition nationally. The demand for its expansion to other areas, the initiative of some districts outside the project area and the help sought by local NGOs, as well as the level of support from some district councils and leadership all point to the value attached to this programme. However, the 1995 review team identified several constraints, including the low status of the literacy unit in the parent ministry. This affects its financial standing and staffing levels. At lower levels, instructors are volunteers and this is not easily sustainable. Collaboration of the unit with other actors and sharing experiences with them has not received enough attention. Production of more materials, writing new orthographies, further training of instructors, and improvement in methods all need to be tackled (Cottingham et al 1995).

There have been some efforts towards collaboration in the field of adult literacy for adult education in general. The Uganda Joint Action for Adult Education (UJAFAE), the result of such efforts, brought together eight member organisations, namely, National Adult Education Association, Institute of Adult and Continuing Education, Kiira Adult Education Association, Kamuli Adult Education Association, Tororo Community Initiated Development Association (TOCIDA), Directorate of Community Development, Development Network of Indigenous and Voluntary Associations (DENIVA) and the National Women's Association for Social and Educational Advancement based in Iganga District. There is also the Literacy Network for Uganda (LitNet) linking organisations engaged in adult literacy, governmental, non-governmental and commercial.

The new development trend in Uganda today gives community adult and non-formal education good prospects. From what was a highly top-down and centralised approach to development, the country is increasingly moving towards a self-reliant and community-based participatory approach. This is in line with the on-going process of decentralisation and civil service reform, which is turning the district administrative unit into a key unit at which future development efforts in Uganda will focus. This new development will demand more capacity building and basic educational activities at the local level.

Conclusion

Starting with indigenous processes of lifelong education, adult education in Uganda has a long history. Formal adult education arrived with the missionaries and developed slowly during colonial times. Much influenced by international trends and development issues, it only really began to flourish after the Second World War. The good progress made before and after Independence in 1962 was destroyed during the military regime. The period 1980 to 1985 generated a ray of hope when several adult education institutions and programmes were revived. Under the NRM there have been some successes in the development of adult education.

The challenge of recovery from the shattered national economy continues with increasing participation of non-governmental organisations (NGOs) and community-based organizations (CBOs). It is estimated that nearly 2000 localised, national and international NGOs are currently registered in Uganda. They operate on a wide range of small and medium scale income-generating and service-oriented projects. A good number of them are engaged in education and literacy, awareness creation, advocacy, lobbying and agriculture. The proliferation of NGOs and CBOs operating in the rural sector has created an urgent need for community education and training in various skills such as small and medium scale enterprise and entrepreneurship development, community development work, rural development management and training of trainers. Development of adult education today should be guided by this demand. Some responses have come during this period from government institutions and non-governmental organisations. However, a lot remains to be done in the area of financing, policy and co-ordination of adult education activities in the country.

3
The Political Economy of Adult Education in Uganda

Daniel Babikwa

Introduction
This chapter discusses the political economy of adult education in Uganda. It specifically analyses the theoretical underpinnings, meaning, application and relevance of political economy to the field of adult education. The chapter attempts to clarify some of the important theoretical issues underlying education practice in general and in Uganda in particular. Whilst it is not the intention of this publication to dwell on education theory per se, it is not possible to discuss the political economy of education without analysing the key theoretical assumptions informing educational practice. Using a discussion of what Habermas (1972) termed 'knowledge-constitutive interests' the chapter sets out to locate theoretically the central assumption of political economy and the socially critical thought that education is not neutral (Freire 1970, Giroux 1983 and Youngman 1986).

Habermas and the theory of knowledge
Educational writing from the critical tradition, which also informs the political economy of education, has developed a system of distinguishing three broad orientations or frameworks in education, based on Habermas's three knowledge-constitutive interests as central components of the theory of knowledge. While this classification has its limitations, it also has considerable value, particularly in characterising and explaining different educational processes and their related outcomes and in guiding discussions on educational practice.

According to Habermas (1972), there are three fundamental ways of looking at and using versions of human knowledge or 'knowledge constitutive interests': the technical, the practical and the critical or emancipatory. It is these interests that influence the different types of knowledge and educational processes, and so the nature of education in different settings. It should be noted that the knowledge interests are politically and ideologically motivated.

Grundy (1987:12) describes the technical knowledge-constitutive interest as a fundamental interest in controlling the life and the physical world through 'rule-following action', based upon empirically grounded laws. The technical interest is responsible for educational processes that aim to satisfy physical and economic needs, and to shape learners in line with the world as perceived by the dominant socio-economic and political forces in society. The technical knowledge-constitutive interest underlies actions governed by technical rules based on experience. The interest has been associated with most traditional adult educational programmes which emphasise behavioural objectives, technical content and transmittal educational processes. Educational programmes located in this tradition downplay the role of socio-political and economic factors in shaping social relations and look at social problems as technical; hence the search for technical solutions.

The practical knowledge-constitutive interest is a fundamental interest in understanding social phenomena through interactions based upon a consensual interpretation of meaning. Grundy argues that the practical interest aims at understanding social phenomena, not to formulate rules for controlling and manipulating it, but 'so that one is able to interact with it' (Grundy 1987:12-13). This interest leads to educational processes and outcomes that create opportunities for learners to play active roles in learning programmes in which they consciously and willingly choose to take part. The interest represents a more liberal view of education and approach to learning.

The critical/emancipatory knowledge-constitutive interest is defined as 'a fundamental interest in emancipation and empowerment (of people) to engage in autonomous action, arising out of authentic critical insights into the social construction of the human society' (Grundy 1987:19). This knowledge interest underlies educational processes that seek to transform the situation of those who are socially, politically, economically and culturally marginalised.

Each of the three knowledge-constitutive interests underlies one of the major educational frameworks or orientations outlined by

Kemmis, et al (1983) namely: neo-classical, liberal/progressive and socially critical educational orientations. Political economy of education in general and adult education in particular is rooted in the critical emancipatory knowledge interest.

What must be emphasised here is that knowledge-constitutive interests represent ideological positions that correspond with particular socio-economic formations and inform socio-political actions, including educational practice. Although the orientations should by their very nature constitute part of the subject matter of the political economy of education, political economists writing in the field of adult education have not clarified the relationship between political economy and the different education orientations. The discussion below is intended to clarify some key concepts of political economy and how they are related to key aspects of educational theory.

Political economy clarified

Political economy has been defined as the 'science that studies the social relations that evolve between people in the process of production, distribution, exchange and consumption of material benefits' (Volkov 1985:275) and also as a science that studies the various 'modes of production' (Popov 1984 and Nikitin 1985). Political economy is rooted in Marxist social theory, which contends that society is stratified according to classes of people based on how they relate to the existing means of production. One of the basic tenets of Marxism is that people under different modes of production relate to the means of production differently (Nikitin 1985 and Popov 1985). In capitalism, currently the dominant mode of production in the world, a few people control the major resources/means of production, with the majority not only lacking ownership and control, but also having to rely on those who own the resources to gain access to those resources. The relationship between the classes is often contradictory, involving shifting terrains of domination and subordination (Youngman 1986). This inequitable ownership and control over resources in society implies a skewed power structure in favour of the dominant classes. It thus implies a society with powerful minority owners of means of production and a powerless majority who own nothing but their labour power, which they inevitably market as a commodity in order to survive.

Mode of production and productive forces

The mode of production constitutes 'the unity of productive forces and the relations of production at a given historical stage in the development of the human society' (Volkov 1985). Relations of production are relations that evolve among people irrespective of their will and consciousness in the process of production, distribution and exchange and consumption of material wealth. Depending on the ownership of the means of production, such relations can either be of exploitation of the producers by the owners or of mutual understanding and sharing (Nikitin 1985). Productive forces are a combination of the means of production (constituting all resources available in society, including infrastructure) and the people who have the knowledge, production experience, and labour skills. People are the most important productive force because they set the production process in motion, and without them, the resources/means of production are rendered useless.

Political economists have distinguished four major modes of production namely: primitive communalism, the slave-holding mode (feudalism), capitalism and socialism. Political economy therefore studies not only the different ways in which people relate to each other during the process of producing goods and services for their economic and social well-being, but also their relationship to the major means of production/resources and the products of their labour. The nature of these relationships is largely dependent on the prevailing socio-economic formation.

Socio-economic formation

The socio-economic formation combines three major elements of society namely:
1. The productive forces
2. The relations of production and structure of the economy
3. the superstructure which includes society's political, juridical, ideological relations and notions and the corresponding

institutions and organisations, e.g. the police, the army, the legislature, the legal system, educational system and bureaucracy of government officials (Popov 1985). The superstructure thus consists of both the ideological and repressive apparatus of the state.

In short, the socio-economic formation combines two important aspects of human society namely: the economic base, represented by the mode of production, and the superstructure of the society and state. These major components of the socio-economic formation inform the character and educational goals of a given country.

Education and the different socio-economic formations

Political economists view human beings as a critical productive force with a pivotal role to play in social, economic, political and cultural transformation. In order for people to play this critical role, they must possess the necessary knowledge, skills and attitudes. This is one of the factors that make education a central institution in sustaining a human society. Viewed from a political economy perspective, education is inextricably linked to the economic, social and political structure of society (Freire 1970, Giroux 1983 and Mayo 1998). It can act as a mechanism for class reproduction and/or a site of resistance and opposition to oppressive socio-political and economic structures. This implies that educational goals, content and related processes reflect the people's goals and interests and as such generate outcomes that perpetuate the values and aspirations of the incumbent society. However, the fact that society is viewed as stratified on a class basis, means that it is the values, interests and aspirations of the dominant class in the community that are perpetuated. The central role of education as a state apparatus is thus to inculcate its citizens with the dominant ideology (Althusser 1971, Gramsci 1977 and Mbilinyi 1977). Education therefore has an 'instrumental' role as a tool in the hands of the state to further its ideological, cultural, economic and political interests. This 'instrumental' role has key implications with regard to educational goals, content, methods and outcomes as illustrated in the case of different adult education programmes in Uganda.

Ugandan socio-economic formations and the character of adult education programmes

In order to understand the character of adult education in Uganda, it is essential to explore the history, politics, social and economic dimensions of Ugandan society. These not only shape the character of national goals, direction, aspirations and ambitions but also the form and ideological orientation of education in general and adult education in particular.

Uganda was colonised from the late nineteenth century for approximately seven decades. Prior to the colonisation, the country was characterised by a diversity of socio-economic, political and cultural systems with varying modes of production. The different societies lived under different pre-capitalist modes of production. In the north, east and north-eastern parts of the country, where communities were organised in smaller units, often clans or families, the ownership of means of production was largely communalist in nature and close to what Eurocentric political economists have referred to as primitive communalism (Nikitin 1985 and Popov 1985). Such communities had less complex socio-political structures and some historians have referred to them as stateless (Karugire 1981, Kiwanuka 1972), due to their decentralised nature and a marked absence of distinct social classes and centralised political structures. Among the more centralised societies of the central, south and western parts of the country, a feudal-like mode of production with some elements of slavery and primitive communalism existed. The differences did not, however, necessarily imply the superiority of one socio-economic formation over the others: all Ugandan pre-colonial societies practised subsistence economies geared towards meeting people's basic needs and not to accumulating wealth in the capitalist sense. Communities living under feudal relations, however, had to pay part of their produce as tribute to the feudal lords. It was mainly this payment of tribute to feudal lords that distinguished the different communities and buttressed the pre-capitalist exploitative feudal relations in some of the pre-colonial societies.

The pre-capitalist modes of production were overtaken by western capitalism after colonisation. The colonial government took deliberate steps to integrate the local economy into the international capitalist economic structures. Such steps included the introduction of coffee and cotton as cash crops needed as raw materials in the rapidly growing European industrial sector and the corresponding market both in Europe and in other overseas colonies. The cash crops did not necessarily have direct relevance to people's daily lives. Money was also introduced, not only as a medium of exchange in local transactions, but also as a tool for compelling people to work for the colonial government or capitalist enterprises which were the only reliable source of the badly needed cash. The integration process also entailed the introduction of legal, political and other socio-economic institutions including education, which played a central role in the deconstruction of pre-colonial socio-economic values and the ultimate inculcation of western capitalist socio-economic and cultural values. The education system was one that responded to the colonial interests: it was intended to make indigenous Ugandans not only easier to govern but also employable in the implementation of the colonial agenda.

The practical result was a distortion of the pre-colonial socio-economic, political and cultural structures. It in essence compelled pre-capitalist peasants, hunters, collectors and gatherers in subsistence economies to produce for an international capitalist market, which they did not control, and to work according to the demands and expectations of the system. People were made to produce crops that had no direct relevance to their day-to-day lives other than meeting the exigencies of the colonial capitalist economic system.

Nevertheless, these changes did not lead to a complete transformation of the pre-capitalist socio-economic formations into pure western capitalism. Instead a new socio-economic formation emerged which represented a distortion and an amalgam of elements of the pre-colonial, colonial and post-colonial political economies. As a result, the Ugandan economy has up to the present been a confused mix of capitalist and pre-capitalist structures, relations and mindsets. Whilst for example, many Ugandans lead a subsistence peasant life, often associated with a communalist lifestyle, their attitudes and orientation is deeply individualistic in some key aspects of life, a major attribute of capitalism and some pre-capitalist modes of production.

Reflections on Uganda's adult education programmes

The view that education is an apparatus of the state, intended to inculcate its ideology and values, is well reflected in the Ugandan adult education and training programmes. The goals of education, the content, methods and outcomes all bear this out. Whilst Ugandan society is practically pre-capitalist, in reality, capitalist values and aspirations reign high among people. This is demonstrated in, among other things, the high degree of aversion to socialist political ideology which emphasises communal values. Such aversion was exhibited in the resistance to the Nakivubo declaration by the UPC government to move 'to the left' (Lubwama 1999) in which Milton Obote proposed governing Uganda along socialist principles.

This aversion to socialism can be associated with the influence of capitalism that began with colonisation and which many Ugandans have continued to view as the right ideology. Capitalist ideology discourages actions that can be interpreted as political, with the potential to lead to radical changes in the character of the prevailing socio-economic formation. Socio-economic problems are thus depoliticised and reduced to technical matters to be addressed by more technical knowledge and skills. Education as a response to socio-economic and political problems is in turn adopted as a technical activity devoid of any political/ideological bias.

The influence of such a perspective on education, educational goals and processes is great. For example, it accords education a more instrumentalist role to 'equip' learners with technical knowledge and skills to perform specific technical tasks or fix problems. This view of education is rooted in the neo-classical educational orientation. This is informed by the technical knowledge-constitutive interest underlying technocratic educational planning, transmittal teaching methods and a hierarchical view of the learner and educator which runs through many of the adult education programmes in Uganda. This technocratic view of education is based on the neo-classical hierarchical view of knowledge and knowing. Here the researcher, the educator, or development worker is seen as endowed with the right knowledge and capacities to conceptualise issues on behalf of learners, research participants or communities with whom they work (Usher et al 1997). It is this assumption that is manifested in many adult education programmes in Uganda including literacy, agricultural extension, community health and others.

The paradox of functional adult education in Uganda
The government-run Functional Adult Literacy programme (FAL), which is currently implemented in more than 75% of the districts, and several other adult education programmes are good examples of the neo-classical, hierarchical view of education.

Adult education programmes in Uganda have, for example, often been developed following an expert-led technocratic centre to periphery model which Popkewitz (1994) refers to as the 'Research, Develop, Disseminate and Adopt' (RDDA). This expert-led model assumes a linear programme development and implementation process and does not allow for ongoing recursion, reflection and review of educational processes. The Functional Adult Literacy programme is a case in point. Approached from the two key angles of political economy and educational theory, it reflects the philosophical and ideological confusion characteristic of a distorted socio-economic formation. This mix-up is manifested in the way contradictory development and educational ideologies coexist and articulate themselves in the programme origins, aims and specific objectives, content, and methodology.

The aims and objectives of the programme reflect three contradictory ideological and theoretical positions. On the one hand, the first two aims of FAL – to 'encourage acquisition of knowledge and attitudes in reading, writing and numeracy, based on the needs and problems of the learners in their community'; and 'to create awareness among learners concerning causes and possible solutions to their problems' (GOU 1996) – are deeply neo-classical, reflecting a predominantly technocratic view of education as a tool to fill-up learners with knowledge, skills and attitudes. On the other hand, although the third, fourth and fifth aims of FA – emphasising active participation in personal and community development; use of a problem-solving approach; and appreciation and enjoyment of the benefits and opportunities acquired through the mastery of literacy skills – appear rooted in the liberal progressive education orientation, the discourse carries clear emancipatory educational overtones.

The objectives display among other things a mix of contradictory educational ideologies in apparent consonance with the distortion and mix in the socio-economic formation mentioned earlier. The neo-classical reduction of education to an instrument for achieving pre-determined goals, itself representing the conservative view of education and change, is surprisingly punctuated by overtones on participation, personal development, appreciation and enjoyment, attributes closely associated with the neo-liberal progressive education ideology. In the same vein, the discourse of participatory problem-identification and solving depict an underlying belief in education as an emancipatory process, a view strongly associated within the critical educational orientation, emphasised by educators using political economy lenses. The scenario demonstrates the levels of theoretical and ideological inconsistency characterising some of the adult education programmes in the country. This is not to imply a polarisation between educational ideologies but rather to highlight that in situations where it is appropriate and necessary to bring together different ideologies within a particular programme, the scenario should represent a synergy and not a contradiction.

In addition to the observations on aims and objectives the programme content reveals that whilst socio-economic and political issues like gender, politics and land, form part of the content of FAL, their centrality in the programme remains doubtful. It is instead the desire to equip learners with technical knowledge and skills in agriculture, animal husbandry, co-operatives, marketing and health promotion that turn out to be the central concerns of FAL. The anomaly is demonstrated further in the overemphasis on transmitting facts and technical knowledge to learners with no serious effort to transform the socio-political and economic dynamics of society, the existing power relations or to level power gradients. These are basic to the socio-economic challenges the programme aims to address.

Apart from gender related issues, other power relations based on class, ethnicity and religion are either glossed over or left out completely. These are important aspects of Ugandan society, which largely constitute the foundation for the perennial conflicts and contradictions that characterise it. Equally important, the programme leaves the colonial legacy intact by failing to address or ignoring issues related to the control over land and other natural resources, which serves to perpetuate the prevailing situation of poverty and deprivation.

The above scenario represents two major gaps in Uganda's adult education programmes including the FAL programme: lack of conceptual/philosophical clarity on the part of those who designed the programmes, and absence of a clear national ideology to guide education and national development.

Challenges of instrumentalist adult education

It is clear from the above discussion that adult education in Uganda is largely instrumentalist. It is also prone to a wide range of problems.

Education viewed as a tool to achieve pre-determined technical goals represents high-level instrumentalism that only serves to perpetuate the ideology of the dominant class, in this case capitalism. Different adult educational programmes in Uganda have manifested this tendency in no subtle terms. This is demonstrated not only through the education/training content but also most vividly through the use of behavioural objective, technology-based training structures, strategies and methods. Babikwa (2003) in a study of community-based educational programmes in rural Uganda noted that the tendency by adult education programmes to state their objectives in behavioural terms leads to undue emphasis on the learning of facts and technical knowledge, supposedly to transform behaviour. The problem with this lies in the inclination to reduce educational processes to a technical activity to achieve a narrow goal, i.e. particularly to change a specific behaviour. This neo-classical approach to education ignores the socio-economic, political and ideological nature of education and in essence treats social situations simplistically. Here, people's problems are viewed from a technical perspective as lack of technical knowledge and skills in production, the right technology and markets, and a result of illiteracy, poverty and ignorance. The responses that emerge are thus technical, seeking to 'fill the gap' or effect a 'quick fix' through technical means while ignoring the complex nature of the problems. In the case of FAL, this is manifested in the desire to equip learners with skills not just in literacy and numeracy, but also with practical skills in health and agriculture.

In the area of agricultural education and extension, educational 'interventions' are often based on the defective assumption that farmers lack the appropriate knowledge, attitudes and skills to do the right thing or practise the correct behaviour. This interpretation of people's problems as technical has far-reaching ideological, methodological and practical implications for adult education. Because it ignores the political dimension of social problems, it indirectly perpetuates the existing socio-economic and political order because it fails to empower programme participants to critically engage the root causes of their problems so as to develop appropriate strategies to address them. In addition, frontline workers in the fields of adult education, agriculture extension, community health and community development operating within this framework are turned into conduits for transferring 'packages' of what government, NGO or CBO programmes view as appropriate skills and knowledge, using transmittal methods in order to achieve the stated programme outcomes (Babikwa 2003, Hilbur 1997). It must be noted that the achievement of such outcomes is largely influenced by the context, which implies that even with all the efforts focused on the ultimate goal, if contextual factors are not attended to, the outcomes may remain a mirage that may never become reality in the project's lifetime.

In educational programmes founded on behavioural goals, failure to change behaviour by learners is derogated as 'resistance to change', rather than as a genuine political action against contradictory class relations, and a contestation of ideological impositions characterising the methods and approaches employed. As a result, poor people are alienated, depicted as unco-operative, uninterested or lazy. Such a view often refers to the resisters as 'laggards, with attitudinal barriers' (Pretty 1995:188). This scenario is rife in a number of community-based/adult education and related programmes in Uganda. However, as Babikwa (2003) observes, farmers' failure to adopt new farming practices is not necessarily an indication of personal and collective weakness on part of the farmers. Such behaviour is, more often than not, a sign of resistance to the technocratic training practices, the capitalist development ideology and the associated belief in growth and modernisation as the way to economic development.

Ideologically, many adult education programmes in Uganda are influenced by capitalism, the dominant economic ideology. Many of these programmes, including functional adult literacy, are based on neo-liberal and conservative economic principles. Such principles involve among other things, overemphasis on economic goals with minimal concern for the socio-political and ideological aspects of society, an obsession with meeting people's basic needs and addressing problems instead of looking at the strategic needs and the systemic causes of these problems. The new trend in agricultural education, for example, emphasises training in farming as a business, including agribusiness and farm business education (see MAAIF 2001). Plausible as this may sound, particularly in Uganda's poverty stricken subsistence economy, it largely ignores the socio-economic dynamics of production. For instance, issues of access to land, the major means of production, and the socio-cultural and gender dynamics of production do not receive adequate attention in the training programmes. In the area of adult literacy, the idea of functionality only seems to serve the interests of the established socio-economic order, largely influenced by international neo-liberal economic demands.

Technology-based training structures, strategies and methods

The structure of the training in different adult education programmes in Uganda exhibits the neo-classical notion of a separation between theory and practice (Higgs, 1998). This assumes that theory is superior to practice and should therefore come first. This attitude has quietly but effectively influenced the way adult educators organise and approach training activities. The character of community-based adult education and training programmes in Uganda reveals that many such programmes structure their activities into distinct segments of 'theory and practice'. Information and facts about the subject characterises the theory part, with the practical part focusing on field demonstrations. This is evident not only in agriculture, where extension workers often teach theory to farmers before transferring action to the field in the form of demonstrations, but also in Functional Adult Literacy.

The theory is often taught at the beginning of the training workshops/seminars in school-like educational settings, obviously based on a neoclassical assumption that good learning takes place when theory precedes practice (Kemmis and Carr 1986). The underlying assumption is that, equipped with the right theory, learners will find it easy to translate learning into action. Learners are thus made to demonstrate what they have learnt theoretically, on the assumption that demonstration will equip them with the necessary experience and capacity to implement the practices on their farms.

This erroneous approach undermines the capacity of adult education programme's to lead to concrete sustainable results. Whilst work on the demonstrations is practical, the method employed is transmittal, 'showing and telling' the farmers what to do, without engaging them in a way that makes them critical and co-constructive co-participants (Lotz and Ward 2000). Demonstration as a training method/approach does not nurture a participatory spirit and, practical as it appears, it remains an autocratic didactic method. The learner can accomplish the process without becoming empowered to become an independent actor, as he/she merely follows what the trainer/educator does. When the educator is not there to follow, the learner may be rendered powerless.

At the same time, demonstration as a method and the accompanying assumptions about the importance of technique makes adult educators believe that they have to become experts, able to provide all answers to all questions (Babikwa 2003). This is one of the ways in which neoclassical educational practices give educators a false sense of power, while at the same time disempowering their learners. This orientation elevates educators as the sole possessors of knowledge and undermines the emancipatory intent associated with collective 'active-meaning-making', as the flow of learning becomes largely a one-way process. This has key implications for adult education in a community context. It perpetuates a sense of false confidence among facilitators that prevents reciprocal learning between them and learners, while at the same time undermining learners' confidence (Freire 1970). These training structures and strategies thus not only create dependent learners and technocratic educators but also perpetuate the traditional hierarchical social relations between learners and educators that lead to increased social differentiation.

The foregoing discussion represents some of the key contradictions characterising adult education programmes in Uganda. The neo-classical orientation dominates, even in programmes that are in principle motivated by critical emancipatory intentions. The neo-classical view of education as a technical process contradicts the basic tenets of political economy of education, which emphasise the socio-political emancipatory role of education in society. The use of transmittal training methods, often applied in service of a critical emancipatory intent, exposes the contradictions underlying these programmes and compels one to wonder how strong the emancipatory intent of the programme really is.

Such contradictions in methodology and approaches can be associated with the traditional approach to schooling in Uganda which represents deeper ideological, socio-economic, cultural and historical tensions, at the macro and micro levels. At the macro level, Uganda has been part of the international political economy for more than a century. The country was under direct colonial tutelage and has been for almost half a century under neo-colonial dependent regimes that have maintained the colonial autocratic, ideological, political and socio-economic structures, including the neoclassical educational orientation.

At the micro level, the politically and economically motivated post-colonial conflicts and wars have led to successive back and forth shifts in national goals and intentions, including education. There is no evidence of any serious deliberate efforts to decolonise the state structures, institutions and associated mindsets. The successive post-colonial governments have, for example, maintained the same educational values and approaches. Whilst it is true that the last fifteen years of the twentieth century saw a semblance of some deliberate intentions by the NRM government to change the status quo in education and other socio-economic structures into more emancipatory configurations (GOU 1992, GOU 1995), the political, social and ideological contradictions of the past have continued to be manifest in the inconsistencies characteristic of the educational disposition. This echoes the critical emancipatory contention that education is a product and a reflection of the socio-economic and ideological context of the society in question (Carr and Kemmis 1986, Giroux 1983, Youngman 1986).

Conclusion

It can therefore be concluded that the character of adult education programmes in Uganda is strongly influenced by neo-classical and neo-liberal capitalist socio-economic and political values. Such values have influenced the conceptualisation of adult education as a technical tool in the service of capitalist aspirations at the micro and macro levels. This pursuit of capitalist/economic ambitions with partial or total disregard of the socio-political and ideological forces within Ugandan society has played a central role in undermining the emancipatory goals of adult education, which include social action for political empowerment and transformation.

Unless adult education programmes in Uganda focus beyond neo-liberal economic goals and incorporate a genuine transformative agenda to change the dominant socio-economic, political and ideological mindsets, adult education will not be able to lead or spearhead the achievement of the national goals of socio-economic and political empowerment, poverty eradication and sustainable development.

4
Government Policy and Strategies for Adult Education in Uganda

Demetrius K. Obbo

Introduction
This chapter examines government policy and strategy for adult education in Uganda. Firstly, it presents a definition of government policy and how it is used interchangeably with government plans and strategies. Secondly, it examines the government White Paper on adult education and other policies that are relevant to adult education. Finally, it suggests future action by government and other stakeholders to promote adult education in Uganda.

The concept of policy
The concept policy is very important in development circles. This is particularly true among senior government officials and chief executives of organisations and other groups where top leadership is concerned with providing guidelines for the implementation of activities. The concept also occupies considerable space in institutions of higher learning. As a result, there is much debate as to what constitutes a policy from practical and educational levels.

In this chapter, a policy refers to a set of guidelines which determine and underline the way individuals or groups of people think and behave in a certain social, cultural, economic and political environment (Commonwealth Secretariat 1998: 3). It is an agreed position or a course of action to be followed by a government, an organisation or a party of any kind. A policy is therefore a practical acknowledgement that the people or objects for which the policy is made form a significant proportion of a national population or the target object. The policy can provide a supportive and informative environment for its target.

In the Ugandan situation, the concept of policy has been used interchangeably with other concepts such as plans and strategies. For example, many government officials may refer to government plan documents or documents containing strategies as the 'policy of government'. This is not totally wrong, because plans and strategies are key ingredients of any policy; but by themselves they do not constitute policy.

A plan is a scheme that intends to translate a given policy into action. A plan document will therefore contain a number of programmes and projects that will be implemented over a given period of time. For example, in Uganda, the Poverty Eradication Action Plan (PEAP) has four major programme areas, which are generally referred to as PEAP pillars:
1. Rapid and sustainable economic growth and structural transformation
2. Good governance and security
3. Increased ability to the poor to raise their incomes
4. Enhanced quality of life of the poor (MGLSD 2002 p.vii).

In this respect, therefore, a plan is carrying out a government policy because it consists of major courses of action in the programmes and projects that are expected to transform society.

Strategies are a major feature of a policy but again, they are not the policy itself. In this chapter, strategy is used not only to refer to the tactics of efficiently applying techniques and methods of implementing programmes, but more importantly to the rules, regulations, procedures and objectives that shape services and programmes. A strategy, therefore, contains different activities for different groups of actors. It contains specific approaches that are best suited to address a given problem of the target group. It also states how long each programme will operate, where it will be offered and which methods of evaluation will be used to assess it.

A policy, especially a government policy, is therefore actually a basis and framework for its strategies and plans. It is a manifestation of the political will, commitment and direction of the nation. It addresses the major concerns and issues that are crucial to the different areas of action. An action plan is developed from the policy. Strategies may also be developed indicating how specific programmes for different population targets may be implemented.

The national policy on adult education

The clearest policy statement on adult education in an official government document was in the White Paper on Education adopted by the National Resistance Council (then the Parliament) in 1992. Another document that gives some clear guidelines is the 2001 National Adult Literacy Strategic Investment Plan (NALSIP).

White Paper on Education 1992
According to the Government White Paper, there are at least five target groups for adult education:
- Young people who have never been to school.
- Primary school drop-outs, rural peasants, urban workers and other unskilled persons who should be given basic functional literacy.
- Primary school leavers who need apprenticeship or vocational training to make them employable and self-reliant.
- The population as a whole, to give awareness education through the mass media, newspapers, radio, television, co-operative and trade union activities and any other activities including drama
- Working men and women who require varied opportunities for continuing education to improve their skills and elevate their professional and academic standards for upward mobility in their places of work (MOES 1992: 15).

These five categories, in that order of priority, are the main targets for non-formal and adult education in Uganda. In the process of democratising of education proposed in the White Paper, these groups should have access to basic education so that they can aquire a minimum level of learning, knowledge, skills and values. This would enable everyone to realise their potential and to contribute constructively towards local, community and national development.

The strategy for achieving this is through the eradication of illiteracy; organising post-literacy and permanent functional literacy; providing livelihood skills and apprenticeship; providing continuing education for those holding Uganda Certificate of Education and Uganda Advanced Certificate of Education; and health care.

In order to achieve this objective, the government has identified the following strategic programmes:
1. Eradication of illiteracy through the National Council for Non-formal and Adult Education, National Teachers' Colleges, Primary Teachers' Colleges, National Curriculum Development Centre and national literacy campaigns.
2. Post-literacy adult education to provide organised systematic learning opportunities for adults. This will enable them acquire varieties of modern productive skills and techniques. The strategy for this is to set up a national council for non-formal and adult education with district committees to work with local communities. A directorate of non-formal and adult education will be set up within the Ministry of Education to, among other things, liase with the national council and the national campaign for literacy and basic education.
3. Apprenticeship education for the youth to provide livelihood skills to school drop-outs. The strategy for achieving this is to work through community polytechnics and other vocational training centres that will make local communities and local councils centres of implementation and mobilisation of resources.
4. Continuing and life-long education to provide improved educational opportunities for meeting the learning needs of school leavers, drop-outs and adults in the world of work. The strategy for achieving this is to enable Uganda National Examination Board to revise its regulations and conduct appropriate examinations.
5. Distance education through radio, television, the internet and rural press. The strategy for this is to set up radio and television channels and internet facilities, as well as training staff specially for education programmes (MOES 1992: 176-185).

This summary of the Uganda government policy and strategies for adult education raises a number of fundamental questions. First, what issues really form the core of adult education and have these issues been adequately identified and analysed? A look at the White Paper shows that relevant issues were identified and analysed through the

Education Policy Review Commission during the late 1980s. One of these issues was the inability of the existing education system to provide relevant knowledge and information for productive life to the citizens. Other issues included the inability of poor and vulnerable groups to demand for services. These issues have also been identified in the development of the national literacy strategic plan.

Secondly, what was the major focus of adult education in Uganda in the late 1980s? Is adult education today still focusing on those issues or on poverty eradication, which is the overriding goal of the government of Uganda today? Since the late 1980s, poverty has been the major issue affecting the population and it is interesting to note that poverty eradication is the centre of focus for adult education.

Thirdly, how is the policy being implemented? Many different organisations are involved in implementing different strategies of the adult education policy, including non-governmental and religious organisations. Some of these, namely, the Church of Uganda, the Catholic Church, the Young Men's Christian Association, the Young Women's Christian Association and the Uganda Moslem Supreme Council have adult education programmes with specific strategies. However, these activities are not effectively co-ordinated without a national council for non-formal and adult education being in place. There have been reports of confusions in terms of duplication of efforts. A good example is the implementation of educational programmes for the girl child.

National Adult Literacy Strategic Investment Plan 2002
The National Adult Literacy Strategic Investment Plan 2002/03-2006/ 07 (NALSIP) was developed to achieve a 50% improvement in literacy levels between 2002 and 2007. The plan seeks to contribute to the making of 'a literate, well informed and prosperous society' in line with the national vision 2025 (MGLSD 2002 p. viii). NALSIP was designed as part of the Poverty Eradication Action Plan, to make a substantial contribution to the four pillars.

The strategic objectives of the plan are:
1. To strengthen national commitment to the programme and incorporate district, sub-county and community level adult

literacy action into overall development frameworks.
2. To provide adequate and equitable access to literacy education to all women and men.
3. To empower the marginalised and vulnerable groups in society through functional adult literacy to participate fully as equal partners in development programmes.
4. To establish a sustainable management framework that will provide direction to the programme for effective performance.
5. To improve the capacity of literacy educators for the Adult Literacy Programme.
6. To improve the quality of learning in the literacy programme through better delivery systems.
7. To establish an effective and sustainable research programme for systematic research-development-diffusion process in all aspects of NALSIP.
8. To provide an effective framework for the collection, documentation, sharing and utilisation of information pertaining to all aspects of the Adult Literacy Programme.
9. To mobilise additional resources for the sustainability of the Adult Literacy Programme and quality implementation of its activities (MGLSD, 2002 p.v).

To achieve those objectives, the plan was designed to venture into the following new areas:
1. Providing information, communication and advocacy to enhance national commitment and incorporate district, sub-county and community level adult literacy action plans into overall development planning.
2. Developing a national accreditation framework.
3. Enhancing access to literacy services for people with special learning needs.
4. Establishing community/village libraries to promote a literate environment for the neo-literates.
5. Research and Programme Development.
6. Building a monitoring and evaluation system to create 'a culture of information'. (MGLSD, 2002 p.v).

The plan was designed to increase access to adult literacy education through a phased expansion at an annual diminishing rate of 100%

between FY 2002-2003; 75% between FY 2003-2004; 50% between FY 2004-2005; 25% between FY 2005-2006 and 10% between FY 2006-2007. A total of 3,500,000 adult literacy learners were to be reached through 180-216 literacy contact hours per learner.

A Social Development Sector Strategic Investment Plan developed shortly afterwards, realised that the target set in the NALSIP was too high and lowered it to about one-third of the above. In view of the financial and other implementation constraints being experienced, this new target may indeed be more realistic. UNESCO in fact estimates that Uganda will not have reduced its adult illiteracy rate by 50% even by the year 2015, the target adopted for all countries in the Dakar Framework for Action 2000.

Other policies relevant to adult education

In Uganda, different ministries and agencies provide adult education, without a co-ordinating mechanism or focus. The policies and strategies or plans of the different sectors therefore have elements of policy that are relevant to adult education, even when they are not specifically referred to in those terms. This section briefly reviews some of them.

The Poverty Eradication Action Plan (PEAP)

Uganda's Poverty Eradication Action Plan (PEAP) is the equivalent of the Poverty Reduction Strategic Paper (PRSP) developed in other countries. It is Uganda's national planning framework for the struggle against poverty. Launched in 1997, 'It provides overall goals for government policy and programmes. It establishes principles to guide investment plans and the management of the economy' (MFPED 2002: 4). PEAP sets out a framework for tackling the complex causes and dimensions of poverty (see p.xx). Fifteen strategies were developed for achieving the objectives.

The fact that NALSIP was developed as a contributing activity to the four PEAP pillars shows that government considers adult education relevant to poverty eradication. This has made it possible for adult literacy programmes to have access to the privileged Poverty Action Fund, a fund that, unlike funds from some other sources, cannot be diverted to other purposes.

The Plan for Modernisation of Agriculture (PMA)

Over 80% of Uganda's population is directly involved in and derive their livelihood from agricultural production. Improvement in agricultural production and productivity is therefore a top priority both with the people and the government. The main target beneficiaries of PMA interventions are therefore the subsistence farmers who constitute the majority of the poor in rural areas.

The Plan for Modernisation of Agriculture seeks to transform agricultural production for greater productivity and to re-orient subsistence farmers from producing predominantly for household consumption to producing for the market. Poverty eradication through agricultural transformation and sustainable natural resource-based livelihood is the overall goal of PMA. It sets out to achieve the following objectives:

- To increase incomes and improve the quality of life of poor subsistence farmers through increased productivity and increased share of market production.
- To improve household food security through the market rather than emphasising self sufficiency.
- To provide gainful employment through the secondary benefits of PMA implementation such as agro-processing factories and services.
- To promote sustainable use and management of natural resources by developing a land use and management policy and promotion of environmentally friendly technologies.

The strategies that were developed to achieve those objectives include: supporting the dissemination and adoption of productivity enhancing technologies; ensuring that all intervention programmes are gender focused and gender responsive; and promoting a two-way (bottom-up and top-down) planning and budgeting process by empowering local governments and enabling them to influence public policy and allocate public resources to alleviate local-specific constraints in a non-sectoral manner.

It can be seen from this that the success of the PMA objectives and strategies will largely depend upon some form of adult education. In order to transform their farming culture and adopt technologies that will enhance productivity, the majority of farmers need new practical knowledge. Ensuring gender focused and gender responsive intervention programmes also requires changes that will come mainly through education. The promotion of a two-way planning and budgeting process also requires local government officers to acquire appropriate skills. Under PMA, education is provided through extension education. The link between this and adult education has recently been confirmed by the introduction of courses in adult education methodology as part of the degree programme in Agricultural Extension Education at Makerere University.

National Health Policy
The overall goal of health sector policy is the attainment of a good standard of health by all people in Uganda in order to promote a healthy and productive life. In order to achieve this, the policy aims to reduce the incidence of disease, to monitor and control fertility and to the reduce the disparities that exist in these between different regions of the country. It also aims at ensuring access to a minimum health care package. The strategies adopted to achieve the policy objectives include health education through various channels: these are mainly forms of adult education.

The health policy's strategic plan has guidelines that are disseminated all over the country through the fast growing FM radio network.

The health care programmes involving health education and promotion have an element of adult education. For example, adult education methods are relevant in promoting safe motherhood through the mother-baby training package, equipping and integrating traditional birth attendants, promoting responsible sexual and reproductive behaviour and the use of the reproductive health service by men and women.

The Ministry of Health and its several agencies such as the AIDS control programme have also utilised the media to promote health education by relaying critical messages that create awareness on the dangers of diseases such as HIV/AIDS and cholera. According to the Uganda AIDS Commission, the impact of the HIV/AIDS epidemic in Uganda has gone beyond the health status of the people. As a result, the government decided to adopt the Multi-Sectoral AIDS Control Strategy. This strategy requires all sectors of society to be actively involved in the fight against HIV infection and care of the people affected, either directly or indirectly. Here, adult education has a major role to play.

The National Gender Policy
The overall goal of the national gender policy is to mainstream gender concerns in the national development process in order to improve the social, legal, civic, political, economic and cultural conditions of the people in Uganda, in particular women.

'It seeks to guide and direct the planning, resource allocation and implementation levels with a gender perspective' (MGLSD, 1999: 2).

The policy has the following specific objectives:
- To provide policy makers and other key actors with reference guidelines for identifying and addressing gender concerns when taking development policy decisions.
- To identify and establish an institutional framework with the mandate to initiate, co-ordinate, implement, monitor and evaluate national gender responsive development plans.
- To redress imbalances that arise from existing gender inequalities to ensure the participation of both women and men in all stages of the development process.
- To promote equal access to control over economically significant resources and benefits.
- To promote recognition of the value of women's roles and their contributions as agents of change and beneficiaries of the development process (MGLSD 1999: 5).

The strategies adopted to achieve the policy objectives include some that are very relevant to adult education:
1. Sensitisation on gender issues at all levels.
2. Promoting a Gender and Development (GAD) approach, based on the understanding of gender roles and social relations of women and men, and the Women in Development (WID) approach that focuses on women specifically.

3. Ensuring that the gender policy will be disseminated, translated, understood and implemented by all sections of Uganda society.
4. Promoting appropriate education, sensitisation and creation of awareness of the responsibility of all concerned parties in each sector to address specific gender concerns between the sectors. This should entail consultation on areas of relevance to identification of gender concerns.

(MGLSD 1999: 6)

Obviously, those strategies make the policy very dependent on adult education for its implementation.

The National Youth Policy

The mission of the national youth policy is empowerment of people between 12 and 30 years of age. The policy's goal is to provide an appropriate framework for enabling youth to develop social, economic, cultural and political skills so as to enhance their participation in the overall development process and improve their quality of life. The goal is to be fulfilled through the following objectives:

- To initiate, strengthen and streamline all programmes and services targeting the youth.
- To promote social and economic empowerment of the youth.
- To build capacity and provide relevant training and information to stakeholders (MGLSD 2001: 20).

The strategies through which the objectives are to be realised are: respect of cultural, religious and ethical values; equality and accessibility; gender inclusiveness; good governance and national unity; youth participation, and teamwork and partnership (MGLSD 2001: 16-17).

All these strategies make use of adult education methods since the primary target for these programmes are the youth who are largely out of school, many of them illiterate, and many living in rural areas. The best way to reach them is through non-formal and adult education, for example through youth meetings and workshops. Other forums are youth groups, associations, organisations or projects specifically designed for young people. Adult education is obviously very relevant for the implementation of this policy.

The Education Strategic Investment Plan
This plan supports the overall government policy on education. Its focus is on formal education with special attention given to assuring universal access to primary education (UPE), increasing enrolment ratios and transition rates, improving attendance and making instructional time more effective. The only areas in the plan where adult education is talked about are the setting up of vocational training institutions and community polytechnics to provide multi-skills training opportunities for primary school leavers.

National Strategy for Girls' Education Uganda
The goal of the strategy for girls' education is:

> All girls in Uganda (including the destitute and girls with disabilities) will have full access to education opportunities and will be supported by their families, schools, communities, government and the private sector to participate fully in gender-balanced education programmes in order to attain their maximum potential as equal and effective citizens. (MOES 1998).

The strategy identifies two major reasons for intensifying girl education in Uganda. The first is that the girl-child in Uganda is entitled to equal access to education as a human right. The second is that the educated girl-child is a lynchpin in the development of any nation. To make this strategy effective, the socio-psychological environment should be conducive to the full participation of all girls in education.

The strategy addresses different barriers to equitable female participation in education, barriers which have been identified in both international and national forums on girls' education. They are categorised as:

- Socio-cultural factors, which give seven barriers: patriarchal culture; harmful traditional practices; traditional division of labour in the home; family instability; some religious beliefs; an insecure environment in and outside schools; and differential motivational scope.

- School-related factors, which give five barriers: inadequate school facilities including lack of comfortable appropriate clothing; inappropriate or inadequate school and college personnel; the absence of trained guidance and counselling personnel; a shortage of relevant alternative quality education opportunities and facilities; and a critical bottleneck to female access to secondary and higher education.
- Political/economic/administrative factors, which also give five barriers: insensitivity to the importance of girls education by the general public; inadequate allocation for resources at all levels to respond to the needs of girls' education; insufficient protection of the girl-child by, e.g. laws on defilement; unavailability of and lack of access to gender disaggregated data and information; and constraints from poverty on choices available to parents.

The Ministry of Education and Sports is the main government agency responsible for the implementation of this strategy. However, there are also numerous partners who work to complement its efforts. Their activities are listed in the strategy document according to the category of barriers each addresses. Thus, 20 partners address socio-cultural factors, 55 address school-related factors and 51 address political/economic/administrative factors.

Clearly, the strategy for implementing the policy on girl-child education cannot be successful without adult education and many of those involved in making it effective rely on the structures of adult education, for example by organising sensitisation workshops on the subject.

An assessment of government strategy for adult education

The lack of a coherent policy on adult education in Uganda is to some extent due to the way adult education is practised. Different government ministries and agencies provide different aspects of adult education, often in an isolated manner without reference to one another's work. There have been a number of calls for the government to set up a co-ordinating structure to promote networking and efficient utilisation of the country's limited resources. It is as a result of such calls that the 1992 White Paper on Education adopted the setting up of an autonomous National Council for Adult and Non-Formal Education as well as a Ministry of Education Directorate of Adult and Non-Formal Education.

These provisions hit an immediate snag because the Ministry that had all along been responsible for adult education was the one in charge of Community Development, not the Ministry of Education. A struggle ensued between the two ministries and has continued until the time of writing. Neither the Directorate of Adult and Non-Formal Education in the Ministry of Education and Sports nor the autonomous Council is yet in place, although of late the Ministry of Education has taken measures to set up the Directorate.

In the Ministry of Gender, Labour and Social Development, where adult education is officially housed, adult education has very little visibility. There is not even a department in charge of adult education. (A department is one of several sub-divisions of a directorate.) There is only a small unit of four administrative officers taking care of the national functional adult literacy programme. There is as a result practically no reference to adult education in this ministry.

There are, however, a significant number of activities that could be seen as adult education in various other government ministries, as exemplified by the brief review of various policies and strategies above. A major concern is that this scattered practice, without any point of reference, has left adult education open to unprofessional ad hoc practice that does not ensure quality and maximum effectiveness. This has raised the issue of the professional development of adult education, discussed in Chapter 7. The existence of government institutions providing professional training in adult education may be a good sign for its future.

Apart from government ministries, agencies and institutions, a significant number of non-governmental organisations are involved in various forms of adult education. Government practice is to let such organisations operate with a large amount of freedom and to actively encourage them to work as partners of government. In certain sectors, especially health and agriculture and even formal education, clear guidelines have been laid down to facilitate this partnership. This is not so clear in adult education, although NALSIP has some vague general statements about such collaboration. Civil society organisations involved in adult education have been calling for this deficiency to be rectified.

Government strategy for adult education has to a great extent been characterised by inadequate commitment. Even in the mother ministry, it sometimes does not have a clear budget-line. When there is a budget-line, it is often the most vulnerable to budget cuts. Only the NALSIP budget, financed under the Poverty Action Fund, has for the last two years been safe from such cuts. The lack of commitment is equally manifest in the local governments, which have a key role to play under the current decentralised system. Some of these have never had a budget-line for adult education or only one for adult literacy under the NALSIP.

Conclusion: the future of government policy and strategy for adult education

The position of government policy and strategy for adult education described here shows that much remains to be done. Adult education is accorded a low profile in comparison to formal or school education. Although some provisions for promoting development of adult education were enshrined in the 1992 education policy White Paper, strategies to implement them have not been fully put in place. Although the directorate and different departments responsible for primary and secondary education are fully funded and facilitated, neither the National Council for Adult Education nor the Directorate of Adult Education has been established.

It seems that it is not adequate for elements of adult education policy to be hidden away in an education policy whose main focus is on formal education and in other sector policies. The different elements of an adult education policy need to be brought together in a comprehensive policy document that can be negotiated with the different actors for final adoption. The development of such a policy will clearly define the place and role of adult education in society and the responsibility of society towards adult education. It will also consider the problems, needs and aspirations of adult education comprehensively and promote the establishment of appropriate structures and institutions to meet them. Finally, it will encourage the beneficiaries of adult education to participate actively at all levels of national life.

If adult education is to prosper there is a need for serious action among the sympathisers of adult education. First of all, a case for adult education needs to be developed. Youths and adults who are actually the main players in both economic and social development of Uganda now need the knowledge and skills to increase their levels of productivity. So government must realise that increased spending on adult education is just as necessary as it is for primary and secondary education.

The role of informing government is squarely in the hands of lobbyists and advocates. All stakeholders in the adult education arena should come together to present their case. One way could be to prepare a draft policy and strategies for adult education in Uganda. The process would involve first a comprehensive review of existing government policy and strategies related to adult education. It would also consist of reviewing other government policies, plans and strategies that have an effect on adult education. Finally, it would consist of reviewing policies of other countries and international agencies towards adult education. The process should, as much as possible, be participatory, consultative and inclusive of all stakeholders at all levels.

The prospects for action seem to be good because, at the time of writing this chapter, various stakeholders have started working together towards the development of just such a consolidated policy.

5
The Role of the Civil Society in shaping Adult Education Practices in Uganda

George L Openjuru

Introduction
Civil society organisations (CSOs) have played and continue to play a great role in educating adults in Uganda. This chapter reviews their role in shaping the country's adult education practices. Beginning with definitions of civil society and adult education, it covers the activities of faith-based organisations, international and national non-governmental organisations (NGOs), and co-operatives.

The concept of civil society
As with the term 'adult education' civil society means different things to different people in different places. According to Fowler (1996: 19), society can be divided into three sectors. The state is the first sector, and the profit-making organisations (businesses) the second. Fowler wrote: 'According to the management science definition, civil society, which functions within the voluntary sector, is the third sector and its role is to pursue personal or social interest, beliefs and concerns.'

Fowler explained that civic organisations have the responsibility to reform or change the way society works or to alter the way its costs and benefits are distributed.

Alfred Stephan (1988, cited in Nyang'oro 1993: 55) looked at civil society as 'an arena where manifold social movement – and civic organisations from all classes – attempt to constitute themselves in ensemble of an arrangement to express themselves and protect their interests'. Chzan (1992, cited in Nyang'oro 1993: 56) defined civil society as 'an organisation which is distinct from the society ... but it is that segment of the society that interacts with the state.' The implication of this definition is that a civil society organisation is one that has a connection to or interacts with the state while maintaining its independence. In this relationship with the state, civil society organisations must not have the intention of replacing the state.

This definition excludes political parties, whose missions are to replace the state. Any organisation which does not interact with the state is also excluded. This could disqualify those civil society organisations, which, because of the nature of some African governments, have decided to leave the state alone. Most NGOs operating in Africa and in Uganda in particular have very little interaction with the state, taking as their main concern the development of the community they are serving. All they need from the state is registration, which gives them the authority to work. On the other hand, by registering them, the state gets what it needs from them – the right to regulate their activities.

From these definitions, the following general characteristics of CSOs can be identified:
- They are a social space with a range of cultural, political, economic, and other dimensions.
- They are different from the state sector, and find their relevance in a kind of antithetic relationship with the state.
- They are fundamentally an associational domain. That is, they function through organised collective expression.
- They require an enabling context to exist and function fully, but do not necessarily need approval from the state, as this is not a precondition for the existence of a civil society.
- They exist as a medium of communication between the state and the people in respect of public policy and public policy options, and social values.
- They serve as moral reference points in community value systems.

The most outstanding factor in this definition is that civil society organisations are non-state organisations, which interact with the state as a voice for the voiceless. In this chapter, civil society organisations refers to all non-state, non-market (not for profit or business organisation) and non-political voluntary organisations working in Uganda.

What is adult education?
According to the Hamburg Declaration on Adult Education, 1997:

> Adult education denotes the entire body of ongoing learning processes, formal or otherwise, whereby persons regarded as adult by the society to which they belong develop their abilities, enrich their knowledge and improve their technical or professional qualifications or turn them in a new direction to meet their own needs and those of their society. Adult learning encompasses both formal and continuing education, non-formal learning and the spectrum of informal and incidental learning available in a multicultural learning society, where theory- and practice-based approaches are recognized. (UNESCO, 1997b: 1).

So, in this chapter, adult education refers to all forms of education offered to a person considered an adult in Uganda. This definition is also used to identify the activities of the CSOs engaged in adult education in Uganda.

Civil society organisations in adult education in Uganda
In Uganda, with the exception of adult literacy education, government is not seriously involved in adult education. This gap has always been filled by CSOs, who have for long taken over this responsibility.

CSOs started participating actively in adult education right from the time the missionaries set foot in Uganda, before a colonial administration was established. Both adult education and civil society in pre-colonial traditional African society require very different definitions from those we use today. Education took the form of lifelong learning with no clear distinction between adults and children and civil society as defined above did not exist because it is defined in relation to the modern state. In the absence of a modern state, civil society is a foreign concept of western civilisation. The role of civil society in shaping adult education in Uganda can therefore only be evaluated from the time a colonial administration was established.

Since then, many NGOs, both national and international, have played an important role in educating adults. In 1984, Okech compiled a directory of 79 governmental and non-governmental organisations involved in adult education. Most of these, with the exception of government institutions, qualify as CSOs under the definition used here. The activities listed in this directory included all forms of education organised for adults outside the formal school systems, that is, 'training and short courses not of a full time nature' (Okech, 1984: 6). Under our definition, these qualify to be referred to as adult education.

Although there are now many organisations involved in educating adults, very few admit that they are doing adult education work because they do not really know what constitutes adult education. They only know about training or extension and community development work. Kwesiga noted this when he said, 'a worker in an organisation related to primary health care, agriculture, trade union, co-operative, etc. blinks if you call him brother in adult education' (Okech, 1984: 2). The few who do admit to doing adult education work, are those dealing with adult literacy education. This is because of the widely held view that adult education is only concerned with adult literacy. In addition to failing to realise they are doing adult education work, those involved often have no professional training in teaching adults, which means that they are not doing their work correctly. Some only have a few weeks' training in facilitation or training of trainers' skills. The rest just gamble.

Religious institutions

Religious organisations, now popularly referred to as faith-based organisations, were the first CSOs to offer learning opportunities to adults in Uganda. The Christian missionaries, both Catholic and Protestant, are particularly credited with introducing social services, including health, education, and community services. In education, they also taught adults, making them the pioneers of adult education work.

The missionaries started by teaching adults how to read and write (literacy). They later extended their teaching to vocational and leadership training. The purpose of teaching literacy was to enable the new faithful to be able to read bibles and prayer books on their own. The literacy classes were referred to as reading classes. The adult learners were taught how to read and write using the rote methods of singing and learning by heart phrases in the bible and prayer books. In the long run, people did actually learn to read. The missionaries produced printed material in local languages to teach literacy and to help the newly literate to consolidate their reading and writing skills more easily.

The vocational skills training included carpentry and joinery, brick-making, blacksmithing, and many other skills. The missionaries taught adults how to build houses using bricks. Leadership training was meant to introduce new social skills that could be used to improve the life of the new converts and to enable these converts to take up leadership roles and responsibilities in the church. The church offered training for its lay workers to prepare them for service in the church as catechists and bible teachers. These then taught their fellow adults facts of the new faith and how to read and write. They also had the responsibility for making new converts and building the faith of the old converts. In this respect, they became the pioneer teachers of adults in Uganda. Okech (1984: 70) said that, the aim of Christian missionaries' educational programmes was 'to develop the whole person morally, intellectually, and physically', a view of education that draws largely from the liberal/humanist philosophy of adult education (Elias and Merriam, 1980).

The teaching of adult literacy by Christian missionaries had a great impact on adult education in Uganda. The church never referred to their training programmes for adults as adult education, just as today most organisations involved in community livelihood skills training do not consider these as adult and community education unless they involve adult literacy. The church still continues to refer to its non-literacy education as community development work and not adult education work. This is in spite of the fact that the main strategy used in so-called community development work is actually through educating adults in the community.

The danger of this limited view of adult education as literacy work alone is that it makes it seem as if there is no professional requirement to perform any other form of adult and community education activities. This has certainly contributed to the marginalisation of adult education in Uganda.

The Christian churches did not explicitly promote adult education because this was not their primary concern. Nonetheless, they were the torchbearers of adult education activities in Uganda, because their educational activities were first targeted at adults and because they continued to offer vocational training programmes for youth and women who were considered adults. This was also at a time when there were no other organisations offering educational programmes and opportunities for adults who had dropped out of the formal school system. The church or church-based and church- related organisations such as the Mothers' Union, the Young Men's, and Women's Christian Organisations, have also played and continue to play a very active role in educating adults in Uganda. Participants were mostly selected through the church systems and classes were organised within the church facilities. Some of these educational activities were done as part of the church community services activities.

The influence of the church on adult education practices

The influence of the Christian churches can be seen in two ways. Firstly, they kept the need for organised learning programmes for adults alive in this country and it remains the biggest champion in initiating educational programmes for adults. Secondly, the Christian churches promoted a concept of education for development that is now very prominent in adult education thinking in Uganda. One of the church's educational aims was the 'development of the whole person to fight against ignorance, poverty, and disease'(Okech 1984: 73). What has been added to this idea of adult education for development is the concept of a participatory approach.

The church funded most of the adult education programmes they were offering to the people of Uganda and for most of the programmes, participants were not expected to pay fees. This set a tradition that regards adult education as a free service for the beneficiaries, a service for which they don't have to pay money. Instead, they come expecting to be paid for their participation in terms of transport refunds and allowances. This is still the practice of most NGOs who are active in adult and community education in Uganda and has been made possible through sources of finances that are very similar to those of the church. While the church used church collections and donations from abroad, the NGOs use financial aid from donors. The effect of this culture is that adult education activities such as community education become difficult to undertake without external funding.

The church focused adult education programmes on the less privileged of society, when formal school education was being given to the children of chiefs and kings. School education emphasised the betterment of the individual as a person and not as a unit of production required to improve economic productivity or stimulate economic growth and development. Church adult education aimed, and still aims at a broader target, the betterment of the individual, household, and community. This view of adult education as a tool for improving the livelihood of the community members made adult education become largely a rural-based community development activity.

Another significant contribution of the churches to adult education was the provision of educational facilities. Both the Catholic and Protestant churches have built a number of training centres that are very suitable for adult education activities. Examples of these in Kampala include Cardinal Nsubuga leadership (Catholic) and Lweza (Church of Uganda) training centres and there are similar centres in many other dioceses. Even in rural areas, church buildings are used for literacy classes for government and NGO adult literacy programmes. These church buildings are in most cases well located in the rural communities. Private business people and other organisations followed the churches' good example by building similar facilities where many NGOs and government departments organise learning programmes for adults through short courses, training workshops, and seminars. Often the facilities are in places where they provide the only suitable venue: without them, the training programmes would not be possible. They have undoubtedly played a great role in promoting adult education activities in Uganda.

Not all educational provisions for adults by the church were offered free of charge. The type of programmes for which fees were collected included skills training programmes such as vocational training for youth. The fees were used to cover the cost of the training. The non-fee programmes were usually aimed at the general welfare of the entire community and not at providing an individual with marketable skills like tailoring and carpentry. These were, and still are, paid for by the people coming to be trained. So individuals also made contributions to their own education in areas where the benefits were seen to be more personal than communal. There are still some church-run programmes, which train youth in the same manner.

The Christian churches have also continued to play a leading role in adult education through various church-based NGOs like: Soroti Catholic Diocese Integrated Development Organisation (SOCADIDO), Catholic Relief Services (CRS), Adventist Development and Relief Agency (ADRA), a Seventh Day Adventist Church based NGO, and Karamoja Diocesan Development Office (KDDO), a Church of Uganda based NGO. This looks like a change in strategy by some dioceses, away from directly getting involved in development work through the normal church structures to forming NGOs that do development and adult education work on the church's behalf. However, some dioceses have maintained the old structure of working through diocesan offices, such as the diocesan planning and development offices or social development offices.

Other faith-based organisations such as the Muslim faith and the Bahai faith have made similar contributions to adult education. The main focuses of their educational programmes are in most cases the spiritual and vocational skills development of an individual. Their programmes are predominantly for the advancement of their faith and preparing people to work for the religious organisation in propagating their faith. In some cases the organisations have developed facilities where educational programmes are conducted, e.g., the Bahai have an institute in Gulu and Mbale where members of the general public can also conduct educational programmes.

NGOs' contribution to adult education
Non-governmental organisations became popular during the 1980s.

In looking at them, we can extend the traditional definition of civil society to include some international NGOs who are largely development organisations. In this perspective of civil society, there are many organisations which have over the years played a salient role in promoting adult and community education in Uganda, especially at a time when government was not very able to perform community development services, including adult education.

For ease of discussing the activities of the NGOs in adult and community education, they are grouped into three broad categories: international NGOs – those with international connections or originating outside Uganda; national NGOs; and local community based NGOs. Within each of these categories, there are three sub-classifications. These are: NGOs clearly identifying themselves as adult education civil society organisations; those that are associated with adult education because of some aspect of their work involving literacy; and last, those who do not think of themselves as having anything to do with adult education.

International NGOs

Among international NGOs currently working in Uganda, there are none that identify themselves purely as adult education NGOs (the first sub-classification). Most identify themselves as development organisations. However, they do their work through community education programmes involving educating the local community, giving them new knowledge and skills and changing their attitude on certain issues, e.g. child nutrition and health.

The international NGOs in the second sub-classification are those involved with literacy education. They include ActionAid Uganda (AAU), Adventist Relief and Development Agency (ADRA), Netherlands Development Organisation (SNV), Agency for Co-operation in Research and Development (ACORD), World Food Programme (WFP) and many others.

Their main adult educational activity is adult literacy education and, as already mentioned, any activity outside this, such as community education in the form of AIDS awareness campaigns, environmental education, health education, community development education is not thought of as adult education. This is more evidence that adult education is narrowly perceived by most CSOs in Uganda, and may explain why there is too much focus on adult literacy as the only adult education activity in Uganda.

Some of these international NGOs have made a tremendous contribution to adult literacy. ActionAid Uganda (AAU), a British-based NGO which works internationally promoting rural development initiatives, is the biggest provider of adult literacy programmes among the international NGOs. It has adult literacy programmes in Bundibugyo, Mubende, Apac and Soroti and Mubende Districts. Their literacy programmes, which started in 1989, eventually developed into a new and very radical approach to teaching adult literacy which went beyond conventional literacy goals. The idea of introducing the literacy project was to facilitate the community development process by educating the population: the literacy component was meant to support other projects in the AAU programme – which, incidentally, AAU did not consider to be adult education. The expectation was that a literate population would be easier to work with and could more easily be involved in their own development process since they would be able to read and write on their own. Literacy was also used as a tool to keep a meaningful and prolonged contact with the community as the literacy programme included discussions on other development problems affecting the community.

It is clear that literacy as taught by AAU and other development agencies is not only about reading and writing. Within literacy education, AAU includes AIDS education, environmental education, income generation, health education and many other related topics which can generally be referred to as community education. The only problem with calling this literacy education is that people who can already read and write are left out of the programmes, yet they could benefit from them as much as the non-literate.

Additionally, AAU was entirely responsible for developing a new approach to teaching literacy known as REFLECT an acronym for Regenerated Freirean Literacy through Empowering Community Techniques. Uganda was privileged, due to the activities of AAU, to be one of the three countries where the two years of action research which resulted in the REFLECT approach was conducted; the others were El Salvador and Bangladesh. As its name suggests, REFLECT is an approach to teaching literacy which aims to involve and empower communities by helping them to acquire literacy and analytical skills which people can use to analyse their local environment and seek solutions to their day-to-day problems.

The fact that Uganda was one of the countries chosen for research in the technique has enabled many organisations in Uganda to be trained in this very participatory approach to teaching literacy. The REFLECT Co-ordination Unit (RCU), which is responsible for training and dissemination of the REFLECT approach in Africa, is based in Uganda and has trained very many REFLECT trainers here. This is not only encouraging the use of the REFLECT approach in Uganda, but also the proliferation of literacy activities in the country, as more literacy facilitators have been trained in REFLECT to work in the community, more literacy circles have been established, and more adults provided with learning opportunities.

The work of AAU in Uganda has generated a lot of literature on adult literacy work in Uganda, particularly on the process of developing the REFLECT approach in Bundibugyo. This has raised the international profile of adult education and educators in Uganda. There is no doubt that adult educators in Uganda have been involved in a very innovative process in the field of adult literacy work. As a result of their participation in the development of the REFLECT approach Ugandan adult literacy educators are visible on the international scene.

The interest generated by REFLECT popularised the work of Paulo Freire a renowned Brazilian adult educator. Most adult education workers in Uganda, including the government department engaged in adult literacy work, make reference to Freire's work. Along with the Freirean philosophy of education is the now very popular concept of participation and empowerment. With this came the concept of the bottom-up approach to development, which recognises and respects learners' views and knowledge and input. This is a philosophy that is currently influencing the work of adult educators, as well as other development workers in Uganda.

The Adventist Development and Relief Agency (ADRA) is another outstanding international NGO active in adult literacy education in Uganda. As with AAU, the policy of this organisation is to teach literacy as a prerequisite to training in livelihood skills. Both these aspects of literacy and training in livelihood skills are adult education programmes, which ADRA does consider as adult education activities. ADRA has a big literacy programme covering several parts of Uganda. Their strategy of literacy and livelihood is a very motivating process as the learners have a strong reason to keep learning. This explains their low drop-out rate of only 20 per cent in a class population of between 40 to 70 learners (Katahoire, 2002: 110, 111). In this, ADRA, like AAU, is championing a new strategy for adult literacy education in Uganda.

The ADRA Adult Education programme is referred to as the Functional Adult Learning Programme (FALP). The initials are the same as those of the government Functional Adult Literacy Programme (FALP) but, importantly, the wording is different: ADRA does not call its programme an 'adult literacy programme' but an 'adult learning programme'. This is very constructive programme naming, showing that it is not just literacy that is part of learning, but also livelihood skills. The use of the word literacy, although politically attractive, has a very limiting influence on the perception of both learners and literacy teachers, who both end up seeing adult education only in terms of literacy. The ADRA example can be seen as a very positive contribution to adult learning in Uganda. The line ADRA has taken, though still at an early stage, will lead to a much broader definition of adult education being accepted and used as a way of reaching out to and opening opportunities for the marginalised poor.

In the third sub-category of international NGOs, those who do not identify with adult education, are NGOs who do community development work like ACORD, World Vision, CARE, Plan International and many others. It is not possible to discuss each NGO's programme in this chapter and ACORD has been arbitrarily chosen as an example of this group.

ACORD does community development work through training or giving skills to people regarded by their societies as adults. They conduct skills training programmes for women and youths, they train local council and community leaders in planning and leadership skills, and they are involved in Aids awareness campaigns and environmental education in different communities in Uganda. They use a variety of adult education methods, including but not limited to theatre and drama, short residential training, seminars, and workshops held at the community level.

The greatest influence of these adult education activities of the international NGOs is that they are popularising adult education for development work, which is largely community education. Most, if not all, NGOs providing learning and training programmes for the community are doing it for development. This has downplayed other aspects of adult education such as continuing education in Uganda. The influence of these NGOs, who work mostly with rural communities, has also tended to direct adult education programmes, including literacy, to the rural areas. As a result, there are very few organisations that provide adult education programmes for the urban population. For example, there are no serious adult education programmes for industrial workers or the urban poor in low paid jobs.

Adult education has in effect ignored the important aspect of helping society to cope with global changes. Because of the training influences of mostly international NGOs and the demands of donors, adult education tends to focus on rural poverty alleviation only. There are of course some businesses covering for these deficiencies by exploiting the people's need to learn. This is not adequate for a country, which needs a national programme for training and retraining of the workforce in skills which make them employable in response to government policies of increased production and private investment. Upgrading the skills of the workforce is just as important for the economy as alleviating rural poverty.

These NGOs make wonderful contributions to adult education work. However, because they do not consider that they are doing adult education work, but rather that they are doing community development or social work, whatever they are doing is not credited to adult education. Instead it is recognised as training; yet, training is just a small aspect of adult education. As a result, the training and the trainers do not benefit from the full professional knowledge base of adult education, which could make their work more effective. The second problem with this view is that it leaves a supposedly professional field with specialised skills open to people who are not trained. Most development work aims at providing knowledge, changing attitudes and behaviour, and developing new skills. A person teaching development work needs to have professional skills in measuring learning and changes in behaviour and attitude, in addition to knowing the methods of teaching adults as a special category of learners. It is not possible to do these things with a few weeks of training or a trainer's workshop. Unprofessional work gets done and it is adult education and adult educators that pick up the blame for wasting resources.

Adult education remains a marginalised field of practice in Uganda where it seems that only practitioners of adult education recognise the work of adult education and educators outside literacy.

It is adult educators who have the responsibility to correct the development workers' misconceptions and convince them that they may need to learn adult education and not just training skills to help them perform better. Those who have the privilege of being in the profession of adult education either by accident or default could also do more to educate and enlighten the public about the extent of adult education and convince them that there is more to providing any learning programme for adults than can be given in a one week's training of trainer's workshop.

In spite of some misguided perceptions about their role in adult education, the activities of these development NGOs have enabled adults to have opportunities for learning new skills, which is, after all, adult education's primary concern. The skills they learn are helping to improve life in the community where the adults have a lot of responsibilities.

There are many other international NGOs doing literacy and adult education work in Uganda and not all can be mentioned here. The few that have been mentioned in detail have made a significant contribution to adult education in Uganda, through their very innovative approaches to literacy and adult learning. Another major contribution made by all the international NGOs involved in adult education, particularly in literacy, is financial. The financing of adult education in Uganda has largely been done through the activities of NGOs, who solicit money from donors to fund their programmes. Without the activities of the CSOs, there would have been much less money for running adult education programmes.

National NGOs
In this chapter, by national NGOs we refer to indigenous NGOs with a national coverage. There are many national NGOs involved in some form of adult education activities. They work at two levels. The first level is made up of NGOs that do community development training for the selected communities in which they have chosen to work. These NGOs work directly with the community at the grassroots level. At the second level are the NGOs that train other organisations in development work or organisational development, e.g. Community Development Resources Network (CDRN).

Like the international NGOs, there are local NGOs that clearly identify themselves as adult education organisations and those that do not. Those identifying themselves as adult education organisations include:
- National Adult Education Association (NAEA)
- Kiira Adult Education Association (Kiira AEA)
- Literacy and Adult Basic Education (LABE)
- Adult literacy and Basic Education Centre (ALBEC)
- Kamuli Adult Education Association (Kamuli AEA)
- Literacy Network of Uganda (LitNet)
- Uganda Joint Action for Adult Education (UJAFAE)
- Uganda Adult Education Network (UGAADEN)
- Uganda Literacy and Adult Learners Association (ULALA)
- Karamoja Adult Education Association (Karamoja AEA).

These organisations and many others directly identify themselves as adult education organisations and mark themselves out very clearly by having the words 'adult education' in their names. The national NGOs do more than adult literacy education. Some train adult educators to work at the community level.

The National Adult Education Association (NAEA) is an active promoter of adult education. Among it various activities, NAEA, runs a certificate course for adult educators through distance education. This is a one-year programme leading to a credit-bearing certificate in adult education (CAE). (This certificate was originally offered by AALAE.) The people trained by NAEA work at the community level, facilitating a number of adult education programmes. The training and certificate provide educational opportunities for some adults, in addition to increasing the number of qualified adult educators at the community level.

The training of professional adult educators in Uganda is a rather recent development (see Chapter 7). The contribution of NAEA is therefore a very significant one since it not only starts people into the profession of adult education but also motivates some to consider further qualifications. For example, many people who have taken NAEA's certificates are now moving to Nsamizi Institute of Social Development to train in adult education at diploma level. In due course, they may join Makerere or another university for degree programmes in adult and community education.

NAEA also does a lot in the other areas of adult and community education, including environmental education, and education for sustainable development. Their approach to these shows the importance of adult education in environmental sustainability: it is only through education that society's environmentally damaging activities can be changed. If other NGOs or CSOs recognise adult education's role in this, they can do much more in bringing about environmentally sustainable development in Uganda. While NAEA is leading the way, not many NGOs have learnt from them that their environmental education programmes are adult education activities which should benefit from using teachers with full professional training.

One of the oldest adult education NGOs in Uganda is Kiira Adult Education Association (Kiira AEA). It was founded in 1976, and its aims include:
- The promotion of adult education as a practice which deserves serious attention

- Co-operating with governmental and non-governmental organisations with the interest of progressive learning for overall self-improvement in the standard of living
- Participating in making rural people well informed of and able to understand government policies
- Improving methods of productivity for effective practical contribution in local and national development process
- Tackling functional literacy as a focal point for expansion of social and economic development, etc (Okech, 1984: 84).

Kiira AEA works directly with the community, focusing on literacy and community education. It played a great role in the development of new adult education organisations such as Kamuli Adult Education Association, and many other CBOs. Kiira AEA continues to be one of the leading adult education organisations in Uganda. Together with NAEA and IACE, they started the Uganda Joint Action for Adult Education (UJAFAE), a partnership organisation whose membership is made up of 15 national and international organisations involved solely in adult education.

Literacy and Adult Basic Education (LABE), which was started by students of the Institute of Adult and Continuing Education, then the Centre for Continuing Education, has grown into a powerful national adult education organisation which makes a tremendous contribution to the field. LABE has specialised in training literacy instructors, and the production of literacy materials for use by community based organisations. In this way LABE helps to build the capacity of the community based organisations involved in adult literacy education to perform their work effectively. One of LABE's most significant contributions was to spearhead the formation of the Literacy Network for Uganda (LitNet) through which organisations involved in literacy work share ideas and experiences, lobby and do advocacy for literacy. LABE won the prestigious UNESCO Noma Literacy Award in 2002 for its exemplary work.

Another organisation that has specialised in offering educational opportunities for adults is Adult Literacy and Basic Education (ALBEC). Like LABE, it was founded by students who were doing a diploma in adult education at IACE. ALBEC trains adults, who are mostly refugees from Sudan, Rwanda, Burundi, Ethiopia, Congo, and Eritrea. They offer English for beginners and some basic educational programmes. They also offer continuing education programmes for adults who are assisted to sit for Uganda National Examination Board (UNEB) Primary Leaving Examination (PLE), Uganda Certificate of Education (UCE), and Uganda Advanced Certificate of Education (UACE). Some of the learners who came to ALBEC have succeeded in joining university education, while the organisation has helped refugees to fit into the Ugandan community.

ALBEC's adult education provision is unique because it provides diverse learning opportunities for adults who would like to continue with their education and is not doing adult education just for community development. ALBEC's kind of offering needs to be encouraged throughout the country so that adults go beyond literacy. There is a need to recognise, develop and institutionalise ALBEC's valuable educational arrangements for adults.

These and the other CSOs who clearly identify with adult education work have played and continue to play a great role in promoting adult education in Uganda. They have made adult education known in its own right as an option for community development work and career development. They have established an environment in which professional adult education work can be done and recognised by both government and donors. They have identified adult educators as a specialised group of people. Most of these CSOs came into existence during the 1980s and the greatest impact of their work can then be seen during those years, when adult education, especially literacy as a strategy for social development, came to be recognised by government.

NGOs who do not identify themselves as adult education organisations still do a lot of work either at the community level or building the capacities of other CSOs. These include:
- Community Development Resource Centre Network (CDRN)
- Uganda Rural Development and Training (URDT)
- The Young Men's Christian Association (YMCA)
- The Young Women's Christian Association (YWCA)

The Community Development Resource Centre Network (CDRN)

was founded in 1994 to provide services to other development organisations. CDRN promotes community development work through a participatory process in order to avoid the top-down approach to development, which excludes the poor. They also do advocacy work. They explain their work as 'Promoting Civil Society's efforts to reduce poverty among women, men and children in Uganda through organisational and institutional strengthening' (CDRN 2001: 5).

Like CDRN, Uganda Rural Development and Training (URDT) organisation is also active in strengthening the capacities of CSOs working in development. They do this through training workshops and organisational self-review.

The Young Men's Christian Association (YMCA), the Young Women's Christian Association (YWCA) are two linked international organisations, which have largely been indigenised in Uganda, and offer a number of vocational, and training programmes for young adults. They have branches throughout the country. Although they have been indigenised, they have maintained their external connection with their mother organisations abroad.

There are too many other CSOs active in adult education to be mentioned here. Some were formed before Independence, e.g. the Uganda Council for Women formed in 1947, to co-ordinate among other things 'literacy work, home improvement, and promoting the status of women' (Okech 1984: 63). It was followed in 1978 by another women's organisation with one of its objectives being "to work for the eradication of illiteracy especially among women" (Okech 1984: 64). Although most of these early organisations have closed down, new ones have come up in their place. The CSOs involved in community development have undoubtedly had a great influence on adult education in Uganda.

Co-operative unions and workers' unions

From the early 1950s, the co-operative unions have been very active in educating adults, especially their farming members. Most were growers' co-operatives and in 1984 Okech listed twelve from different parts of the country. Most of these co-operative unions collapsed during the political instabilities of the 1970s and the 1980s. Efforts are now being made to revive them.

The co-operative unions taught their member farmers book-keeping, modern farming methods, marketing skills, financial planning, and management. The co-operative union's educational programmes took the form of short courses, workshops, and residential and non-residential programmes and study groups (Okech 1984).

The fundamental principles of the co-operative educational programmes were to promote the economic interest of members by encouraging better farming methods in order to produce greater yields or improve productivity, getting loans for members, and marketing their products (ibid 1984). The co-operative unions' educational programme leans towards the progressive and behaviourist philosophy of adult education. The co-operatives were required by law to put some funds aside for the education of their members and, as with church adult education, the members paid no fee for the programmes. The co-operatives also built educational institutions to train members and trainers in extension work. In this, they further reinforced the tradition of free adult education.

The trade unions have also been very active in educating their members. In the early days of independence, they had an important educational institution, the Labour College, founded in 1958. The activities of the trade unions were co-ordinated by the Uganda Trade Union Congress and are currently organised by the National Organisation of Trade Unions (NOTU). Trade union activities suffered set-backs, first with the government's closure of the Labour College, whose premises are now used by the Law Development Centre, and then through Uganda's general social and economic decline of the seventies and eighties. However, like many sectors in Uganda, trade union and workers' education have again revived and there are many vibrant educational activities, some with support from external funding.

View for the future

Though civil society in Uganda has done a lot in shaping the practice of adult education, there is still a lot that they can do. Civil society

needs to work towards creating conditions where people's demand for adult education can be heard and acted upon. They need to:
- Fight for appropriate policies, which recognise that education is a right for all persons young or old.
- Co-ordinate the efforts of all civil society organisations working in adult education.
- Develop new strategies to extend the benefits of adult learning to those currently excluded.
- Promote a culture of learning.
- Do research and document the adult education experiences in Uganda and their impact on the economic growth of the country, as one way of influencing policy makers to recognise the contribution of adult education to national development.

These and many other activities still need to be done in order to strengthen the practice of adult education in Uganda.

Conclusions

This chapter has used a few selected examples of civil society organisations to show the role different civil society organisations have played in strengthening adult education in Uganda. The organisations selected are involved in different aspects of adult education such as community education for poverty mitigation, organisational and institutional development for adult and community education, providing vocational and continuing educational opportunities for adults. Some offer programmes to improve the productive capacities of their members. Without the activities of these organisations, adult education would have no significant profile in this country. While this is true, adult educators still need to enlighten the CSOs about the benefit of gaining professional adult teaching skills in doing community development work through community education. They also need to understand that whatever the description they give to their various programmes, what they are in fact doing is adult education.

6
University Adult Education in Uganda

Yolamu N. Nsamba

Introduction
This study of university adult education in Uganda is a critical examination of the entire process as it has developed with a detailed assessment of both positive and negative contributions of various actors over a period of nearly fifty years. First it makes a critical assessment of the concept of university adult education as it was perceived by the pioneers of this service, how local conditions affected its provision and how far opportunities for its development were exploited. The study discusses the options that existed, the rationale for making deliberate choices, their significance and impact.

University adult education in Uganda evolved in a very specific historical context, a context that led to deliberate government repression, including the sad history that turned a service to the country into an anti-state subversive activity. The post repression era and the challenges and opportunities that it presented in terms of institutional reform and development are discussed as well as the exploitation of the emerging technologies and partnerships in the provision of university adult education. Finally, the chapter looks at the consequences of widening the provision of university adult education and the challenges of maintaining standards in the face of mass provision to a large student body.

Liberal university adult education in extra-mural studies packages
After 1945 an upsurge of nationalism and armed rebellion against colonial rule made most British colonies ungovernable. Ex-servicemen who returned from soldiering in the Second World War fuelled demands for independence. As colonies became ungovernable, a paradigm of British rule shifted from repression of the colonised people towards a search for native leaders to whom political power

could be handed during the anticipated neo-colonial era. This included a new look at concepts of colonial education.

Repression as a policy of British colonial rule was exemplified in the recommendations of The Uganda Development Commission appointed by the Colonial Government in the 1920s. It states an uncompromising dictum to use education to repress the population. Its recommendations opposed 'any extensive education for the general native population and ... consider[ed] that it should never proceed beyond a standard which enables a native to learn a trade by which he [could] earn a living' (Report of the Uganda Development Commission, Government Printer, Entebbe, 1920: 34). Natives were to be educated to become commodities for the labour market (Jackson 1997: 47). The Commission's recommendation was aimed at reducing natives to mere articles of commerce in the colonial economy (Freire et al. 2000: 66). Education was reduced to a materialistic necessity to produce suitable workers and its values of improving the quality of life and inspiring both individuals and the community were lost to the policy makers (Jackson 1997). The commissioners argued that 'unless literary education is complete, or is accompanied by technical training, the native is apt to regard himself as a superior being for whom the ordinary duties and responsibilities of life have no significance' (Uganda Colonial Government 1920).

The commissioners told government to provide: 'facilities without delay for a thorough technical education, whereby the creation of a class of really competent craftsmen will be assured.' It suggested medical schools, a school for carpenters, masons and other artisans including training for mechanics, turners, blacksmiths, users of agriculture implements, veterinary workers, printing machine operators, text composers, surveyors and forest workers. Vocational education prescribed in this manner resembled the education recommended in Great Britain 100 years earlier for the British working class. It sought to deny Ugandans, 'access to knowledge associated with power' and knowledge, which according to Freire develops, consolidates, and sustains democratic institutions.

Although no coherent policy was worked out for adult education to tutor and raise a local political elite for the self-governance of the colonies, a form of liberal adult education was introduced in Uganda to establish democratic institutions and systems of governance well known in the United Kingdom. It was to fill the vacuum of leadership as colonial forces retreated. Adult education came with, 'the marks of its foreign origin ... prejudices and ... deformations, which include lack of confidence in the people's ability to think, to want to know [and]... it ran the risk of falling into a type of false generosity [characteristic] of ... oppressors.' (Freire et al 2000: 59)

The concept of university adult education

A concept of university adult education that must include liberal adult education has been defined as courses students attend out of interest in a particular subject for personal and social development rather than for vocational objectives. In Great Britain the culture of university liberal adult education has its origins in the Victorian self-help movements among the poor who created learning facilities including workers' trade unions, institutes, libraries, evening classes and correspondence courses to educate themselves beyond the minimum schooling then available to them, so as to enrich their lives, their families and the whole society (Turkett 2002).

As an aspect of lifelong learning that secures participants an economic future, university adult education must enable civilised society to develop the spiritual side of people's lives, active citizenship, community participation as well as strengthening the family, neighbourhood and nation. This suggests learning for both capacity building and leisure. Lord George Wigg in 1950 expressed scepticism about introducing liberal adult education in the African colonies in a prophetic statement in the House of Commons:

> I am not sure at all that the ... university colleges ... have a concept of adult education that commends itself ... I do not think that there is an understanding of what we have done in [Britain] during the last 100 years, nor is there an imagination to use that experience and apply it to ... African needs ... if one picks up the product of adult education experience such as the tutorial class or extension lectures as used by the older

universities in this country and try those out ... they will fail. (Hansard 1950: 1452)

This concern, reflected in the current recommendations of the Non Award Bearing Continuing Education of the Higher Education Funding Council for England, has universal implications. University liberal adult education must advance knowledge rather than establish practices. (NABCE 2002)

When J.W. Harris founded the Extra-Mural Department at Makerere University in 1953 and became its first resident tutor, he does not appear to have been fully conscious of the 'heritage' of what is considered legitimate university adult education. He was ignorant of the issues that Lord Wigg raised and lacked professional competence to introduce university adult education as a distinct body of knowledge into the university environment and to secure for it a legitimate and recognised professional status. All he did was to translate his perceived notions of university adult education and package them as an extra-mural studies programme. Having made a false start in June 1954 he declared: 'In planning for Uganda, one is faced with the truism that this country is not London, nor Cambridgeshire, nor yet is it the West Indies or the Gold Coast. In all these areas, there are successful and well established Departments of Extra-Mural Studies.' (Harris 1954: 6) This praise of ongoing extra- mural work in the colonies had never won the admiration of Lord Wigg.

To claim success for an institution that had not established credibility in the eyes of its critics was misguided. Without adequate knowledge, Harris got on with the job and wrote: '... social educational conditions in Uganda, with its fifty years of close contact with European civilization, are obviously not exactly parallel to those in West Indies or even in the Gold Coast, with their generations of links with Britain'. (Harris 1954: 8) It would, therefore, also have been very useful to have the advice and co-operation of those with long experience in administration and education in Uganda and East Africa. 'But not all this experience was really necessary. University extension work is a relatively unfamiliar idea even to English people. In order to find out the reactions of people to a completely new idea, there was really no alternative to putting the new idea into actual practice.' (Harris 1954: 8)

This stand presents a misconception. Harris perceived the 'new idea' that he was so anxious to put into practice in a manner that failed to match that concept of adult education which Lord Wigg knew but found inadequately catered for by university adult education initiatives in Africa. To Harris it was 'spreading a tradition of integrity and independence of thinking and of devotion to accurate analysis and research as applied to the problem.' (Ibid. p.13). We shall return later to the two issues that he mentions, analysis and research, and examine Makerere's performance in these. But it is clear that he was thinking of what is known as liberal adult education for his extra-mural programmes.

Liberal adult education has many aspects. 'A liberal adult education programme involves working towards a set of objectives that include freedom, humane aspirations, spiritual enlightenment, self realization, cultivating the qualities of leadership, working towards reform of society, developing an ideology of non-ideology, building tutor autonomy and a sense of integrity, objectivity in the study and analysis of issues and events.' (Harries, 1982. p. 49)

Harries raises the following weaknesses of university liberal adult education, to which extra-mural work is related. First is the inability to meet demands for standards due to recruitment procedures which allow sub-standard students onto courses, admission in the middle of courses, inadequacy of written work, absence of proper examination, non-verification of achievement, lack of intellectual discipline and lack of commitment. Secondly it is beset by an 'irrationality' of approach, which promotes individual idiosyncrasies of tutors. Thirdly there is failure to manage the educational resources rationally to achieve ends which the opportunity cost should justify. Fourthly is the tendency to be elitist and to cater for a minority interest, ignoring the deserving under-privileged. Lastly is the lack of values towards the satisfaction of practical utilitarian ends and the tendency to ignore involvement with concerns for the manpower needs of society. (Harries 1982)

The Makerere University concept of adult extra-mural studies showed two problems: it did not address the stated objectives of liberal adult education and it failed to cope with the weaknesses inherent in it. Of the nine odd objectives to which liberal adult education aspires it focused on only one, objectivity. As J.W. Harris wrote, '...the ultimate aim of university extra-mural teaching is the development of habit of mature thought and judgement and the encouragement of a thinking educated (social) class ...' (Harris 1954: 276).[He seems to have been unaware of the possible weaknesses.

The fact that at this time the Colonial Office had embarked on a policy of de-colonisation coloured the concept of university adult education introduced in Uganda at that time and Harris's packaging of university adult education was calculated to justify extra-mural work to the Colonial Welfare Development Fund that paid for it. As Harris confesses: 'Sometimes supporters of this work have used the phrase "education for self government". The Universities themselves might make a slightly less spacious claim and also one less likely to agitate unduly the practical political officers of a paternal colonial government he was anxious to please.'(Harris 1954: 275)

J.W. Harris's selective pursuit of the objectives of university adult education gave it a role that left a lot to be desired when set against the spectrum of the objectives of traditional liberal adult education as described by Jenkins Harries. Also, his claim that the extra-mural package of university adult education he introduced in Uganda was based on the British model is not accurate: it is pegged to only one out of the nine objectives of the British model. As an operative of the Colonial Office he used top-down communication channels, dispensing services by those who knew best to the ignorant colonised peoples. He rationalised and defended his approach that university extra-mural departments elsewhere had for long recognised the necessity for stimulating the demand for study amongst non-university men and women. Instead they waited for demand to become articulate in overseas areas such as East Africa, where the initiative came from the university side rather than from the people.

University adult education clientele

The Makerere University Extra-Mural Department originally assumed that demand for study amongst non-university men and women in

Uganda was lacking. At that time there must have been no more than 1500 people who had a college education. A survey of the Ugandan elite conducted in 1957 showed a total of 1697 registered members of the elite – those educated to at least Cambridge School Certificate standard. By 1962 this figure had risen to 300 graduates, 7500 holders of Higher School Certificate or its equivalent and 11,500 holders of Cambridge School Certificate or its equivalent. This rate of growth indicates that in 1953 there must have been at least 3000 people qualified for a university education who would have benefited from the extra-mural package. Mr Harris noted that among the Department's clientele almost all students had at least a few years of secondary school education and a number had been to universities. The department's clientele was therefore drawn from people who had sufficient education and had attained a level of competence and motivation necessary for them to benefit from programmes of university liberal adult education. There was a curious fact in '.... the age composition ... over half the total are between 25 and 30 years, and that the whole age-distribution is surprisingly reminiscent of that in many Workers Educational Associations (WEA) class groups in England.' (Harris, ibid. p.5)

Yet no lessons were drawn from the British experience of university extension of mobilising a possible clientele. An informed approach to extra-mural work in Uganda could have set university adult education on firm ground and on a rational and systematic base. Instead Mr. Harris started by sending circular letters to people he imagined might be interested in extra-mural work and advertised his classes in the press. His report lists the government departments he collaborated with to do publicity. To these he adds other agencies namely Kampala Radio, the Uganda Society, East African Literature Bureau, East African Libraries and the British Council.

University adult education work was approached as if it was administered by a new government department using top to bottom communication. It was never established on an independent base of its own and no alternative media of communication were considered. It simply adopted methods used and taken for granted by the colonial civil servants. The Resident Tutor travelled 1000 miles every week, (quite a lot of mileage to cover on murram roads) and he could not have spent less than 30 hours on the road every week. He was exhausted by such travelling and had little time left for actual university adult education work. He set a precedent for future generations of extra-mural tutors at Makerere, who over the next thirty years also travelled around the country in similar style, organising programmes of doubtful university adult education value. There was hardly any cost-effective use of the resources availed to the university adult education extra-mural studies department.

Lost opportunities and wasted funding

The Colonial Welfare Development Fund, the Carnegie Foundation and in later years DANIDA, funded university adult education. Funding always had conditions attached and utilisation prescribed. For instance in 1970 Denmark granted several million Krona for the construction of a residential college on the model of the Danish Folk High Schools. These were developed in Denmark during the nineteenth century by Grundtvik with the idea of establishing the 'living word and a school for life', built on the concept of detachment from the external world in order to eliminate task interference and aid serious scholarship. However, the idea did not travel well. The Extra-Mural Department failed to fully understand that residential facilities for adult learners were critically important in enabling them to live together, to build strong interpersonal relationships, attain in-depth focused learning and undergo qualitative personal changes.

The Residential Centre building at Makerere University, modelled on a Danish Folk High School, stands as evidence of well-intended egotism on the part of the donors and folly on the part of the recipients and a senseless use of resources on the part of both. It betrays the futility of transferring to the third world institutions and technology as a development strategy. In the Folk High School building lecture rooms remained empty for several years. At a loss about what to do with the new building, Director Daniel Okunga behaved like Mr Harris and wrote circular letters to various people announcing that the Centre was going to mount a certain unknown quantity and quality of courses. This announcement drew the reaction of the Permanent Secretary in the Office of the President, who cautioned that whatever courses were mounted they should not duplicate the effort of already established institutions.

What went wrong? The 1966/67 Kironde Report had established the terms of reference for a Centre for Continuing Education, which was to co-ordinate the work of the old Extra-Mural Studies Department with that of the Residential Centre, as well as with a new department to cover correspondence courses and mass media. Through these organs the Centre was to offer university education to adults, secondary school leavers and primary school leavers. In summary the Centre was to provide university continuing education in the English language for persons who had received some formal education. In December 1967, Resolution No. 2133 of the University Council endorsed the report's recommendations and at this point it would have been quite easy to get the University Council to commit funds to a well articulated proposal. In 1967 the Department of Extra-Mural Studies was renamed the Centre for Continuing Education, but Daniel Okunga and his colleagues failed to develop either an operational plan or a project proposal to implement them and to seek funding for the Centre.

The unlimited scope recommended by the Report required a working plan to tailor it to the available resources. Mr Durand, Principal Assistant Secretary, Finance, Ministry of Education, in 1972 advised as follows:

> The present dilemma in which the Centre for Continuing Education finds itself is that the policy which it is asked to implement is greater than the resources with which the Centre has been supplied. It is therefore necessary to define the policy in more detail so that resources of personnel and finance are made available to match a clearly defined policy. (Durand 1972)

On 16th June 1975, a meeting was convened to co-ordinate the programmes proposed by the Centre. Representatives of the Uganda College of Commerce, The Institute of Public Administration, Nsamizi

Training Institute, the Ministry of Public Service as well as both the National Teachers' College Kyambogo, and the Uganda Technical College, Kyambogo were invited although the last two did not attend the meeting. In the absence of a clearly defined policy, the Centre for Continuing Education was left at a loss as to what it could legitimately do with its new building because the other institutions already offered many courses in the areas of study that it proposed to teach. (Minutes of the Meeting of Principal and Directors of 16th June 1975). The Board had only one defence as to its non-use of the new building and this was that some of the facilities were incomplete.

The use of the building continued to be controversial. Deliberating on it in 1978, the Board of the Centre for Continuing Education noted 'with concern the pressure that had been put on the Director of the Centre in the use of the building and would like to stress that the Centre's activities and students should take priority in the use of the building.' (Min. BC 110/8/78 The Centre's New Building). A huge library stood with dust-coated bare shelves. Adult students never used the lecture theatres and the lecture chairs were covered in a mantle of dust and cobwebs. Expensive sensitive radio hardware to equip studios for mass educational communication was never installed and remained huddled in a dark room. The studios themselves remained dark vaults frequented by rats. The residential facilities meant to accommodate adult students were turned into an undergraduate hall of residence named Complex Hall after being unused for eight years. It is still an undergraduate hall at the time of writing. There was yet another example of the futility of transfer of inappropriate technology: printing presses sent to the University by UNESCO for printing materials for adult education. Two presses became wrecks and broke down before they printed any university adult education work.

It has been the curse of administrators of adult education that they have been unable to meet the needs of the learners with the funds donated to Africa. Often large sums of money are spent on the officials of the implementing agencies towards capacity building in the form of training courses, seminars, workshops, study visits, research, and procurement of motor vehicles. Barely 30% of the donated sums of money ever reach the target groups. This must be a subject of further investigations. The impacts of adult education that we see today could have been different if the planning of adult education had targeted the rightful beneficiaries. (Afrik 2000: 28).

But it was not merely the fact that money failed to reach the rightful beneficiaries that caused the problems. In the case of adult education at Makerere University the entire planning process was flawed. For instance, when the Extra-Mural department was converted into the Centre for Continuing Education in 1967 the relationship between the Centre and the university was left undefined. Isaac Ojok noted:

> It is not clear which faculty the Centre for Continuing Education fits in because nobody in the university has yet come out to spell it out; at any rate, it is not itself a faculty. This rather loose association with the University that the Centre for Continuing Education enjoys, worries most of those who work under its umbrella, including the Organiser; within the Centre for Continuing Education there is, unlike in other departments no systematic hierarchy of promotions for those who work in it ... the Centre for Continuing Education, like its predecessor, the Department of Extra-Mural Studies is often misused as a stepping stone to getting fat salaried jobs or higher status (Ojok and Onyango 1969).

In this badly planned and poorly structured Centre, poorly planned correspondence courses were introduced. '... though it is accepted that these courses enable the Centre to serve a wider clientele, it is now clear that far too many courses were introduced with little regard to cost and expertise. These two factors have been the cause of great strain on existing staff and have left standards less good than one would like to see. The financial resources have proved inadequate for the courses we run' (Okunga 1974). The courses offered ran into very serious difficulties and the capacity to correct the problem that Director Daniel Okunga identified did not exist. This was noted in the executive meeting of the Centre attended by senior colleagues of the Department: '[there were] problems being faced in the writing of sets in English where the writer is too slow, Sociology where the writer is incompetent, and Man and His Environment where the writer has moved away to Mbale.' (Min. EC 4/2/75, The CAS Course)

Alternative approaches to university adult education

University adult education at Makerere University has been characterised by failure to develop the partnerships necessary to expedite the development of university liberal adult education. Opportunities to work with non-governmental organisations such as the churches were never developed. Equally, opportunities to work with state organisations such as the army were lost. Both the churches and the army were transplanted into the country with astonishing success nearly one hundred years ago. The local population accepted them and the values for which they stood were internalised over time. Again no lessons were learnt from their experiences of education. Many of the potential extra-mural clientele were products of missionary schools but out of 308 students there were only four priests and no soldiers.

The values of liberalised university adult education in the extra-mural packages at Makerere University were not new to Uganda, as J.W. Harris seemed to suggest but had been introduced by earlier intensive missionary activity which included adult literacy and vocational training and which Makerere University failed to exploit. Similarly, no lessons were drawn from Britain's one hundred years of extra-mural work. In Britain, the churches had provided liberal adult education before the universities; non-conformists used it as part of their liberating mission. Ben Rees (1982) discusses the religious dimension of early university adult education in Britain and narrates how Albert Mansbridge was inspired to start the Workers' Adult Educational Association by the spiritual values of education rather than by any feeling of class solidarity. His main supporters were similarly inspired, including the Anglican Church leader William Temple, who for a short time during the Second World War was Archbishop of Canterbury. The link between the church and university extension in Britain was not considered. Instead, the Extra-Mural

Department made an empty claim that they were working towards 'social progress ... a chance to further knowledge and understanding necessary for participation in the process of democratic change – extra-mural could play an important part in the preparation for self government.' (Rees 1981: 80.)

Before Independence, adult education at Makerere did nothing to combat the overt and covert British colonial intentions that pursued objectives incompatible with liberation and social progress clearly sited in the repressive recommendation of the 1920 Uganda Development Commission. No one heeded Lord Wigg's calling for social progress instead of repression during the Kenya Mau Mau insurgency. As early as 1946 he had subscribed to the liberal tradition and suggested a programme of adult education for the askaris [African soldiers] in the King's African Rifles in East Africa. He had also expressed fears that 'moves towards self-government before ... [laying] a permanent educational foundation were fraught with menace. He argued for the English language to be taught to the askaris. The circumstances at that time were that English was a language for command and any African who spoke it to a white man qualified for a belting.' (Fordham 1970: 60)

While nationalists were equally suspicious of their people learning English, for different reasons, it is important not to lose sight of the argument behind the objections to educating the askaris and the implications of that decision. In the end Lord Wigg did not convince the Colonial Office and he sadly noted: 'Thus little was done about teaching English and less about teaching Africans how democratic institutions worked but time had run out.' (op. cit.)

Repression of university adult education

Ten years after Uganda's independence, what Lord Wigg anticipated became manifest. The soldiers of the Uganda army who had been denied an education and brought up in the repressive tradition seized power. They were hostile to democratic institutions as well as to education in general and university adult education in particular. Like their colonial military officers, they 'belted' anyone who dared to address them in English. Their objection to English was not a matter of national pride. It was fulfilment of the military tradition established in East Africa by the British. The military that clearly had a role of leadership in the country had been deliberately denied educational opportunities. As Lord Wigg wrote: 'East African Development might have been different if the army and the Colonial Office had [adopted] ... the educational policy set out in a White Paper published during the War, entitled Mass Education in Africa' (Wigg op. cit.).

Uganda's history in the mid-sixties saw an ill prepared military emerge into the forefront to cope with a deteriorating breakdown of law and order but without the knowledge to do the job within a democratic framework. As their influence increased, particularly after the 1966 constitutional crisis, the fragile makeshift liberal hegemony that university adult education had engineered receded into the background. The events that surrounded the 1966 Commission of Inquiry attest to repressive tendencies, intolerance, polarised political attitudes and subjectivity. Students and lecturers no longer respected the value of a liberal approach to problem solving. They welcomed the emerging repressive hegemony and looked to it as a tool to silence dissent. An opportunity was lost to teach the people of Uganda to manage dissent by institutionalising it into democratic institutions mandated to debate and resolve differences before they degenerate into armed conflicts. This set Uganda on the tragic path of resorting to military means to resolve conflicts.

> Rather than encouraging scepticism, extra-mural classes became indoctrination sessons where resident tutors preached a doctrine and built themselves political bases. ... It does not pay to dismiss this accusation as far-fetched simply because the Government of Uganda at the time strongly denied it. The fact is that the resident tutor of an area has the opportunity to become a carrier of political views and rumour because he travels widely, and he is in a position to encourage not only critical attitudes towards government policies but also to propagate alternative proposals. There is a strong possibility that the divorce between politics and education, which is supposed to exist according to British views on education, is

seen as a pious fraud in Uganda (Williams, 1968 p.3130.

The professionalism and tutor autonomy of the extra-mural staff was hollow. It had never been part of the extra-mural package of university adult education that the Colonial Office prescribed. It failed to groom a cadre of lecturers committed to a liberal adult education tradition. Staff recruited were not professional adult educators. In 1975 despite the recommended minimum qualifications for university academic staff being a Master's degree, the Centre for Continuing Education, 'have nine out of twenty-one members of the teaching staff with first degrees only' (Min. EC/7/2/75). The irony of the situation was that Director Daniel Okunga was planning to attend a three-month course in Canada on Comparative Education – a course that would never give him any grounding in adult education. None of the degree holding staff had qualifications in adult education. Others were far below the Makerere University staff qualifications threshold.

The staff development situation was utterly hopeless. In 1978 Emmanuel Kaibandira noted, 'As far as I know, Mr Kwesiga is the only person qualified to teach would-be adult educators.' (Letter Referenced CRs/1.78 of 19th June 1978.) Despite this yawning gap in staff competence and qualifications, departmental policy on staff development to allow three members of staff to be trained in any one year remained firmly in place. In the absence of an aggressive staff development policy the Department did not attract young potential adult educators and it became severely understaffed. The eighth meeting of the Board of the Centre for Continuing Education noted that there was, 'an acute staffing problem. Out of 22 academic staff tutors' posts we have only 8 staff posts that are filled. In our 7 regions we have only three Resident Tutors and two are without Organisers.' (Min. BC/108/8/78).

And yet as far back as 1969 the recommendations made by Ojok and Onyango were simply ignored and never translated into a viable staff development policy for university adult education. Those recommendations had suggested:

... the organisers and Resident Tutors should undergo formal training in adult education works if they have to work efficiently. The present system of trial and error is utterly self-defeating. The C.C.E should therefore embark straight away on drawing up training programmes for its staff first, before embarking on an ambitious plan of training other adult educators. Such training should take into account short study tours abroad or within Africa. Other members of staff in lower cadres should also be encouraged to do in-service training locally to promote efficiency. (Ojok and Onyango ibid.)

The manner in which the lecturers approached their work, as we have seen above, lacked professionalism. Hence the Department of Extra-Mural Studies was accused of operating in an atmosphere calculated to silence dissent. William's (1968) stilted reporting at this time indicates that his academic colleagues responsible for this were in sympathy with the views of the party in power, most likely for purely opportunistic and not objective reasons. He couches this in the phrase 'propagate alternative proposals'. The financial provision, promises of jobs and related favours which resident tutors knew came from the government compromised the quality of university adult education. There was no established independent platform for a healthy and authentic institution of university adult education.

The inability of the lecturers in the Extra-Mural Department to do the jobs they were expected to do by the university is betrayed by their failure to generate articles for an Adult Education Journal. A Makerere University Adult Education Journal was proposed on 29th May 1975 with the mission to publish articles 'strictly distinctive to adult education'. The journal was to benefit from research and publications grants that the University Senate had committed and recommended in Min. 223 at its 17th Meeting of 29th August 1973. Yet two years passed without the Centre for Continuing Education taking any meaningful action. (Min. EC/3/2/75, Minutes of Publications Committee). The publications committee did not suggest any effective way to generate the necessary articles in a sustainable manner. No wonder colleagues in sister university departments taunted the Centre staff with questions about what the Centre did.

A truly liberal university adult education programme must develop its own independent roots but this the Centre, grafted onto the colonial administration and later the government of Uganda, had not managed to achieve. By the mid sixties both the government and the opposition doubted the authenticity of university adult education. The scenario resembled the one that existed in the Caribbean Department of Extra-Mural Studies at the University College, Mona, Jamaica, grafted onto the nationalist movement during the late forties. Philip Sherlock, its first director, advocated a nationalist oriented extra-mural programme in the interest of nationalism. His 'resident tutors considered themselves as engaged in a type of "guerrilla warfare" in regard to nation building' (Gordon 1979: 49; Harris 1954: 5). The result of this misguided endeavour was the failure to obtain the support of the university community which in turn jeopardised the department's ability to obtain solid financial support from the government and the public. Hence the inevitable financial cuts that affected its programmes, and sceptical government attitudes as to whether it deserved any financing at all. There was no integrity within its inner structure because it failed to adhere to the full breadth of the extra-mural heritage of liberal adult education.

While fellow academics doubted the quality of university adult education the soldiers launched a hunt for the lecturers and resident tutors and many fled the country and remained in exile or simply took a low profile and abandoned their professional charge. In 1977 Director Daniel Okunga, assisted by his secretary, narrowly escaped the deadly arrest by Idi Amin's notorious State Research Bureau operatives and fled the country, while Radio Uganda named him among the wanted conspirators. Those captured faced the firing squad, including the Chief Inspector of Schools; an Archbishop of Uganda was also arrested and murdered.

One month later, when the author of this chapter reported to Gulu as Resident Lecturer, to replace John Obokech who had also fled the country, he was advised by a friendly administrator to keep a very low profile: the Governor of Gulu would neither understand nor appreciate the kind of work he was to do for Makerere University. He was also warned that anti-government elements were being systematically eliminated and that he should be very careful of his movements. Within one week he was hunted out of his house in Gulu town by a group of armed drunken soldiers.

Partners in provision of university adult education

Two categories of partners have provided support for university adult education at Makerere University. The first category is the donors and other international partners who are covered in Chapters 8 and 13. The second category is that of other departments of the university that have co-operated in the provision of adult education or provided programmes of their own for the wider community. The Board of the Centre for Continuing Education noted 'with gratitude ... ready participation by members of the intra-mural departments of [Makerere University] in the Centre's work' during 1978 (Min. BC/111/8/78).

Over the years, Makerere University has lost its monopoly in university adult education. Ugandan universities that participate in research and manpower development include the Uganda Christian University, whose students include a large number of adult entrants, and the Uganda Martyrs University, Nkozi, which has a growing number of extension programmes.

The Makerere University Business School teaches skills to improve business people's performance. The course, developed under a World Bank programme, targets middle to top management cadres and enhances skills for successful managing. The school operates 'bus clinics' at which businessmen discuss problems in their operations. The Uganda Management Institute offers university level courses to adult learners in management skills and awards diplomas and Masters degrees that have a strong research component. Nkumba University, Ndejje Christian University, Mbarara University of Science and Technology, Bugema Seventh Day Adventist University, Kampala University, Kampala International University and Namasagali University all participate in some form of university adult education, including specifically adult education courses, extension courses in their area, and enrolling adult learners in normal courses.

Departments at Makerere University such as Soil Science in the Faculty of Agriculture have embarked on aggressive fieldwork and extension work to make knowledge once the preserve of universities more widely accessible. Lecturers train farmers in troubleshooting to discover deficiencies in soil that show declining productivity; farmers learn university subjects tailored to their requiremens. The Faculty of Law has been instrumental in training paralegal operatives in the basic legal practices in Uganda. Law is demystified and rendered accessible to all those who are trained. The Department of Extension in the Faculty of Agriculture very often applies the skills of its staff to increase extension services outreach. NGOs and departments of universities collaborate in providing the necessary teaching. Tools of social analysis developed at university have been used to promote 'transformative' research. This is research that is essentially Freirian in that it promotes people's participation. The tools developed and in common use include Focus Groups and Participatory Rural Appraisal (PRA)

Widening mass provision of university adult education

In its bid to survive, the paradigm of university adult education at Makerere University has shifted towards what has come to be termed 'Widening Provision'. This concept describes a 'development activity, which leads to wider participation in higher education for groups previously disadvantaged in this respect.' This was inevitable due to the growth of eligible and qualified people who were denied access to university education for lack of adequate space. At the start of university adult education there was a baseline of 3000 potential consumers of university adult education but this has greatly changed. Current demand is very high.

African countries in the early post-colonial years had stuck to colonial patterns of adult education provision but were soon forced to change. Departments of extra-mural studies that had been set up continued at the national universities but with changing functions. In response to the demand by enrolled students, they trained personnel for certificates, diplomas and degree awards.Sadly these qualifications were slow to advance their holders' employment opportunities because their equivalencies and worth were difficult to establish with potential employers. They served merely as stepping-stones. Universities introduced departments of continuing education and extension for health, population, life, and environmental programmes. The universities also established open learning distance education and correspondence. The Commonwealth of Nations supported these initiatives. (Afrik 2000: 21-22.)

At Makerere University school drop-outs, i.e. people who failed to qualify for university education, became beneficiaries of these programmes. The university started to offer correspondence education that ranged from the equivalents of Ordinary Level School Certificate, to two courses namely the Makerere Intermediate Certificate and the Certificate of Adult Studies. To ensure that the qualifications offered were of an acceptable standard, entrance requirements were modified:

> We have therefore been obliged to satisfy demands for equivalence: we have made careful comparisons with HSC results, and now select more rigidly on predicted ability. We have also been obliged to prepare our people more positively for the mature age entry examination to the university (Clarke 1970: 33).

These courses represented a move to specialised professionalism of university adult education and could no longer claim to be aimed at providing a 'liberal adult education'. The quest for professional legitimacy resulted in the development and growth of fully-fledged diploma and degree courses in adult education at Makerere University.

Makerere University has yet to consider Experiential Learning Assessment, an arrangement by which students are able to earn academic credit for the knowledge they have from work, outside activities and life experiences. Faced with a large student body that has overcrowded the campus, there are not enough lecturers to cope with the teaching loads. The new university requirement that the minimum qualification for lecturers must be a doctorate is forcing many lecturers into either spending more hours pursuing personal doctoral studies or simply abandoning university teaching. Yet these are men and women with many years of research and university teaching. The solution to this problem may lie in Experiential Learning Assessment.

While Makerere University adult education may not have the capacity to conduct such assessment and award appropriate credentials, the university would do well to seek partners from abroad to assist it with the exercise. It cannot afford to ignore the known benefits of Experiential Learning Assessment:

- It enables more employees to obtain qualifications
- It increases the self-esteem and confidence of the lecturers.
- It will promote partnership with the providers.
- It will minimise training costs that are not cost effective since the money is spent on members of staff who are already qualified for their jobs.
- It will eliminate time that lecturers are to spend away from their teaching duties.

(Michelson 1997: 144).

Finally, Experiential Learning Assessment will assist the university to cope with what is described in adult education literature as 'massification' – an enormous expansion of student demand for university education – currently compounded by the lecturers' quest for doctoral qualifications. Yet room is very limited. Hardly 30% of qualified applicants may be admitted. The situation at Makerere University is not isolated but is happening all over the African continent; for example, at the University of Botswana out of 12,000 applicants only 4000 could be admitted (Oduaran 1997: 33).

The need to cater for school drop-outs who have missed the chance of higher education but now see their need of it, is greater than ever before. This demand is real and needs to be given a realistic monetary value to ensure appropriate planning and facilitation to match the negative effects of massification with the provision of quality programmes. Occurring in the era of accelerated mass communication, massification can benefit from the technological advances of the twenty-first century. Thousands of students apply and qualify to enrol for courses at the available universities. The need for university adult education has reached unprecedented dimensions and universities in Uganda must be equipped to meet this challenge by taking advantage of new technologies and new methods of university adult education management.

There is a big demand for second chance learning opportunities so that the unfortunate people who missed out on schooling are enabled to catch up and keep abreast of development and technology. Specific needs must also be addressed, including acquisition of further qualifications for those who need them, personal development and self actualisation, artistic creativity, intellectual stimulation and enjoyment, social status improvement, family quality upgrading, enlightened community leadership and national patriotism. Adult university education – continuing and even lifelong education – can fulfil these needs The basis for these developments is adequate pluralistic policies that need to be put in place to establish an enabling climate.

7
Challenges of developing Professional Adult Educators in Uganda

Patrick K. Kagoda and Anne R. Katahoire

There are many opinions about, but little research pertaining to the characteristics or training of adult educators. Most attention is on the learner. Adult educators are somehow supposed to look after themselves. Moreover so many came to adult education through the legendary back door one wonders if there is a front entrance (Brookfield 1985).

This chapter explores the challenges of developing professional adult educators in Uganda. This is an area where there seems to be a noticeable scarcity of literature not only on Uganda but also elsewhere. Out of a collection of over six hundred conference papers covering a period between 1993 to 2001, compiled by the Adult Education Resources Center Web Page, only three were found to be related to the professional development of adult educators. Part of this scarcity of literature on the subject may be the result of the continued debate as to whether there is an adult education profession and whether emphasis should be placed on the professional development of adult educators. This chapter argues that there is a need to develop professional adult educators and explores the challenges of developing professional adult educators in Uganda.

The adult education profession

Adult education as a practice can be said to be as old as mankind. However its existence as a profession in the sense that law or medicine are professions, and as a discipline of academic study is more recent, especially in Africa. Brookfield (1985) observed that the awareness of adult education as a professional practice in America is usually dated to the founding of the American Association for Adult Education in 1926. Despite the formation of the Association, debates as to whether adult education should be considered a profession have continued to date. Liveright in 1964 observed that while adult education could not be classified as a profession, it clearly met the criteria of a 'profession in transition' or an 'emerging profession'. He argued that adult education could lay claim to techniques based on general principals of adult education, even if it could not cite a generally accepted code of ethics and lacked control over its practitioners. Liveright observed that while the original practitioners in the field came from other professions, they were increasingly getting involved in special adult education training and research suited to the field. He argued that, like professions such as law, medicine and social work, adult education was developing as a helping profession because of its primary focus on the human being. Knowles (1980) argued that adult education was a relatively new field of social practice that was still in the process of forming an identity separate from youth education, social work, counselling and related fields of social practice.

The argument that adult education is indeed a profession has continued to be echoed by others working in the field of adult education. Bown and Okedara (1981) in their editorial introduction to *An Introduction to the Study of Adult Education* argued that adult education is an emerging field of study and that like other professions it is a discipline worthy of academic study. They noted that like other professions adult education has a specific clientele, namely the adult learner, and that although adult education may be allied to other fields such as sociology or psychology, it has a core subject matter that can only be researched and taught by someone fully qualified as a professional. This core subject matter includes among others: the historical, philosophical, psychological and sociological foundations of adult education, the psychology of adult learning and of the adult learner, programme planning and evaluation in adult education, the political economy of adult education and development, adult education and sustainable development and research design in adult education.

While arguments for the professionalisation of adult education were being advanced, there were counter arguments against it. Hallenbeck (1948) observed that 'adult educators are born not made'. Others have argued that the professionalisation of adult education destroys the very nature of adult education as a helping occupation.

Their argument is that adult education thrives best on the notion of the 'gifted amateur'. Others argue that no one should be denied the opportunity to practise adult education because of lack of training. Carlson (1977) argued that 'attempts to certificate or credential adult educators threaten the notion of "friends educating each other"'. Boshier (1985), however, argues that, as adult education becomes less marginal and is adopted as an instrument to facilitate attainment of social, economic and cultural goals, it is too important to be left to untrained amateurs, no matter how gifted. Deliberate efforts should instead be made to ensure that as many educators of adults as possible are professionally trained.

The development of education of adults in Uganda

In Uganda, adult education work as it is known today can generally be said to have started between 1945 and 1949. Okech (1984) observed that the most 'significant and systematic' educational programmes for adults organised by the colonial government were those it ran through its Public Relations and Social Welfare Department. Under this programme, demobilised veterans were trained in skills such as brickmaking, mud-stove making and other vocational skills. They were then expected to go and demonstrate these skills to the rural communities. In a sense, this programme was a one-off effort to train a specific group of adults in specific skills, and for a specific purpose. It cannot therefore be seen as a deliberate effort on the part of the colonial government to develop educational programmes for adults. The significance of the effort however lies in the fact that it was the first time for the government of the day to get involved in the provision of education for the adults in Uganda. This effort was followed by others such as the training, by the Ministry of Health, of a large pool of men as hygiene orderlies in hygiene practice.

Later, in 1954, Nsamizi Institute of Social Development was opened, basically as an educational institute for the education of adults. Its major task was to train multipurpose grassroot and middle level/ front line workers (Okech: 1984). Nsamizi was opened as a Local Government and Community Development Centre. It ran short courses for, among others, community development and welfare workers. It was also used for purposes of inducting officers going and coming from overseas to adapt to the new life or environment. After independence other institutions like the Law Development Centre, the Institute of Public Administration and Agriculture and Co-operative Colleges were established and so the running of courses for this cadre of staff at Nsamizi was terminated; instead the Centre remained with courses in Community Development and Welfare. In 1970 a two-year diploma course in social development was launched, followed in 1975 by a one-year certificate course in the same subject. Many of the frontline workers engaged in the education of adults in the past and to some extent even today were trained at Nsamizi.

At around the same time as Nsamizi Institute of Social Development was established, a Department of Extra-Mural Studies was also established at Makerere University. This was set up in 1953, to take the university to the adult community and to encourage the community to participate in the learning and teaching activities of the university (Kwesiga 1983). Initially, the educational programmes it organised for adults were mainly conducted off campus and many of them were organised up country. The educational programmes consisted of public lectures, day and residential courses and evening classes under the supervision of university resident tutors.

After Independence, however, the role of the department expanded to include other educational programmes for adults conducted through mass media (radio, TV, correspondence and newspapers) and longer residential courses. These included courses for upgrading teachers, Certificate of Adult Studies and others. Because of this new and expanded role, the Extra-Mural Department was renamed the Centre for Continuing Education (CCE).

Clark (1967) a former Director of the then Extra-Mural Department at Makerere University listed a number of educational activities organised for adults, which were being carried out in the country at that time. They included: weekly classes and short courses organised by the Adult Studies Centre; functional literacy and 'fundamental education' courses organised by the Community Development Department; technical and vocational education under the Ministry of Education; specialised courses for co-operative officials, social workers, etc. organised by the Milton Obote Foundation, and workers' education courses organised by the Labour College and other organisations like the YMCA and YWCA. In addition to these activities, Clark further referred to 'a mass of fringe activities...which (made up) ...the pattern of education for adults in Uganda.' These included film-shows, informal talks, debates, concerts, festivals and exhibitions. It is important to note, however, that although all these were educational activities organised for adults, the staff who ran these programmes were trained in fields other than adult education.

While these scattered efforts were initial attempts to focus on the learning of adults in Uganda in an organised way, they did not serve as the beginning of the professionlisation of adult education in Uganda. As Clark noted, these efforts were largely 'scattered and uncoordinated.' Secondly, the focus of the programmes was not on adult education; they were not based on any recognisable body of knowledge in adult education or even on adult education principles and practices. The staff engaged in these adult education activities, especially those from the then Community Development Department, were not adult educators in any sense of the term. They were largely civil servants, from non-adult education professions, doing their job. They did not even think of themselves as adult educators. Kwesiga (see Okech 1984) observed years later, that educators of adults in organisations related to primary health care, agriculture, trade unions and cooperatives were the kind of people who would 'blink if you called them a brother in adult education.' Meaning they did not consider themselves adult educators as such.

The development of professional adult educators
While in Uganda and in Africa in general, the training of professional adult educators in universities is a recent practice, universities, especially in the USA and Britain, have been doing so for several decades. A study carried out by Griffin (1983) revealed that there were over 200 professors of adult education and about 2038 doctorate holders in adult education in USA alone. Despite this, adult education continued to be regarded as a 'come and go' profession for many years, mainly because the profession lacked qualified, full-time

practitioners, an issue that, as noted earlier, has been addressed over the years. A survey of adult educators conducted by the Learning Resources Network (LERN) in 1983 in the U.S.A indicated that:

> The typical practicing adult educator [was] new to the position, [had[little or no course work in adult education, [came] from a field outside of adult education and [was] likely to leave it in five years (Brookfield 1985).

Training approaches and methodologies

In Uganda, the majority of the people who are engaged in the education of adults often start off as volunteers. While some of them leave the field after a few years, others decide to stay and become full-time educators of adults. Those who decide to stay often realise that they need some form of training in the field if they are to do their job better. These are the ones who go on for further training to become adult educators.

Early recruitment to the field of adult education in Uganda was based on the content and nature of educational programmes being organised for adults. Later, however, a number of those engaged in the education of adults sought more specialised training in the UK and the USA. On their return to Uganda they became the first trainers of trainers in adult education. The short courses they started later developed into longer-term training programmes for adult educators.

Bown and Okedara (1981) made some useful distinctions relating to people who work in the adult education field. They distinguished between; 'adult educationists', 'adult educators', and 'educators of adults'. They defined adult educationists as basically the theoreticians in the field. These have undergone professional training in adult education, conduct research, and are qualified to train other trainers of adults. 'Adult educators' on the other hand, are the trained cadres who participate in the actual education of the adults. Bown and Okedara refer to this category as 'practitioners', while other authors have referred to them as the 'ones in the trenches'. Not only are they engaged in the education of adults, but their work is based on proper adult education methodology, principles and practices. The 'educators of adults' are involved in the education of adults, but they do not base their education of the adults on any recognisable principles and practices of adult education. The majority of them are volunteers in the field. Some may not even know that they are adult educators or refer to themselves as such. Several authors argue that this category of workers constitute the majority of the people in the adult education field. They include the village craftsman, the literacy instructor, the tailoring instructor and others.

Currently, there seem to be two main methodologies used in the training of educators of adults, namely on-the-job experience and short-term, in-service courses. Longer-term courses leading to the award of diplomas and degree certificates (Merriam 1985) and online professional training (Hawk W. B., 2000 ERIC) are for adult educators.

According to Merriam (1985), on-the-job experience is the major means through which practitioners become 'competent' or 'proficient'. This is mainly because 'most enter adult education through a "back door" from some other field, role or agency.'

> Proficiency in the role thus develops through trial-and-error, through modelling another's behaviour, through consulting with colleagues and co-workers, and through self-directed study. (Merriam 1985: 37)

Short-term, in service training is the second major way through which the training of educators of adults occurs in Uganda. This training is mostly carried out by NGOs like LABE, NAEA, Action Aid and to some extent the Ministry of Gender, Labour and Social Development. It is intended for the large numbers of volunteers and part-time workers in the field of adult education. Here, as Merriam noted, the employing institution or agency, professional associations, resource centres, colleges and universities, and private consultants usually sponsor the training.

They are short-term, seek to achieve specific goals, which are usually job-related, or situation-specific, and may offer Continuing Education or other credit units (Merriam, op cit.,).

The long-term, full-time training in institutions of higher learning such as Makerere University, Nsamizi Institute of Social Development and to some extent the National Adult Education Association are for adult educators as opposed to educators of adults. This kind of training leads to the award of various certificates, diplomas, undergraduate and post-graduate degrees. The training introduces the learners to specialised topics in adult education such as 'adult learning', 'organisation of the field', 'programme development and administration', and special courses in related areas.

Online professional training is the latest methodology for training adult educators. Online training is becoming increasingly popular, mainly because previously many adult educators were 'having difficulties finding training opportunities in areas vital to adult education, such as principles of adult education and learning, second language acquisition theory, teaching methodology and the use of technology in instruction' (Hawk W. B., 2000). Advances in Internet technology and the increasing accessibility of the Internet have enhanced the popularity of online training.

> Internet-based training offers more structure in both the content and delivery of the training, including the guidance of a facilitator or team of facilitators... Internet resources can include everything from online journal articles to real-time chats on specific topics to models for materials and curriculum development (Hawk 2000, op cit.).

Online professional training is an area which is new, but which promises to revolutionise the training of adult educators all over the world. The modern trend in higher education is to move away from stand-alone universities to networked universities, from teacher-led learning to student-led learning, from full time students to dual mode students, from onsite-learning to online-learning and from locally oriented universities to internationally oriented universities.

The professionalisation of adult education in Uganda

The second decade of independence brought issues of development to the forefront in Uganda. There was a growing realisation of the need for various development workers to be trained in skills of communicating effectively with adults. Adult education gained momentum in the neighbouring countries and some Ugandans underwent adult education training there. In 1982, Makerere University's Centre for Continuing Education conducted a needs assessment survey on the training needs of development workers and the provision of extension services in Uganda.

The survey was followed by discussions and consultations with organisations and individuals involved in the education of adults and in development work in the country. The survey and consultations revealed valuable lessons. Firstly many government ministries and non-governmental organisations were spending considerable resources in rural extension work, but their noble efforts were being hampered by lack of proper training for the extension personnel. Secondly, most rural development programmes were poorly planned and managed and in most cases these programmes were never evaluated. Furthermore, many development workers were failing in their work partly because of not taking into consideration all the different forces which affect the development process. Rural problems were being treated in isolation whereas they were part of a wider complex of realities. More importantly, in learning situations adults were often treated like school children and they resented this.

All these problems convinced CCE that there was a need to start longer-term training programmes in adult education and development. Before these training programmes were started, however, CCE in 1983 decided to start off by running a series of pilot non-certificate courses, each lasting 10 weeks. The German Adult Education Association (DVV) made the series possible through a generous grant. These pilot training programmes were a forerunner for the diploma and degree courses in adult education and development, which were later launched. The pilot programmes were meant to stimulate discussions, comments and suggestions about the future training of adult educators. During the five cycles of the ten-week courses in adult education and development, many valuable lessons and ideas developed and these were later incorporated in the diploma course, which was launched in 1988/89.

Pandak (2000) suggests that the introduction of a distinct body of knowledge into the university is a signal that a particular area of practice is actively seeking legitimating and 'professional' status. At Makerere the introduction of the short training programmes in adult education and development and later the diploma and degree marked the beginning of the professionalisation of adult education in Uganda.

The diploma in adult education was primarily aimed at people who were already carrying out or intended to carry out some kind of adult education or development work. The course was designed to enable the participants to work with communities in educational and other developmental programmes, regardless of their physical, economic and social situation and to exhibit concern for individual adult learners and other adults in the communities. For nearly two decades Makerere University's CCE was the only institution in Uganda involved in this kind of professional training of adult educators.

Over the years, however, those trained through these programmes started their own training programmes, drawing on adult education methodology, principles and practices. These organisations include, the National Education Association, Literacy and Adult Basic Education (LABE), NWASEA and Nsamizi Institute of Social Development.

Literacy and Adult Basic Education (LABE), for example, which was started by graduates from the diploma in adult education and development course at Makerere, has developed specialised literacy training. LABE's core activities now cover the training of literacy trainers and instructors, the production of training materials, developing the management capacity of district level NGOs, developing literacy plans with key players, civic education and training of literacy workers who are engaged in teaching basic English to adults.

Towards the end of the 1980s the National Adult Education Association introduced a certificate course in adult education. The certificate is run through distance education and more than five hundred trainees have been through the programme. Nsamizi Institute of Social Development, which pioneered training in social development, has in the past trained the majority of staff employed by the department of community development, which is in charge of adult literacy and basic adult education work in the country. There is now an effort to strengthen the adult education component by introducing a diploma in adult education at the institute.

With these new initiatives in place, there was growing demand for more advanced training at degree level. So the department of adult education and communication studies at Makerere University decided in 1996 to introduce a Bachelor degree in adult and community education and to gradually phase out the diploma in adult education. The main objective now was to create a cadre of well-trained decision makers, designers and implementers of adult and community education programmes. While a critical mass of frontline workers was being developed at the lower levels, a gap still existed at the higher levels of policy makers in adult education. The Bachelors in adult and community education was thus designed to equip learners with sound knowledge, skills and attitudes in adult education, community development and contemporary socio-economic issues related to the development process of adult education. The graduates of this programme are expected to work with communities and adult learners of different types in order to facilitate a quick process of community development and social transformation.

The programme is designed so that at the end of the three-year programme graduates should be able to relate and apply the concepts, principles and theories of adult education and community development to practical Ugandan situations and other third world countries. They should also be able to exhibit a positive attitude towards adult and community education, demonstrable in their interest, willingness and readiness to work with communities in educational and other developmental programmes regardless of the community's physical, economic and social situation. They should also be able to demonstrate their concern for individual adult learners and other adults in the community. The graduates should also be able to demonstrate practical skills in assessing community needs, designing educational and other developmental programmes in response to the identified needs, implementing and evaluating adult education and other development programmes, facilitating adult learning and training in different environments, designing and carrying out a research project in adult and community education and producing a scientifically acceptable report.

Challenges of training of adult educators in Uganda

While adult education as a profession continues to develop in Uganda, it also continues to face major challenges. The Directory of Adult Education Agencies in Uganda, compiled in 1984, revealed over one hundred agencies in Uganda involved in the education of adults. This number has more than trebled over the years. The majority of those working in these agencies are recruited and they learn on the job. Most community-based organisations, too, recruit community workers who learn on the job and these form the bulk of educators of adults in Uganda. Some agencies make a deliberate effort to organise training workshops for their employees, others do not. The fact that the majority of educators of adults are untrained is a challenge in that their lack of training compromises the quality of their work and in the long run the overall development of the communities they seek to serve. Efforts by government and some training organisations such as LABE, NWASEA and NAEA which carry out training of frontline workers at the grassroots level are scattered and unco-ordinated. There is no unified curriculum that encompasses the diversity of adult education programmes being run in the country, while at the same time emphasising the core of the adult education discipline.

Adult education in Uganda is composed of diverse activities and programmes whose extent and magnitude is not always easy to determine. This continues to make it difficult to bring the different practitioners in this field together. Various attempts in the past to form a National Association of adult educators have been viewed with suspicion. This has made it difficult to argue a case for resources and for recognition in the face of national planners whose idea of education is normally bound up with a more or less unified structure under a Ministry of Education.

Partly because of this problem but also partly because of problems related to terminology and definition, it has become difficult for adult educators and practitioners to speak the same language and to recognise that theirs is a common destiny in the service of mankind. Kwesiga (see Okech 1984) observed that the language around the field of adult education is littered with all sorts of terminologies that in the end leave one confused and wondering whether the neighbour is truly of the same profession. What seems to bring those involved in adult education together is the content they deliver and not the target group or the methodologies they employ in organising learners and facilitating learning. While emphasis in co-ordinating programmes should be more on methodology, the majority of adult education programmes and practitioners are organised around content.

Adult education being a relatively new profession has to fight for recognition. This has become more apparent in Uganda with graduates from the Bachelors of Adult and Community Education joining the job market. Most of these are employed by NGOs or CBOs. Government on the other hand continues to advertise for social scientists and formal educators to do the work of adult educators. Graduates of BACE often express concern that the qualification is not understood or known in the world of work. This calls for a great deal of sensitisation and advocacy work.

Another big challenge remaining is how to incorporate the advances in technology into the training and professionalisation of adult educators in Uganda. As already noted, many untrained people are continuing to join the adult education profession. Their lack of training compromises their work and therefore the development of the communities they serve. Yet opportunities for training and therefore professionalisation remain few and far between. A major suggestion being made to meet this challenge is to increase opportunities for online training or 'E-learning'.

E-learning is making connections among persons and resources through communication technologies for related learning purposes. E-learning is flexible in the sense that it is independent of time and place, as long as there is an Internet connection. It allows students to follow different learning paths, supports individual, peer coaching and group work, supports several communication tools, and the use of different learning materials with different degrees of interactivity.

Makerere University is currently evolving an E-learning project. The long-term objective of the project is capacity development in the field of E-learning aimed at the promotion of ICT in all areas of education and research at Makerere University. E-learning will, however, demand new teaching and assessment skills, including skills such as coaching skills in a virtual environment, and online test/examination skills.

8
Economics and Financing of Adult Education in Uganda

Anthony Okech

Introduction
The title of this chapter borrows from the title of one of the UNESCO Institute for Education reports arising from UNESCO's Fifth International conference on Adult Education, Hamburg, 1997, code-named CONFITEA V. Some of the analysis tools used in this chapter have been inspired by that report (Madhu Singh 1999) and by other documents from that conference.

In its key document, The Agenda for the Future, CONFINTEA V states:

> The costs of adult learning must be seen in relation to the benefits that derive from reinforcing the competence of adults. ... The education of adults contributes to their self-reliance and personal autonomy, to the exercise of basic rights and to increased productivity and labour efficiency. It is also positively translated into higher levels of education and well-being of future generations. Adult education, being a human development and productive investment, should be protected from the constraints of structural adjustment (UNESCO 1997: 26).

The view expressed in this quotation is that adult education is a productive human development investment. Financing adult education is therefore an investment in human development that produces benefits. Some of the benefits produced are listed in the quotation. According to CONFITEA V, these make it important to protect the financing of adult education from constraints such as structural adjustment.

In Uganda, the financing of adult education, like the financing of other services, must have suffered to some extent from structural adjustment programmes. However, it is important to establish how much funding priority was accorded to adult education even before the structural adjustment programmes. It is also important to establish what other factors may have affected the funding of adult education.

This chapter will accordingly try to establish the level of funding priority adult education has enjoyed among the different financing agencies in Uganda, to see the implications of the financing for the practice and development of adult education in Uganda, and to assess the cost-effectiveness of the provision as a human development and productive investment. It is hoped that this will provide researchers and practitioners with ideas that can be used in making a case for adult education in the competition for scarce resources. In the process, the chapter will give some idea about the equity of allocation and make some comparison of cost-effectiveness between the different programmes.

This chapter is not about absolute quantitative figures. While some figures are given, the chapter relies more on indicators of the level of funding relative to its adequacy, and of benefits accruing from the investment. This, it seems to the author, is even more important than a mere listing of concrete figures. The chapter will then attempt to show how the funding and benefits compare.

Challenges of discussing adult education financing

The first challenge in talking about the financing of adult education in Uganda is finding a commonly agreed understanding and demarcation of adult education. Although this problem is not unique to Uganda it is particularly difficult there because there is no policy or structure that in any way groups together activities known as adult education. As earlier chapters have shown, adult education as an area of specialisation is still in its formative stages. This chapter returns to the Hamburg Declaration quoted in Chapter 1 for a definition to use:

> Adult education denotes the entire body of ongoing learning processes, formal or otherwise, whereby people regarded as adults by the society to which they belong develop their abilities, enrich their knowledge, and improve their technical or

professional qualifications or turn them in a new direction to meet their own needs and those of their society. (UNESCO 1997: 1)

This definition admittedly covers a broad area that transcends the distinction some writers have made between 'adult education' and the 'education of adults'. Ignoring that distinction, we here divide the broad area into two main categories based on the breadth of the target group and address some identifiable components within the two groups.

The two categories under which the financing of adult education will be examined are: (a) adult basic education and extension, and (b) continuing and further education. In the first category the components covered include adult literacy, other adult basic education and extension education. The second category includes various forms of continuing and further education. Both categories may be offered in any setting or delivery mode: formal, non-formal and informal, face-to-face or at a distance.

The second challenge is the difficulty of having access to information on the financing of adult education. This difficulty is due in part to the complexity of activities that constitute adult education. The diversity of provision, without focus or co-ordination, complicates the effort to identify the budgets or expenditure dedicated to adult education. In many cases, budgets that serve adult education are not in budget-lines explicitly designated as adult education. In the current decentralised system, many local governments do not have such a budget-line at all, as was discovered during the evaluation of adult literacy programmes in Uganda carried out in 1999 (Okech et al. 2001). Adult education carried out in the sectors of health, agriculture, commerce, industry and others is not referred to as adult education and the budget dedicated to education is often not differentiated from other activities in the sectors.

Even some civil society organisations involved in adult education often have adult education as part of other activities and may not necessarily have a distinct budget for it. When these organisations do have distinct budgets for adult education, it is often more specifically for adult literacy. In such cases, it is more possible to identify the expenditure on adult education.

There is, however, another barrier: the secrecy that seems to surround information on finances. Both government and non-government organisations are usually reluctant to reveal information on their finances. This is in spite of the fact that they are handling funds for which they are accountable to the public or their membership. The difficulty in obtaining financial information may be partly responsible for the lack of researched information on the economics and financing of adult education and related activities. The only significant financial analysis – the 1999 evaluation of adult literacy programmes – was, naturally limited to adult literacy. (Okech et al 2001)

Types of financing

Education is funded in five main ways in Uganda: directly by the people who pay fees and other costs; by the government through various mechanisms; by local non-profit making non-governmental organisations; by foreign and international agencies; and by commercial enterprises. This pattern of funding applies both to formal and other types of education and particularly to adult education.

Financing by individual adults for their own education has tended to focus on the further and higher education levels, where it has increased significantly in recent years. Many adults have enrolled for both general and specialised programmes at post-primary, post-secondary and university levels. The opening up of university education in Uganda to non-government sponsored students during the last decade has resulted in thousands of adults re-entering the education field, through both the face-to-face and the distance learning modes.

At the adult literacy and basic education level individual financing has been low. There has of late been some change in this situation with private enterprises starting to offer adult literacy, basic and continuing education for a fee, especially in the urban areas. The response has been good although such provision is still very little.

The government and NGOs are mainly engaged in functional adult literacy and adult basic education, including health, civic and agricultural extension education. Government financing comes from tax revenue, while some national and local NGOs raise finances from membership fees and income-generating activities. In most cases, however, these NGOs rely heavily on external funding. Many government programmes are also still run mainly on external funding.

Financing of adult basic education and extension education

Government provides adult basic education through its functional adult literacy programme and other non-formal adult education programmes. This section will first look at adult literacy, which has usually been most readily identified as adult education, and then at other forms of non-formal basic education and extension education.

Adult literacy

As earlier chapters have shown, it was religious missionaries who first introduced adult literacy and non-traditional education in general during the second half of the nineteenth century. The colonial government in Uganda had very little role to play in the provision of education during the first fifty years of its rule. It gradually started being involved, first in formal education and later also in adult basic education. Government involvement in adult education picked up more after the Second World War with one of the aims being to occupy demobilised soldiers and keep them out of mischief. This is when the government first made some notable input in adult basic education, but it was apparently still not very much.

After obtaining independence, the government of Uganda, like many other newly independent governments of Africa, embarked on an effort to ensure education for its citizens and to do away with illiteracy. In 1964 it therefore launched a nationwide mass literacy campaign. This was a fairly big effort, involving holding writers' workshops to develop a literacy primer and reader in each of the selected twenty-two Ugandan languages, producing the materials, mobilising thousands of volunteer instructors and opening up literacy classes in all parts of the country. Although it is not possible to access the actual figures of expenditure, this was certainly a big investment in adult literacy, probably the highest, comparatively, that the government has ever made at one time.

However, although this was a relatively significant investment, the fact that the campaign relied entirely on unpaid volunteer instructors raises a big question regarding the adequacy of the financing. It is true that, so soon after independence, there was still plenty of nationalistic enthusiasm. People had a sense of patriotism that prompted them to give their time generously for the development of their newly independent country. One could, therefore, say that the volunteer instructors were able to put in their best even without pay. The important thing was for them to have adequate facilities and materials.

One type of facility that the government provided for adult education was the community centre, built in every rural sub-county and urban division. The centres were multi-purpose but one of their most important functions was to serve as a venue for adult literacy classes. Of course, one centre per sub-county was accessible to only a fraction of the population of the sub-county as distances within sub-counties at the time covered up to 30 kilometres. Adult literacy classes were therefore held at many other venues, including schools, religious buildings and other borrowed premises where available, or under the shade of a tree.

The lack of facilities placed adult literacy in the situation of a marginal activity of little importance, even when it had been launched as a mass campaign. This was reinforced by the fact that adult literacy depended on unpaid volunteer instructors. Adult literacy indeed occupied such a marginal position that it was among the government programmes that disappeared almost completely in the social and economic disruption during Amin's regime in the seventies.

It was during this period, when government adult education programmes were at their lowest, that NGOs started coming up in Uganda to make whatever little contributions they could towards filling the gap. The Kiira Adult Education Association started operating in 1976, followed by the National Adult Education Association three years later. The only inputs that these associations could make were in kind contributions of the members' time, skills and property such as land or houses that could be used for learning activities. They not only kept the spirit of adult education alive, but also ushered in a new era of civil society involvement in the provision of adult education. From their roots sprang the great blossom of civil society organisations that one sees in the field of adult education in Uganda today. Unlike today, Uganda was then largely cut off from the rest of the world and these organisations could not obtain much external support.

With the departure of Amin in 1979, Uganda became gradually more accessible to the outside world although to a very limited extent during the civil strife in the first half of the eighties. Uganda was thus to a small extent able to participate in the Programme for the Eradication of Illiteracy in Africa adopted by African ministers of education in Harare in 1982. The UNESCO regional office in Africa (BREDA) supported the effort in African countries by providing financial and technical skills for training and developing literacy plans. Support by BREDA to Uganda increased during the second half of the eighties with the more peaceful conditions that came after the National Resistance Movement came to power in 1986. Other external support also started coming in, particularly from the German Adult Education Association (DVV), which signed a formal co-operation agreement with the Makerere University Centre for Continuing Education, Kiira Adult Education Association and the National Adult Education Association. However, government revenue remained so low that it was not possible for government to finance adult literacy, which was, therefore, not included on the new government's priority list until the early nineties.

In 1991 the government accorded adult literacy higher priority and allocated a nominal budget to re-launching government literacy activities. What was more important was that this was a signal for external support to government adult literacy programmes. UNICEF and DVV came in to support the re-launch of the activities through a pilot project whose preparation had also received support from UNESCO through technical assistance. This was the beginning of renewed financing of adult literacy in Uganda, which grew slowly until it received a sudden boost by being included under the government's Poverty Action Fund in 2001.

The 1999 evaluation of adult literacy programmes in Uganda did an analysis of their costs and cost-effectiveness (Okech et al. 1999 and 2001, Chapter 8). An earlier review, in 1995, to evaluate the pilot project that had run from 1992 to 1995 had also computed the costs of the project, calculating that the total estimate of the project during that period had been just over US$1 million. The 1999 evaluation estimated the amount spent by the central government and donors on the programme from 1996 to 1999 as US $640,000, bringing total expenditure to between 1992 and 1999 to US$1.7 million.

The evaluation found that the percentage of central government expenditure in comparison to donor expenditure had over the period reduced from 50% to about 30%. Since donor funding was not increasing, this meant that there would have been a decline in expenditure on adult literacy. The growing gap was to some extent covered by local government contributions in the decentralised system that was introduced in 1997. However, the level of budgetary allocation to adult literacy by local governments (districts and sub-counties) was very low, ranging at sub-county level from about US$1,000 to as low as US$25. As noted above, in some cases there was even no clear budget-line for adult literacy.

During the same period, NGO investment in adult literacy and adult education in general increased. The most prominent contributor in the field of literacy was ActionAid Uganda, first through its functional adult literacy programme in Mubende and then through the REFLECT programme in Bundibugyo and other districts. By the time of the evaluation REFLECT, which had started as a pilot project in Bundibugyo, had been scaled up and was being taken up by other organisations with support from ActionAid's REFLECT Co-ordination Unit based in Mubende. The evaluation also studied the Netherlands Development Organisation (SNV) which had launched the Women's Empowerment Programme in the north-western districts, Save the Children UK, which had a literacy programme in the same area, the Soroti Catholic Diocese Development Organisation (SOCADIDO) in

Eastern Uganda and LABE, a literacy development and support organisation, which was operating an annual budget of several hundred thousand dollars supported from various external sources.

Other national NGOs benefiting from external support were able to run adult literacy programmes. A small number of organisations networked as the Uganda Joint Action for Adult Education (UJAFAE) were benefiting from DVV support, some of which was used for literacy. Several other faith-based organisations (apart from SOCADIDO) were running small-scale literacy activities, for example, the Community Education Programme of the Karamoja Church of Uganda Diocese, the Young Men's Christian Association (YMCA) and the Young Women's Christian Association (YWCA).

In spite of all these sources, the amount of money being put into adult literacy was still very insignificant compared to the need. The 1999 evaluation report calculated that all the programmes were together reaching only about 4% of the five million non-literate adults. In 2002 the National Adult Literacy Strategic Investment Plan (NALSIP) painted an even bleaker picture when it stated that all adult literacy programmes were reaching 4.3% of the 6.9 million non-literate adults (MGLSD 2002, p. vi). It is against this background that the government developed and started implementing NALSIP in 2002. This plan put adult literacy financing in a privileged position under the Poverty Action Fund, a fund that is protected from diversion to other uses. Government funding of adult literacy suddenly shot up about twentyfold.

However, in spite of the financial boost that functional adult literacy received as a result of being included as a key strategy under the Poverty Eradication Action Plan (PEAP), the funding still remains inadequate. The government adult literacy programme still depends on unpaid volunteer instructors, lacks facilities and still largely operates under trees, has very inadequate allocation for training instructors and lacks the means to carry out effective supervision. In realisation of the very limited funding available, the government ministry in charge of the adult literacy programme came up during 2003 with a new sector wide strategic investment plan that has reduced the targets to about one-third of what NALSIP had proposed.

Agricultural extension, co-operative education and health education

All adult literacy programmes have what are referred to as functionality components that include agriculture, health and co-operative education, among others. However, these different aspects of non-formal basic education have their homes in other government programmes and ministries. Their financing therefore needs to be discussed in the context of these other programmes and ministries.

Agricultural extension education has traditionally been carried out mainly by the government ministry in charge of agriculture, a ministry that has obviously always undertaken many more activities than agricultural extension education. In the 1984 Directory of Adult Education two of the five objectives given by the ministry itself were relevant to adult education, namely, 'teaching farmers good husbandry practices' and 'popularising the production of good quality cash or export crops'. These were translated into activities through 'teaching and training farmers at district farm institutes' and 'door-to-door extension work' (Okech 1984: 11-12).

Although agriculture is considered to be the most important economic activity in the country, the sector received a surprisingly small percentage of the national budget. Its budgetary allocation has grown from just 1.0% of the national budget in 1998/99 to 2.3% in 2002/2003 (MFPED 2002: 87). Because of the heavy emphasis on the provision of physical inputs, not much of this rather limited budget actually goes into the kind of extension education that reaches the small farmer. The 'door-to-door extension work' that is supposed to be one of the activities is hardly implemented anywhere. Of late, the extension education function has been removed from the mainstream activities of the ministry and handed over to specialised agencies, currently the National Agricultural Advisory Services. The Poverty Eradication Action Plan 2001-2003 reported that instead of the 80% of all households that were to be reached by agricultural advisory services, only 10-15% of household were benefiting (MFPED 2001: 149).

There are a number of organisations, both national and international, that invest in various forms of extension in Uganda.

Agriculture is such a key concern to over 80% of Ugandans, especially the poorer sections of the community, that most organisations working for development in Uganda have a component of agriculture among their activities. A few organisations, however, engage only in agricultural development. Among other activities, they invest in agricultural extension education, although only in selected districts and on a project basis. A noteworthy effort is that by the Sasakawa Africa Association, which, together with the Global 2000 programme of the Carter Center, has been implementing the Sasakawa Global 2000 extension programme in Uganda. This programme was reviewed in 2002 and found to have made a significant contribution (Plucknett et al. 2002).

The Uganda National Farmers' Association is a national organisation that has branches in all districts of the country. It works to mobilise farmers for improved production and greater productivity. Agricultural education is accordingly one of its main activities. It raises financing for its activities both from the membership and from external support.

The ministry in charge of agriculture has often also covered forestry, animal husbandry and fisheries. The composition of the portfolios held by this ministry is, however, one of those that have changed a number of times since independence. All these areas of activity involve a certain amount of extension education, wherever they may be housed at any given time, usually as departments or directorates. The amount of financing for their activities is necessarily not much when, as currently, animal industry and fisheries is with agriculture in a ministry that has only 2.3% of the national budget. To appreciate the extent to which the budget is inadequate, it is useful to keep in mind that the total national budget, for a country with a population of over 24 million, amounts to only about US $1.5 billion (MFPED 2003).

For over a decade, there has been increasing focus on environmental education through both formal and non-formal and non-formal education. Environmental education in Uganda is closely related to agricultural and forestry activities, because such a large percentage of Ugandans depend directly on these resources for their livelihood. The lead government agency for this is the National Environment Management Authority (NEMA). Established in 1994, NEMA is a specialised agency linked to the Ministry of Water, Land and Environment and has the mission, 'To promote and ensure integrated and sustainable environment management in Uganda'.

Education is one of the ways that NEMA promotes to ensure integrated and sustainable environment management. In 1997, it commissioned Anthony Okech of IACE to develop a national Non-formal Environmental Education and Community Training Strategy (NEMA 1997), which is also available on the NEMA web page (nemaug.org). This strategy focuses on environmental education for adults and communities. NEMA supports the districts, other agencies and non-governmental organisations in the provision of environmental education.

There are hundreds of NGOs and community based organisations operating in the field of environment in Uganda (NEMA 1999) and most of them have some element of environmental education for adults. They invest resources in this from different sources, with most of them benefiting from external financing. In a few cases NEMA has obtained financial support for some community based organisations. Collaboration between NEMA and NGOs is one of the strategies in the non-formal environment education strategy.

Co-operative education in Uganda is also very much linked to agriculture and has therefore been an important category of adult education. The main providers of co-operative education have been the government department in charge of co-operative development and the co-operative unions and societies themselves. For a long time there was a ministry of co-operatives and marketing with a co-operative department whose objectives were: to organise farmers in rural areas for better marketing of their various crops; to educate farmers in co-operative phenomena and related topics and uplift the general standard of living of farmers. Educational activities carried out by the department include day classes, seminars, workshops, in-service training, short courses and occasional meetings. The sources of financing for the department's activities are government, primary co-operative societies through a statutory education fund and several external sources, especially the United States Agency for International Development (USAID), Agricultural Co-operative Development International (ACDI) and the European Economic Community, now the European Union (EU).

The 1984 *Directory of Adult Education in Uganda* listed twelve co-operative unions in Uganda, of which nine were agricultural produce marketing unions (Okech 1984: 79-83). All twelve were engaged in co-operative education for adults through their Co-operative Education and Publicity Officers. Although there has been a decline in co-operative activities in Uganda, the co-operative unions still invest some resources in co-operative education. They are supported in this by the Uganda Co-operative Alliance, an autonomous organisation supporting co-operative education and development.

Health education is one of the most widespread forms of adult and community education in Uganda. It is carried out by the Ministry of Health through its health service delivery points, outreach activities in the communities, specially organised health education activities and the mass media. The ministry carries out training of both health workers and communities in personal hygiene, sanitation, disease prevention and treatment. It has a Division of Health Promotion and Education whose objective is the strengthening of comprehensive and effective information, education and communication programmes. The number of educational activities reflects a significant amount of investment by government and other organisations. Of late there has been a particularly intensive educational campaign in the struggle against HIV/AIDS.

Health education has attracted financing from both internal and external sources. Two United Nations specialised agencies, the World Health Organisation (WHO) and UNICEF, have offices in Kampala through which they have provided much support to government programmes. In its collaboration with various organisations in Uganda, the Ministry of Health set up the public-private partnership in health to increase private health sector participation in all aspects of the National Health Programme. The partners of the ministry in this arrangement fall into three categories. The first is that of private not-for-profit health providers, such as the faith-based medical bureaux,

Catholic, Protestant and Muslim, or other humanitarian organisations, Red Cross, Oxfam, African Medical Research Foundation (AMREF), Save the Children Fund (international) and the Italian CUAMM. The second category consists of private health practitioners including private individual practitioners, professional associations and specialist associations. The third category comprises traditional and complementary medicine practitioners such as herbalists, spiritual healers, bonesetters, traditional birth attendants, hydrotherapists and traditional dentists. Some of the activities in this partnership include investment in health education.

Financing continuing and further education

Adults of different ages undertake various forms of continuing and further education, in both formal and non-formal settings. Continuing education is used here to refer to education that is often undertaken in discrete units, not graded from one level to another but undertaken mainly as work-related refresher courses, skills improvement or to acquire new knowledge and skills in specific areas of need or concern. This type of education takes place mainly in the non-formal setting. Much of this category of education is financed by government, by external funding through institutions and NGOs or by commercial enterprises. Trade unions have significantly financed such education and training for workers, using members' subscriptions and funds obtained from external sources. Individuals also often finance their own participation in such programmes when it offers them the prospects of better economic returns or jobs.

There has been some concern in the national press about the frequency and number of such non-formal continuing education activities. If the views expressed are anything to go by, then one could say that a considerable amount of money is being spent on them. Together with conferences, such educational activities keep many hotels in and around Kampala well patronised. A comprehensive study of non-formal continuing educational activities taking place in hotels would provide an interesting insight into the amount of investment in them.

One gap that should be noted is the absence of any legal provision obliging employers to provide for employee education or training. There is no requirement for employers to contribute to any training or education fund, to provide their employees with any education or training opportunities or even to allow their employees time off for any form of education. It is often only through difficult negotiation that employed persons obtain permission to undertake any educational activities that may require time off their work. In many cases permission is even denied. It is thus at the sole discretion of the employer to decide whether an employee needs continuing education or further training in any aspect. The Federation of Uganda Employers and the trade unions have to some extent tried to promote the realisation of the importance of continuing education for employees, but many employers seem to remain sceptical about it.

Further education is used here to mean the type of education undertaken by schooled adults at various levels, including university level, to attain higher qualifications and so raise their educational status. This is a broader definition than the one used in Britain. The amount of such further education undertaken by schooled adults, especially at post-secondary level, has increased rapidly in recent years. Much of it is undertaken in formal educational institutions. A large number of private commercial institutions have grown up to meet the rising demand. Because of an inadequate framework and insufficient resources for quality assurance, there is much concern about the quality of the education and training offered in many of the mushrooming private institutions. Certificates or diplomas obtained in many of these institutions are often not recognised by employers or the established institutions of higher learning. In spite of that the private commercial educational institutions seem to be doing good business and attracting more investors daily.

While most institutions offer adults their further education programmes in the usual formal way, some have designed flexible modes of delivery that enable adults to undertake formal programmes without being boxed into the rigorous structures of formal education. This has given rise to the growth of distance education provision (see Chapter 9). There is also an increasing number of programmes offered on a sandwich, weekend or evening basis. Most adults finance their further education from their individual resources. There are very few cases of financial support from employers. A few adults undertaking full time higher education at government-sponsored universities benefit from the bursary scheme, but only about 5% of the bursaries are given to them, the rest go to direct entrants from schools. The fact that about 30% of the 30,000 student population in Makerere University are adults returning to studies from the world of work gives an idea of the amount of money adults are spending on further education.

Impact of economic and financial policies and strategies

The economy of Uganda has for almost two decades now undergone a steady process of liberalisation and privatisation. At Independence there were a number of parastatal organs and government corporations and boards running both industrial or manufacturing and commercial enterprises. The independence government not only took these over but also established more state-run concerns and quickly shifted towards a state-controlled economy. As a result, the state controlled and operated many of the key industrial and commercial concerns. This continued until the liberalisation and privatisation process was set in motion during the late eighties.

Liberalisation of the economy and privatisation have had a direct impact on the enterprises in question and an indirect impact on other economic and social activities. The first direct impact was the removal, from most of the enterprises, of the monopoly status they had enjoyed under state ownership. Removal of monopoly introduced competition and so the need for competitiveness. Performance had to improve and managers and other employees needed to have the proper skills. In many cases this required skills improvement training; hence the increased demand for continuing and further education and the readiness to pay for it.

Liberalisation opened up opportunities and stimulated the initiative for Ugandans to start various industrial and commercial enterprises. In the increasingly competitive environment, starting and successfully running enterprises required adequate knowledge and skills. Some entrepreneurs, correctly reading the trend, invested in establishing educational and training institutions, and started advertising them, thus adding a supply-driven impetus to the growing demand for knowledge and skills improvement. Largely, therefore, liberalisation and privatisation can be said to have boosted individual investment in adult education.

Another policy that has had an impact on investment in adult education has been the drive towards poverty eradication through the Poverty Eradication Action Plan (PEAP) and the Programme for the Modernisation of Agriculture (PMA). This drive has led to the increased government prioritisation of basic education as an important foundation for poverty eradication efforts. Some aspects of basic education including, as explained earlier, adult literacy were accordingly included under the Poverty Action Fund (PAF). A number of health programmes, including health education are also under PAF. Agricultural extension education has also benefited, especially through the National Agricultural Advisory Services (NAADS).

Decentralisation, discussed in Chapter 4, has affected financing of adult education by devolving the functions of planning and budgeting to the local governments and the people. One of the objectives of decentralisation was to promote more efficient use of resources and greater accountability. Judging by the reports from many districts, this objective will no doubt need time to be realised. However, there have been positive changes. Some of the funds, including some of the adult literacy funds under PAF, can now be spent only within the sub-counties, ensuring that they at least reach that level. As a result more money is now being spent on the actual provision of adult literacy education.

Decentralisation has also encouraged districts and sub-counties to make their budgets according to their prioritised needs. A number of districts and sub-counties have placed adult literacy and basic education on their high priority list. This has sometimes been the result of encouragement from development partners working directly with the districts, as is now possible under the decentralised system. Such partners often want to see some local commitment before putting in their support. So there have been some cases of increased investment in adult literacy and basic education by districts and sub-counties.

Costs and benefits of adult education

From what has been presented in this chapter, it is clear that measuring the costs and therefore cost-benefits of adult education in Uganda is a very challenging task. It has never been done on a comprehensive basis. However, the effort made in the 1999 evaluation of adult literacy programmes in Uganda (Okech et al. 1999; 2001) is interesting and is recounted here for illustration.

One of the objectives of the study was to estimate the cost-effectiveness of the Functional Adult Literacy (FAL) programme. The study did this by estimating unit costs and unit benefits of the government programme and of some of the NGO programmes; and comparing both with some other standard costs. The assessment of unit costs was complex because, although the amounts budgeted for the adult literacy programme were relatively straightforward, it was not easy to determine what went into actual expenditures on adult literacy. The following reasons were given to explain the difficulty:

- Accounting and budgeting at the sub-county level were not organised in a consistent fashion across the country.
- Other donors had also made contributions, usually at a local level, which were not always easy to track.
- The adult literacy programme is the responsibility of the Community Development Officer (CDO) and Community Development Assistant (CDA) who were also responsible for a number of other activities.

The assessment of unit benefits was also found to be complex because of the several different possible dimensions of benefit. The study attempted to assess the following dimensions of benefit in quantitative terms by:

- The extent to which the learners had learnt reading, writing and numeracy compared with children in P3 and P4.
- The extent to which they had acquired functional knowledge, attitudes and skills compared to non-literates who had not participated in the programme.
- The likelihood of them sending children to school compared with non-literates.

Other benefits that had been covered in the study, such as the following, were considered less easy to measure:
- The increased level of self-confidence when travelling, going to meetings, etc.
- The fact that mothers were now able to read health posters, medicine labels, etc. and in general take care of their children.
- Improved family care.
- Participation in the political process.
- Taking precautions against HIV/AIDS.

The earlier process review of the pilot phase of the government programme had computed the costs in dollars over the period 1992-95 to just over US$1m. With a cumulative total of about 15,700 learners enrolled up to that point, the unit cost per learner was about $67. The 1999 evaluation reasoned that the relatively high costs were because those cumulative totals included a large investment in materials development and printing of primers, teachers' guides and other materials. Since the bulk of such costs are incurred at the start of a programme, the 1999 evaluation could not use the same approach. It focused more on recurrent costs, basing the analysis on computed annual unit costs of participation in the different programmes, which was taken as roughly the same as unit programme completion costs because the government FAL cycle lasts nine months.

The costing then took into account the following cost categories:
- The personnel costs incurred at several different levels, estimating, where necessary, the percentage of working time spent on the programme.
- Specifically instructor costs, excluding the unremunerated costs, since most were unpaid volunteers.
- Equipment and materials distributed during the year.
- Buildings and facilities used for the classes.
- Administration, especially fuel, subsistence and other transport costs.
- Learner costs, excluding opportunity costs, although these had been probed into during the study.

Actual costs were done as closely as possible for each of the cost categories and the study came up with an estimated unit cost per learner (for the 9 month cycle) of US$4.20-5.20 per year. This was calculated using learner enrolments of 137,000 taken to represent 110,000 effective learners, given the attendance rate of 80% that had been arrived at through the study. The study however warned as follows:

> Note that all these figures would be dwarfed by any valuation of the instructors' time involving a system of incentives (however paid), which we have estimated at between US$9 - 10 per learner per year (let alone the opportunity costs of the learners' time which we estimated at US$54 per year). A decision to pay an allowance (whether in cash or in kind) to the instructors – which we see as essential to ensure sustainability of the programme – would transform the calculations. The realistic annual recurrent costs of a sustainable programme, with reasonably committed and qualified instructors, would then be about US$14 per participant per year. (Okech et al. 1999: 168)

The study showed that adults with nine months in the literacy programme seemed to perform better in literacy and numeracy than most children with three to four years of primary education in the same environment. Calculations revealed that four years of primary education at the time cost around US$80. This showed the adult literacy programme as much more cost-effective than the primary school. That study could not, of course, be considered in any way as conclusive. It does, however, give some idea of the cost-benefits of adult education. More comprehensive studies certainly still need to be carried out in Uganda.

Implications, constraints and challenges

The financing of adult education, like that of other activities in Uganda, needs to be considered in the context of the socio-economic conditions of the country. Uganda is naturally well-endowed, with great agricultural potential and other natural resources. The history of Uganda has, however, not enabled the country to take maximum advantage of its rich natural resources. As a result, the country ranks among the very poorest in the world. In such a situation, even with the best policies, legislation and commitment, it would still be difficult for there to be adequate investment in adult education.

As has been shown in this and other chapters of this book, Uganda does not have appropriate policy and legislation in favour of adult education. This has tended to make adult education receive even a smaller share of the investment than it would otherwise have. For some time, the low priority accorded to most aspects of adult education kept away even external funding. One of the first measures that need to be taken towards improving the financing of adult education in Uganda is, therefore, to put in place appropriate policies and legislation. These would not only ensure greater government commitment to financing adult education but would also help to mobilise funds from other sources. For example, employers could be required to make a monthly contribution to an adult education fund from which their workers and even prospective workers could benefit.

Adult education in Uganda has benefited significantly from external funding. The revival of the functional adult literacy programme during the 1990s was possible mainly because of external support. However, the government tended to let the programme depend more on external funding than on government budget. The 1999 evaluation calculated that over the eight years that the programme had run the ratio of government funding to external funding for the programme had declined from 50% to 32% (Okech et al. 1999: 160). The trend seems to be similar in the financing of other areas of adult education.

This is not a healthy trend because external funding is usually for a limited period of time and cannot therefore be relied on for sustainable continuity of the programme. The fear has also sometimes been expressed that external funding often comes with conditionality that may not be in the best interests of the country. In this regard, one could say that adult education in Uganda has been lucky: in spite of relying heavily on external funding, it has generally been able to plan its programmes without much external influence. The strongest influence has come from the fact that different donors have particular areas or topics that they are interested in funding. However, all the areas have been relevant to Uganda and all needed funding.

The increasing investment by individuals in their own continuing and further education is an important development. As explained above, self-financing at the adult basic education level is much less. Those who need adult basic education are the very poor and cannot therefore finance their own education. The increased investment by individuals coincided with the government move to increase support to basic formal education while decreasing support to higher education. In the context of a country with scarce resources, the government move is sensible and needs to be extended to adult basic education to ensure the success of the fast track initiative.

A serious gap in the financing of adult education in Uganda is the failure to remunerate adult literacy instructors for the dedicated work they are doing. The 1999 evaluation revealed that attitudes towards unpaid volunteer work were changing and this was likely to disadvantage the adult literacy programme. Even with the increased investment in adult literacy under the Poverty Action Fund, regular remuneration of instructors has not been included. Leaving a programme to depend on unpaid volunteers does not show high consideration for the programme.

In conclusion, it can be said that there is significant investment in adult education in Uganda at various levels by the government, non-governmental organisations, business enterprises and individuals. Much financial support has also been received from various external sources. However, the financing remains inadequate and there is need to strengthen the funding considerably. One important set of measures for strengthening the funding is an appropriate policy and legislation package that will strengthen and regulate government commitment and oblige employers and other business entrepreneurs to contribute to the financing of adult education.

9
Distance Education and Open Learning

Jessica N. Aguti

Introduction

Distance education is a growing phenomenon in Uganda, as it is elsewhere in the world. Its growth is particularly related to adult education and this chapter examines its role in the promotion, growth and development of adult education in Uganda. Since their beginnings in Uganda in 1967, distance education and open learning have come a long way although they were constrained in the Amin years by the general political, social and economic degeneration of the time. Today, Uganda can boast of a variety of programmes. They are, however, faced by a number of challenges, which can be viewed either as opportunities for further growth and development or as problems that could impede it.

Generations of distance education

The growth and development of distance education is closely tied to the growth and development of Information Communication Technologies (ICTs) and the terminologies used at different periods have been related to the dominant technology of the time. Some writers describe its development as being in generations (Bates 1994:1574, Garrison 1996:17 and Rumble 2001:1). Bates and Garrison talk of three generations, Rumble of four generations. They all, however, agree that these generations merge into one another and are therefore not pure examples of separate generations.

Distance education programmes of the first generation are dominated by a single technology: print, radio or television (Bates 1994:1574, Garrison 1996:17 and Rumble 2001:1). According to Bates (1994:1574), programmes of this generation date back to the days of St Paul and according to Rumble (20001:1) to 1840. Both authors were, of course, considering only written programmes for these dates. First generation programmes are characterised by having very little interaction between the learner and the teacher and also very little among the students. Where any interaction takes place, it is by mail.

Second generation distance education programmes use integrated multimedia approaches. Rumble (2001:1) calls this generation the 'multimedia distance education system' and adds that such programmes became prevalent in the 1970s while Garrison (1996:18) calls it the 'generation of teleconferencing'. Both agree that it includes the opportunity for dialogue between the teacher and the learner and among learners. In this generation, institutions continue to use one-way media like print, radio, TV and cassettes, but begin to incorporate two-way communication, mainly correspondence by mail, telephone and face-to-face sessions (Bates 1994:1575, Garrison 1996:18).

Third and fourth generation programmes are dominated by computer mediated communication. They date back to 1985 when computer technology began to be more widespread (1996:18, Rumble 2001:1). Rumble (2001:1) calls them 'online distance education systems' while Bates (1994:1576) says these are courses based on electronic information technologies. All three authors, Bates (1994), Garrison (1996), and Rumble (2001) agree that courses of this generation are dominated by computer technology and have high levels of interaction between the learner and the teacher and also among the learners. The most typical technologies used in third and fourth generation programmes are 'computer-conferencing or computer networking, and audio- and video-conferencing (including audio-graphics)' and they also include use of television to transmit lessons to remote classes, sometimes with two-way television or by telephone (Bates 1994:1576).

Terminologies

There is currently a plethora of terminologies used to denote distance education, loosely linked to the definitions of generations above. In some instances, these terminologies are used interchangeably but each may have a shade of meaning that makes it distinct from others, for, as Sauve (1996:102) says, 'each definition is formulated according to the context and the authors involved'.

Correspondence education

Correspondence education is the oldest form of distance education. Commonwealth of Learning (2000a) defines it as '...education that relies on print-based, self-study materials with communication through postal services.' The greatest impetus to the growth of correspondence education was the development of the print industry and postal systems. The system consisted of written or printed lessons and assignments which were sent to the learners by mail. The learners would do the assignments and mail them back to the teacher or institution (Bates 1994:1574). There was little if any personal interaction between teacher and learner.

However, as other media began to be used to supplement written correspondence, the term 'correspondence education' was seen to be inadequate. Holmberg (1986:1) says, '...as more people seem to regard correspondence as something that takes place entirely in writing, distance education has been adopted as a more neutral term'.

Distance education

The term 'distance education' was formally accepted in 1982 when the International Council of Correspondence Education changed its name to The International Council of Distance Education. As an international organisation bringing together all institutions and agencies providing distance education, its adoption of a new name gave great recognition to the new terminology and to the forms in which the education was provided. (Holmberg 1986:1, ICDE 2001).

In distance education, much more than correspondence takes place and the terminology describes the second, multi-media generation (Holmberg 1986:1). In other words, instead of relying on correspondence alone, education now used a combination of: print study materials; face-to-face meetings for students at different locations; correspondence communication between learners and the institution; and use of other media like telephone, radio, and TV.

Open learning

The launch of the Open University, UK in 1969 introduced new elements in the provision of distance education and brought the term

'open learning' into use. While qualifying as a 'second generation' provider, the particularly new element was the programme's broad target. Some of the major tenets of the Open University UK include openness to:
1. People, since it would not debar applicants on account of their lack of educational qualifications.
2. Place, in the sense that learning would be home based and not restricted to classrooms or a campus.
3. The use of new methods of teaching and
4. Ideas
(Rumble and Keegan 1982:12)

Its founders saw existing distance education as restrictive and not flexible enough or open enough to permit everyone who desired to receive education to do so regardless of previous qualifications. So this new form of providing distance education was seen as a major step towards democratising education. As Paul (1990:40) says, '...open learning is merely one of the most recent manifestations of a gradual trend towards the democratisation of education'. However, in spite of this desire to be open, no institution has really achieved this total openness. Institutions, including open universities have continued to have restrictions of a various nature (Rumble and Keegan 1982:12, Paul 1990:40).

New technologies and distance learning

The increased access to computers introduced the third and fourth generations of distance learning with new ways of communicating with learners. The new elements gave rise to terminologies like flexible learning, telematic education, distributed learning, on-line education and virtual universities. As will be shown in the subsequent sections, there are minor distinctions, sometimes even confusion, about these different terminologies (Guiton 1999:51, Moran and Myringer 1999:59). Also, the choice of a particular term may sometimes have regional or institutional preferences. For example, according to Moran and Myringer (1999:59), in North America, the terms 'distributed learning', 'technology mediated learning', and 'telematics' are used while in Australia, the term 'flexible learning/delivery' is more popular.

Flexible learning

The typical university student is no longer necessarily an individual going straight from school to higher education. More and more adults are returning to studies (Peters 1994:28, Robinson 1996:6, Berge 2001:6) and require a form of education that is flexible and that allows them to study as they work. Flexible learning is designed to be such a system but as (Guiton 1999:51) says, '...as with most aspects of openness in education, interpretations of flexibility are as elastic as the term itself.'

However, it is agreed that flexible learning is a student-centred education that uses a variety of methods and technology so as to ensure flexibility in terms of:
- Access to and exit from several learning programmes
- Accreditation and portability of qualifications
- Modes in which communication takes place
- Study material
- Time and place of study, and
- Pace at which learning takes place.

(University of Pretoria - Telematic Education 1999:9)
Flexible learning uses a variety of technologies and emphasises interaction. Indeed, Thomas (1995) defines flexible learning as 'the dynamics of the learning process which takes place between the expert, the learner and the learning resource'. In this case, flexible learning is seen to have a lot to do with the interrelationship and interaction of these three.

Two of the major attractions of flexible learning are the pace of learning and the portability of qualifications. Traditional internal university programmes have rigid structures that make it difficult for any student to progress at his/her own pace and to transfer credits from one institution to the other or from one programme to another. This is also a problem that many distance education institutions also still grapple with (Rumble and Keegan 1982:12, Paul 1990:40). Flexible learning is therefore a step towards overcoming this handicap.

Distributed learning

Like flexible learning, distributed learning relies heavily on technology, especially modern technologies and emphasises flexibility. Multimedia is therefore used involving '...workstations, servers, video conferencing ... internet connection, phone lines...' (Meyer-Peyton 2000:85). As a result of the variety of technologies used, distributed learning can take place either synchronously or asynchronously, that is, either in real time as with a videoconference or delayed as with e-mail. The learning can therefore be said to be 'distributed' in the sense it can take place in different places using a variety of technology, enabling learners to participate and interact as they learn (Meyer-Peyton 2000:86).

Distributed learning enables students to study at home as long as they have access to the relevant technology. Alternatively, institutions that offer programmes under distributed learning can establish learner centres equipped with all the necessary technology where students then access courses, information and other support.

On-line education

Another phrase that has come into use with increased access to computers and particularly to the Internet and the World Wide Web technologies is on-line education, also variously called virtual universities or web-based education.

The *World Book Dictionary* defines virtual as 'created and existing only in a computer; artificial' while Jarvis (1999:195) defines a virtual learning environment as 'The use of electronic means to create a situation in which teaching and learning can occur when teachers and learners are separated from each other in space and time'. Bates (2000:173) defines virtual universities in a similar manner when he says, '...a virtual university is an organisation that delivers courses and accreditation to students electronically'.

However, there is controversy around the use of the label 'virtual', for literally translated it means 'non-existent, unreal or artificial'. As Holmberg (2001:28) says:

> This is neologism of doubtful value as 'virtual' in non-technical English means 'not really exact or true'. A virtual promise is not an explicit, real promise...A seminar arranged as a computer

conference is real and university teaching on the net is also real, so why should they be called 'virtual seminar' and 'virtual university'?

Perhaps it is because of this controversy that the terms 'on-line' or' web-based' education are sometimes preferred.

On-line/web-based or virtual learning is wholly dependent on computers and access to the Internet but as these have become more common, it has enabled institutions to offer web-based courses to large numbers of students (Schrum 2000:91, Mason 2001:268).

Rayburn and Ramaprasad (2000:70 -71) identify two ways in which on-line courses are offered: the first by institutions that act as brokers by relying on resources of member institutions; the second by institutions that develop and offer their own courses. The African Virtual University (AVU) is an example of a broker since it relies on courses of other institutions for its programmes. (Aguti 2000:261, Perraton 2000:146).

On-line/web-based or virtual learning:

> ...can include everything from simple information gathering, to a much more integrated training approach which could include audio, video, graphics, animation and/or live interaction with a facilitator and/or other students (Hugli and Wright 2000:220)

The many different designations that have been given to distance education have in many ways reflected the dominant mode of provision which has also varied from region to region. However, in the remaining part of this chapter, the term open and distance learning is used to refer to any one of the different terminologies.

Reasons for the growth of open and distance learning

In Uganda, distance education and open learning had its beginnings in the programme for the upgrading of 'vernacular' teachers to Grade II level. The Ministry of Education and UNICEF financed this programme while Makerere University Centre for Continuing

Education ran it. It began in August 1967 with 1000 teachers. In December 1970, 948 sat the examinations set by the National Institute of Education. Of these, 876 passed (Kaye 1973: 67). This was an extremely high completion rate and on the basis of this, the Ministry of Education ran other programmes. Since then a number of distance education and open learning programmes have been run in Uganda. These will each be discussed later in the chapter.

The major reasons for this increased interest and growth in distance education and open learning are varied but all are closely tied up with adult education. The major reasons are:
- Growing demand for education.
- The changing nature of the college/university student
- Changing work demands

Open and distance learning and the demand for education

There has over the years been a rapid growth in population and this has been accompanied by an expansion in the demand for education (Peters 1996:42, Saint 1992:xi, Perraton 2000:3). By 1962 when Uganda gained its Independence from Britain, the population was only about 7 million people; by 2002 this had grown to about 24.7 million. Of this 24.7 million, about 48% are below 15 years while only 3% are above 64 years (The Population Secretariat 2001:1, Uganda Bureau of Statistics November 2002:3). The majority of the population is therefore of school-going age.

In addition, an increasing number of adults are returning to school and the existing universities cannot meet this demand for education. Alternative means must be found. For example, Makerere University has introduced evening classes and external degree programmes but this is still insufficient. Evening classes only reach those living and working in and around Kampala while only three degrees (B.Ed, B.Com and B.Sc.) are run as external degrees. Programmes available throughout the country are necessary and distance education and open learning are certainly an attractive alternative here. That is why the Government of Uganda's White Paper on Education recommended the use of open and distance learning methodologies to meet the growing demand for education (Republic of Uganda 1992:4).

Open and distance learning for equal access

Although school enrolments have been rising in a number of countries, there are still categories of people who do not easily get access to education. In developing countries, this includes the rural poor and women. In addition, most education systems are highly selective with fewer and fewer people receiving education as one goes up the education ladder (Saint 1992). This situation is contrary to the World Declaration on Education for All which states that everyone has the right to education. Selective systems of education can therefore be said to violate this right.

Distance education and open learning have therefore been used as a means of addressing these inequalities (Rumble and Keegan 1982, Holmberg 1986:30, Rumble 1992:19, de Wolf 1994: Holmberg 1995). They have been used in countries with scattered populations to reach out to those who live in remote areas. New Zealand and Australia are examples; de Wolf (1994:1558) says, '...correspondence schools for out-of-school children were started in Australia, where some outlying "stations" were situated a long distance from the nearest town or village'.

Perraton (2000:136) also says 'In Australia, distance education was developed for school children because of a commitment to educating children in the bush...' It has also been used to give people who may for one reason or the other have left school an opportunity to return. In Sudan and Somalia, distance education and open learning have been used for those displaced by war while in the University of Iowa Extension Services, USA they have been used to meet the education needs of those '...who suffer from physical disability or long illness, which prevents them from attending a normal school' (Perraton 2000:136).

In Uganda, admission into Makerere University is very competitive. The main route is through the Advanced Level examinations ('A' Level) with the minimum entry requirement as two principal passes. However, the number of 'A'-level candidates qualifying is much higher than the number of places available and many of those who qualify are actually left out. For example in 1999/2000 academic year 15,630 'A' Level candidates qualified for admission but of these, only 2000 were admitted as government sponsored students and 7816 as private students. Thus a total of 5814 eligible 'A' Level candidates did not get a place (Epelu-Opio 2000:5). The actual number of those left out each year is likely to be higher because not all those admitted as private students eventually register as university students.

Two other qualifications are acceptable for university entrance: an appropriate diploma certificate; or passing the Mature Age Entrance Examinations. The Mature Entrance Examinations is a special examination Makerere University sets for adults who desire to join the university but do not have the minimum qualifications.

The shortage of places was one of the reasons for the establishment of the External Degree Programme of Makerere University. This was meant to open up access so as to cater for the needs of adults desiring to return to education. Today, in addition to the 'A' Level leavers, Makerere admits to the B.Com External degree course adults who have the relevant diplomas but also those who do not have the 'A' level qualification and have been out of school for a number of years, provided these sit and pass the Mature Age Entrance Examination. The 'A' Level leavers admitted are those who have the minimum entry qualifications but are not admitted into other university programmes. Also, all those admitted for B.Ed and B.Sc. are working adults (CCE 1990).

Open and distance learning for the changing nature of the university student

In many universities, the traditional university student was one who had received twelve to thirteen years of schooling. Many of the entrants were therefore directly from the high schools and were generally aged between 19-25 years. However, this is no longer the case. Many universities today have adults, some of whom may have been out of school for many years and are already working (Robinson 1996:6, Perraton 2000:55, Berge 2001:6). Such students want universities of convenience. Like department stores, universities should be easily available and programmes should be delivered during hours that are convenient for the students '...preferably around the clock' (Levine 1993:4 as quoted by Rumble 2000).

Since distance education and open learning permit a student to study while working and the student is not expected to spend many months in residence, many adults find this a convenient way of studying. Peters (1996 :) says that this form of education does not confine a student and so is less disruptive. Robinson (1996:6) argues in the same way when she says of training teachers by distance:

> Teachers can study while continuing to teach and schools are not depleted of teachers. Moreover it is less disruptive to teachers' lives, an important consideration for mature teachers with families, community obligations and second-income generating activities including food growing (often essential for low paid primary teachers).

Makerere University has registered a higher number of students who are above 21 years of age than was the case before the introduction of evening programmes and external programmes. A huge proportion of the students on the evening and external programmes are working adults who are unable to attend the day programmes because of their work commitments. For example, of all the students admitted for the B.Com (External), nearly 50% are working adults while all those admitted for the B.Ed (External) are working teachers. The B.Sc., which was launched in 2002, admitted 75 working adults and none directly from 'A' Level. None of these students would, perhaps, have had access to university education if the distance education and open learning programmes had not reached out to them.

Distance education for urgent professional needs

Some of the earliest distance education and open learning programmes run were especially designed to meet urgent professional needs. Perraton (1993) documents a number of case studies of teacher education programmes that have been run by distance education and open learning and most of them were designed to meet an urgent need for teachers. Distance education and open learning have also been used to meet urgent professional needs in other fields. For example, Brande (1993:54) talks about the problem of the shortage of skilled people in Europe in the field of Information Technologies. According to him:

> One of the identified solutions to the skill shortage problem is increased training and retraining through technologies. Most studies refer to the need for a new learning concept and propose large structural efforts in distance and flexible learning throughout Europe.

In Uganda distance education and open learning have been used before to meet needs in a number of areas. For example, from 1967, it was used for upgrading teachers, and later for training of clerks for the public service (Kaye 1973: 67). Also, the Teacher Development and Management System (TDMS) is a scheme that was started to train teachers and head teachers for primary schools (Odaet and Higwira 1994, Makau April 2001:1). Prior to the establishment of TDMS, there was no training programme for head teachers in the country. Head teachers were appointed on the basis of seniority and excellence in teaching; yet an excellent teacher is not necessarily an excellent manager or administrator. The Head Teacher Training Scheme was designed to help meet the need for well-trained head teachers for Ugandan schools.

Distance education as a cost effective alternative

Education is today becoming increasingly expensive because of the increasing number of people to be catered for. In many developing countries, education is provided and funded by governments. This is made even more expensive because of the practice of providing accommodation, food, transport and other allowances to college and university students (Saint (1992:xii). This can no longer be supported by most governments, whose budgets are already under pressure, and many are looking for more cost effective measures.

To establish a distance education and open learning programme, there is no need according to Perraton (2000:118, Berge 2001:9) for the kind of physical structures needed to establish a conventional institution. There is no need for halls of residence, for many classrooms or lecture halls, and there no need to pay students travel and subsistence allowances. This could cut down the costs of distance education and open learning although it must be remembered that distance education and open learning require structures that conventional institutions may not. For example, distance education and open learning require high initial investments in terms of technology and student support and in physical and management structures.

Not many cost analysis studies have been done (Orivel 1994:1567) but Perraton (2000:126 -127) presents some examples with indicative comparative costs. According to these studies, distance education was cheaper than conventional education in the case of junior secondary education in Malawi and Zambia; India National Open School, and in Mexico Telesecundaria. Perraton, however, adds that in cases where numbers were very low, distance education was more costly.

It is clear that distance education and open learning are likely to be costly initially because of the high initial investments in developing study materials and establishing student support structures as well as in the technologies themselves. This is one of the issues that has been ignored by a number of policy makers to the detriment of distance education and open learning. It is also one of the problems faced at Makerere University. The cost of the programme is also likely to be dependent on the technology used. Technology that encourages high two-way interaction (synchronous) is likely to be more costly than programmes with only one-way interaction (asynchronous). In addition, for distance education and open learning to be cost effective there need to be high student enrolments. Unless local computer centres are available countrywide, this may be difficult to achieve.

Open and distance learning programmes in Uganda

Distance education is still not well established in Uganda. One major reason for this is that the political and economic chaos of the Amin era (1971-1979) affected the development and growth of these programmes. The late 1980s reopened debate and interest in distance education. Since then, government, non-governmental organisations and individuals have initiated a number of programmes and projects. The government launched a Task Force in November 1999 to look into the possibilities of establishing an Open University of Uganda as one of the measures to implement its 1992 White Paper on Education. This Task Force submitted its report to the Ministry of Education. Hopefully, an Open University of Uganda will be established soon.

Mubende Integrated Teacher Education Project (MITEP)
This is a project that was launched in Mubende and Kiboga districts of Central Uganda, districts that had up to 80% untrained teachers (Thomas, 1993). The community in these districts initiated Mubende Integrated Teacher Education Project to train them. The project was launched in January 1992 with funds from Overseas Development Agency (ODA) and ActionAid United Kingdom (AAUK), a development charity organisation based in the UK. The main aims of the project were to '...improve the quality of primary education in Mubende District' and to assess '...the cost effectiveness of MITEP... in order to assess its worth as a model for replication throughout Uganda' (Robinson and Murphy 1996:15).

To train the teachers, the course was run by distance education using print-based materials supplemented through student support activities. Nine hundred untrained and under-trained teachers were recruited but only 306 completed and passed the Grade III Teachers' Certificate Examinations.

The Northern Integrated Teacher Education Project (NITEP)
MITEP was followed by the launching of a similar project, NITEP, by the Ministry of Education as part of a national programme to rehabilitate the north and north-eastern parts of Uganda which were ravaged by war and civil strife.

NITEP aimed to train up to 3000 untrained primary school teachers. By the time the project was wound up in 1998, a total of 2051 (66%) teachers had been trained and had passed the Grade III Teachers' Certificate Examinations (Wrightson 1998:55).

Rakai Integrated Teacher Education Project (RITEP)
This was another local initiative, this time in Rakai District in southern Uganda. It also dealt with the problem of untrained teachers in primary schools. RITEP received its financial support from the Lutheran World Federation and trained up to 200 untrained teachers in the district. To do this, RITEP used some of the MITEP modules, although the project developed some of its own materials (Odurkene, 1995).

Teacher Development and Management System (TDMS)
This is one of the major strategies for the implementation of primary education reform. Through this, government hopes to train more primary school teachers and school managers on the job, using distance education. In so doing, government hopes to achieve its aims of improving the quality and quantity of teachers and school managers (Odaet and Higwira, 1994 Makau April 2001:4). TDMS also hopes to improve the quality of teaching and learning materials, and to involve the community in school support and management. Some NITEP modules are used, but TDMS has developed a lot of its own materials.

Today, TDMS is spreading throughout the country, to become a national programme. It therefore wound up its activities as a project having trained a number of teachers and head teachers. Table 1 gives a summary of the different educators trained under this scheme.

Health Manpower Development Centre: Distance Teaching Unit
The Health Manpower Development Centre was set up in 1982 as the Ministry of Health's Centre for Continuing Education but in 1987 it changed to its present name. The Centre's main task is to provide continuing education to all those who are involved in health and health-related work. The Centre set up a distance teaching unit in 1985. To run its initial programmes, the unit borrowed and adapted materials from Kenya. Today, it has produced a number of its own courses
and materials and has also set up a number of branches in the north, east, and west of the country. The Centre receives its financial support from the Canadian International Development Agency (CIDA), and

Table 1: Number of Education Staff Trained Under TDMS

Staff Category	Numbers Trained
Untrained Teachers Upgrading to Grade III	8685
Head teachers	7414
Principals of Core PTCs	18
Deputy Principals in Core PTCs	36
Heads of programmes based in Core PTCs	54
Co-ordination Centre Tutors	539
Volunteer Community Mobilisers	13,000

[Source: Adapted from Makau (April 2001: 9,10)]

has an accumulative enrolment of more than 5500 since it was launched (DEP Records Mbale 1998;). To run these programmes, the Centre uses study materials, radio programmes and face-to-face sessions.

This programme has proved quite popular with the health workers although the completion rate is only 11% mainly because the Ministry of Health does not recognise the certificate issued (Bbuye 1999:). So those completing do not get any promotion or increment in salary as a result of completing the course.

World Links for Development (WorLD)
This is a global collaborative learning programme sponsored by the World Bank Institute. The goals of this programme are to:
- Improve and expand educational opportunities and horizons for secondary school teachers and students around the world.
- Narrow the information gap between students in developing and industrialised countries.
- Build bridges among the leaders of tomorrow.

This programme links schools in developing countries with partner schools in Australia, Canada, Europe, Japan and the United States.

A total of 14 countries in Africa and Latin America are involved in this network (WorLD Uganda Records 1999).

Uganda was the first pilot country for WorLD, which was started in July 1996 with only three schools. Now 20 schools are participating with a total of 1000 students and 600 teachers (WorLD Uganda Records 1999). WorLD helps deliver teaching aids for schools, educational resources and references and access to knowledge and information through access to the Internet. To ensure students and teachers benefit fully from its services, WorLD Uganda has run a number of seminars and workshops for both students and teachers. It should, however, be noted that WorLD is still in its pilot phase.

The African Virtual University Project (AVU)

This also started as a pilot project initiated by the World Bank. Unlike most virtual universities, the AVU is a satellite-based distance education programme, transmitting video-based courses. It currently operates in 25 campuses in 15 countries in Africa. In Uganda, three institutions are participating: Makerere University, Uganda Martyrs University, Nkozi and Uganda Polytechnic, Kyambogo.

The AVU's mission is to use the power of information technology to increase access to educational resources in Sub-Saharan Africa. It is particularly committed to increasing enrolment levels for scientists, technicians, engineers and business managers.

The AVU launched its programmes in October 1997 and has since offered basic computer literacy courses, foundation courses in the sciences, remedial instruction and seminars. It has now launched a fully-fledged degree programme in computer science. The study package for the AVU courses includes:
- Video-based lessons. At present, all these courses are originated from universities in Canada, USA and Europe. However, plans are under way to make these courses computer-based and eventually to have them originating from Africa.
- Live interactive sessions (two-way audio and one-way video).
- Tutorial support by local academics.

- Assignments and tests.
- Practicals at sites where applicable.

The AVU also has access to a wide selection of library resources including 1700 journals on-line, most of them full text. These can be accessed at any of the AVU campuses. The AVU also now has a web site that incorporates e-mail, chat rooms, bulletin boards, file sharing and transfer. So far, more than 10,000 free e-mail accounts have been given out. Since launching the programmes, more than 12,000 students have completed the various courses and 2500 professionals have participated in the different seminars and workshops so far run (AVU 2001).

The three sites in Uganda have each participated in a number of courses transmitted. In addition, each site previously offered a variety of other services depending on local needs although Uganda Martyrs' University and Kyambogo University are no longer active in this. For example more than 400 Makerere University students have participated in the courses and more than 250 in the seminars.

Other services being offered in AVU Makerere include:
- Various customised courses mainly in computer applications.
- Training seminars for university staff in the use of e-mail and Internet.
- E-mail services.
- Access to the Internet   (Aguti 2000:262).

The AVU has now become a non-profit making organisation with its headquarters in Nairobi.

External degree programme of Makerere University
Makerere first ran correspondence courses in 1965 when it ran a pilot course 'Good Letter Writing'. However, the first teacher education programme was the Teacher Training Course to upgrade Grade I teachers. Makerere then ran other correspondence courses but by 1980, correspondence activities had deteriorated gravely as a result of the devastating aftereffects of Idi Amin's rule (Aguti 1996:4).

With the hope of reviving the distance education programmes at the University, a plan to start external degrees was included in the 1980-1986 University Plan. However, it was not until 1991 that the

External Degree Programme (EDP) was finally launched with two degree programmes: Bachelor of Commerce (B.Com) and Bachelor of Education (B.Ed) (Aguti 1996:4, 2000:265).

The EDP was launched with the following objectives:
- To introduce degree courses by distance education and so increase university intake in some fields of higher education which meet urgent national needs.
- To produce good quality course materials which would also be used by the internal students and other people in the near future.
- To strengthen the university's distance education organisation on the basis of enrolment and practice.
- To develop Makerere University's capability to offer a good distance education service, which will meet national, community and individual needs at undergraduate and postgraduate levels. (CCE 1990)

Since its launch in 1991, there has not been any overall evaluation of the programme but from different partial evaluations and from the Department's reports and records, it can be surmised that a lot has been achieved. These achievements will now be discussed in relation to the objectives of the EDP.

The Department of Distance Education has helped boost the university intake numbers through its EDP. With its total population of nearly 7000 students, which is 30% of the overall University student population, it is the department with the largest student population. Prior to the launching of the EDP Makerere University admitted only 50 - 60 students for B.Com. and had no student for B.Ed except for students who were studying at the Institute of Teacher Education and registered for this Makerere degree. Even then only about 300 students were admitted each year.

Since 1999, the EDP has admitted more than 2500 students each year and between 1991 and 2002 many have completed the training. A total of 974 teachers have completed and graduated with Bachelor of Education; 1954 have completed but are yet to graduate while nearly 2690 are continuing with the programme. As for the B.Com. a total of 1272 have completed while 2872 are still on the programme.

(See Tables 2 and 3 for the numbers admitted and those completing since 1991.)

It is clear that the EDP has helped to increase student enrolment at Makerere and has particularly helped many adults to receive continuing education. However, there have been no tracer studies carried out to establish the impact of this training on the students' performance, particularly of those upgrading, its impact on the school system (in the case of B.Ed) and on the economy as a whole. This is an area that requires urgent attention.

The EDP uses a study package that includes:
- Written materials including, handouts, textbooks, reference materials and especially produced modules.
- Student study group meetings.
- Face-to-face sessions.
- Audio cassettes and radio.
- Other student support services.

Written materials were supposed to be the core medium of instruction in this programme. However, the rate of development of the study materials has been extremely slow. A lot of study units have been written but only a few have been published. This seems to be a major handicap of this programme for as it is pointed out:

> unfortunately, the EDP still relies heavily on face-to-face sessions as the major form of support. This is partly because of lack of sufficient study materials which should really be the core of the study package (Department of Distance Education 2001:1).

However, whatever materials have been produced are being used by both the external and internal students of the university. In so doing the programme has helped address the problem of lack of reading material in the university.

Another related development has been that some of the lecturers who have been trained in the development of distance education materials have gone further and written and produced other books using the skills acquired in these training sessions.

Table 2: B.Ed (External) Student Enrolment and Completion Figures 1991 - 2002

Year	Admitted	Registered	%	Did Not Register	%	Continuing	%	% Drop out
1991/92	198	148	75	50	25	72*	47	63.6
1993/94	178	132	74	46	26	87*	66	51.1
1994/95	120	89	74	31	26	64*	72	44.2
1995/96	233	132	57	101	43	107*	95	44.9
1996/97	600	450	75	150	25	410*	91	48.0
1997/98	360	300	83	60	17	234*	78	51.9
1998/99	980	693	70.7	287	29	599**	75	38.9
1999/00	2500	1640	65.6	860	34.4	1355**	90	45.8
2000/01	1646	1200	72.9	446	27.0	1051	63.9	36.1
2001/02	1300	900	69.2	400	30.8	809	62.2	37.8
2002/2003	1200	830	69.2	370	30.8	830		
TOTALS	9315	6514		2801		5618	60.3	39.7

* Those who have already graduated
** Those who have completed but not yet graduated

Table 3: B.Com (External) Student Enrolment and Completion Figures 1991 - 2002

Year	Admitted	Registered	%	Did Not Register	%	Continuing	%	% Drop out
1991/92	112	98	88	14	12	49	43.8	56.2
1993/94	194	135	70	59	30	89	45.9	54.1
1994/95	212	207	98	05	02	140	66.0	34.0
1995/96	270	160	82	34	18	153	56.7	43.3
1996/97	1000	620	62	380	38	450	45.0	55.0
1997/98	750	650	87	100	13	391	52.1	47.9
1998/99	750	480	64	270	36	435	55.6	44.4
1999/00	1500	850	56	793	52	549	52.8	47.2
2000/01	1767	1149	65	618	35	916	51.8	48.2
20001/02	972***					972		
TOTALS	7527	4349		2273		4144		44.9

* Those who have already graduated
** Those who have completed but not yet graduated
***Those who picked up admission letters

After the correspondence courses of the 1960s collapsed, the university lost its capacity to run distance education programmes. However, since the launching of the EDP, the University capacity has grown stronger as evidenced by:
- The establishment of the Department of Distance Education in 1992.
- An increase in the number of staff in the Department of Distance Education with some of them undertaking various studies in the field of Distance Education.
- The Department was allocated an entire block for office space at the main University campus.
- The study centres up country are being renovated and the face-to-face sessions and other programme activities are being decentralised.
- As part of the university's growing confidence in its ability to run distance education programmes, a Bachelor of Science (External) was launched in 2002.

The launching of the EDP has certainly helped rejuvenate distance education and open learning activities at Makerere University.

Diploma in Primary Education
The External Diploma in Primary Education was launched in April 1999 at the then Institute of Teacher Education (ITEK), now Kyambogo University. This programme was launched in order to upgrade Grade III teachers to diploma level using distance education. The general aims of the programme are:
- To increase intake in primary education up-grading courses to meet urgent national needs of the teachers in primary schools.
- To provide an opportunity to eligible and interested teachers who cannot pursue full-time courses in the colleges/institutions or universities.
- To develop a more flexible mode of education that caters for a variety of needs, changing circumstances and learning requirements of the teachers.
- To develop manpower for Universal Primary Education.

(Kyambogo University Records)

Students enrolling for this diploma are expected to take a minimum of three years and a maximum of five years. The study package for the programme includes print-based study modules especially developed in a distance education mode, compulsory residential sessions and student group meetings.

Other distance education programmes
Apart from the programmes outlined above, various ministries and NGOs have in the past run radio and television broadcasts. The Ministry of Education has, since 1963, supplemented classroom teaching for schools and colleges. Today the Ministry is working at reviving this service and strengthening the unit. This is particularly important, as other distance education programmes in the country would benefit from a strengthened broadcasting unit.

The Ministry of Information and Broadcasting has also run broadcasts for various target groups and is seeking to strengthen and improve its activities. This is crucial since the White Paper sees this Ministry as central in the development of distance education in the country. For instance, the White Paper states:

> Distance Education through radio, television, and correspondence courses should be strengthened. For this purpose, the Ministry of Information and Broadcasting should set up separate radio and television channels for educational programmes (Republic of Uganda, 1992:184).

In recent years, many new universities have been opened, some of them private, some state run. The increased number of universities has led to an increase in the number of distance education and open learning programmes being run. For example, Uganda Martyrs University runs a Diploma in Primary Education while Kampala International University has introduced a number of distance education and open learning programmes.

Major features of distance education and open learning programmes in Uganda

Looking at all the programmes mentioned here, a number of common characteristics emerge. However, the programmes can also be grouped into two broad categories based generally on their management and organisation: dual mode institutions and projects.

Common characteristics

Some of the common characteristics of the programmes are:
- They are largely government funded or donor funded with the exception of Makerere University EDP, Kyambogo University Diploma in Primary Education, Uganda Martyrs' University ... and Kampala International University..... In other words, the private sector is not yet heavily involved although if these programmes are to integrate other media, and to find alternative funding, the private sector must be brought in much more rigorously.
- Most of them are for retraining and upgrading, teacher training being one of the main concerns. This has gone a long way to meet the demand for trained teachers. However, with the current expansion of the school system, particularly the primary school, and the changes in requirements for jobs outside the education sector, distance education and open learning must get involved in other fields as well.
- Print is still the main medium but some programmes have integrated Information Communication Technologies (ICTs). There are a number of challenges to this but ICTs have certainly generated a lot of interest.
- A few, like the AVU and WorLD are using other technologies but these are project based and donor funded. These programmes have demonstrated that it is possible to utilise IT in the provision of education in Africa.
- The programmes use face-to-face sessions as one of the major components of the learning package.

These characteristics are a pointer to some of the challenges that distance education programmes face in Uganda.

Dual mode institutions

Dual mode institutions are those that run both internal and external programmes. They include Makerere University with its External Degree Programme and Kyambogo University with its Diploma in Primary Education and perhaps later the Grade III Teacher's Certificate and the Head Teacher's Management Training Course. The last two are programmes that were initially run under TDMS but are being institutionalised under Kyambogo University.

In both universities, the programmes are being run under the Departments of Distance Education. In each case, this is a service department collaborating with other departments in the university. The Departments of Distance Education are responsible for the management and administration of the programme while the collaborating faculties are responsible for the teaching functions. In Makerere University for instance, the Department of Distance Education is responsible for: keeping and maintaining student records; receiving and dispatching assignments for marking and eventual distribution of marked assignments to students; identifying and training tutors, writers, editors and reviewers of the study materials in consultation with the teaching faculties; and production and publication of study materials developed.

Athough this arrangement seems quite plain and clear, it has created some problems. First, the demarcation between administrative and academic functions is not that obvious. The case of the B.Com. (External) degree programme best illustrates this. There has been no clear agreement between the Department of Distance Education and Makerere University Business School over what constitutes administrative and what constitutes academic functions. For example, is receiving and keeping assignment records an administrative or an academic function?

Distance education and open learning also require specialised skills and management, which are not often found in universities running internal programmes. Introducing distance education and open learning therefore brings in new demands, creating tensions and pressures. Once again, the External Degree Programme of Makerere University illustrates this tension.

As a fee-paying programme, the External Degree Programme contributes a certain percentage of its income to the central administration of the university. However, the contributions made are calculated on the basis of whether a programme is a day programme or an evening programme. No special arrangement was made for the unique nature of the External Degree Programme. As a result, the Department has been dissatisfied with the way this is being handled whilst the Central Administration seems baffled by the Department's position. Clearly this indicates a lack of clear understanding and appreciation of the uniqueness of distance education and open learning programmes.

Projects
Most of the programmes discussed in this chapter have been run as projects with external funding. This is beneficial, particularly for the launching of the programmes, but sustainability of these programmes often becomes a challenge. For example, in TDMS for phases I - III the bulk of its funding was from external sources (Makau April 2001:21). The question being asked now is how can government sustain TDMS programmes with the inadequate contributions it has been making?

The AVU is another example. In all the three institutions in Uganda that participated in the project phase, the level of activities has dropped because of, among other things, lack of adequate funding. It is perhaps therefore wise while initiating any distance education and open learning projects to build in sustainability right from the initial stages.

Challenges to distance education and open learning

It is evident that distance education and open learning have great potential in Uganda and yet, in spite of beginning as early as 1967, they have not developed as fast as they should. Also, in spite of the high interest in ICTs and the enormous potential this offers, these have also not developed fast. What are some of the bottlenecks to development and growth of distance education and open learning and to integration of ICTs in distance education and open learning in

Uganda? There cannot be one answer to this question. In fact it may be a combination of factors some of which are:
- Lack of faith in distance education and open learning programmes.
- Sustainability.
- Poor social service and technological infrastructure in the country.
- The need for comprehensive planning for the implementation of distance education and open learning programmes.

Lack of faith in distance education and open learning
When the External Degree Programme was launched in 1991, a number of academics within the university openly expressed fears that it was impossible to train high calibre personnel using distance education and open learning. For instance a number of tutors of B.Com. (External) again and again expressed their reservation about the effectiveness of distance education and open learning for B.Com studies. However, over time, this view is gradually changing. Although the B.Com (External) still has a lot of weaknesses as a distance education and open learning programme, its students have performed comparatively well and this may be one of the reasons for the change of heart.

Another reason may be a comparison between the problems of the internal and external programmes. An internal programme with mediocre courses and poor teaching/learning activities is just as bad as a distance education and open learning programme that offers poor services and mediocre courses. How effective is it in an internal programme for a lecturer to address 800 students in an auditorium, never to have tutorials, to set objective questions for an assignment and then wait for students to sit examinations? This is just as bad as a distance education and open learning programme where students have no study materials, no face-to-face sessions and no student support.

For distance education and open learning to challenge these prejudices the onus is on the current providers to work towards more quality programmes; programmes that meet needs and are accessible to its students and all the other stakeholders. Unfortunately, distance education and open learning has to prove its worth!

Quality
The issue of quality in still an unresolved one in all the distance education and open learning programmes run in the country. True, through these programmes a number of different professionals have been added to the system. However, in the case of the teacher education programmes, the enormous increase in primary school enrolments and the growing numbers of secondary schools in the country far outstrip these efforts. A lot more needs to be done as otherwise the schools will continue to be filled by untrained teachers, adversely affecting the quality of school education.

Also, whereas distance education is growing in the country there are still fears that the products are 'not as good' as those trained through the full time residential programmes. Unfortunately, no tracer studies have been carried out to establish the impact of these different programmes. The onus is on the providers of distance education and open learning to ensure that the systems put in place facilitate the provision of high quality programmes.

Drop outs
One of the major reasons for advocating for distance education has been that it opens up access (Rumble and Keegan 1982, Holmberg 1986:30, Rumble 1992:19, De Wolf 1994, Holmberg 1995). Unfortunately, although most distance education systems register high enrolment figures, completion rates are believed to be generally low and drop-out rates therefore unacceptably high (Keegan and Rumble 1982:228, Paul 1990:79, Perraton 2000:12). The distance education and open learning programmes that have been run in Uganda have also faced this problem.

As we saw earlier, in MITEP 900 teachers were recruited but not all the 900 completed and/or passed the final examinations. Only 306 (34%) completed and passed all the examinations and therefore attained the Grade III Teachers Certificate, 384 (42%) failed the examinations while 197 (21.8%) did not complete the course. A failure rate of 42% is certainly very high.

With NITEP on the other hand, 3128 students enrolled for the training programme but of these, 2755 (80.1%) sat for the Grade III Teacher's Certificate Examinations while 373 (11.9%) dropped out. Of these, 1763 passed the examinations after the first sitting and a further 288 after the second sitting giving a total of 2051 (74.4% of those who sat). The completion rate under NITEP was higher than that of MITEP and nearly the same as for the internal students (Wrightson 1998:45, 55).

Since the launching of the programme in 1991, the External Degree Programme of Makerere University has on the other hand had an average drop-out rate of 21% for B.Ed. and 25.4% for B.Com. This is a percentage of those who initially registered. However, when this percentage is worked out for those who were admitted, a much higher drop-out rate of 39.7% for B.Ed. and for B.Com. is registered. (See Tables 3 and 4.) It is nevertheless worth noting that the drop-out rate has been going down each year, except in 1997 when it shot up and then began to drop again.

There has unfortunately been no study carried out to establish either the reasons for the drop out or for improved completion rates. It can, however, be said that since the majority of those registered are adults with a number of responsibilities, and also since students have to pay fees, responsibilities and lack of money may be some of the reasons.

Relating to Policy on Recruitment
Government employs the majority of teachers in Uganda and so their salaries are dependent on what the government policy is. For example, traditionally, primary school teachers were holders of a Grade III Teacher's certificate and so their salary was set at that level. With the opportunities available for upgrading it is becoming increasingly difficult for government to accommodate all the upgraded teachers in the salary budget. This is particularly the case for primary school teachers who upgrade to either diploma or graduate level.

Many of these teachers have upgraded but have had problems being registered and getting their salary adjusted to the new level they have achieved. This is demoralising and is likely to affect enrolments in some of these distance education programmes.

Also, the B.Ed. (External) is offering a number of courses that are not 'teaching subjects'. For example it includes as major subjects Educational Administration and Management, Curriculum Studies, Educational Psychology and Educational Evaluation and Supervision. These are relevant to the teaching service but are not taught in schools. Because the policy is that a teacher must have two teaching subjects, teachers who opt for these non-teaching subjects are having problems being registered as graduate teachers.

The implication of all this is that there must be co-ordination between the Ministry of Education and the universities.

Integrating Information Communication Technologies in the Programmes

Nearly all the programmes discussed in this chapter rely heavily on print materials and have not fully integrated other technologies. The challenge therefore is for distance education and open learning programmes in Uganda to begin to explore the possibilities of integrating ICTs in their programmes. This is critical, especially because of the widespread use of ICTs in various other sectors of society. Everyone in Uganda needs to be knowledgeable in these ICTs if they are to have any competitive edge in the world of education today. One way of achieving this is by integrating ICTs in every distance education and open learning programme.

Sustainability

Nearly all the programmes discussed here, with the exception of the External Degree Programme and the Diploma in Primary Education, have had a heavy reliance on External funding. Although this helped to start and run the programmes to the end of their project lives, it raises the question of sustainability. For as Makau (April 2001:21) says,

> The TDMS project illustrates the need for Uganda to proactively consider long-term sustainability of social development initiatives. External funds constituted the highest proportion of

the resources invested in the project (e.g. over ¾ of Phases I-III...). Uganda needs to consider how dependence on external funding could be reduced.

Even the other programmes continue to be plagued by inadequate funding. This seems to be the case with the Makerere University External Degree Programme, which relies entirely on student fees (Aguti 2000:276) and has failed to produce all the required study materials due to inadequate funding. Yet, as Edstrom said way back in 1973, 'It is unwise to make a correspondence institution in a developing country entirely dependent for its economy on student fees' (Edstrom 1973:98). The case of the External Degree Programme is, however, a very ironical one because the programme actually has an annual fees income of nearly 2.5 billion shillings (about $138,000). With this sum of money, it should be making a lot more progress with its materials development but this is not happening because, after deductions by the University administration, only about 50 per cent of the money is left for the running of the programme. Is this perhaps a reflection of lack of university commitment to distance education and open learning or a lack of understanding of what it all demands and requires?

Distance education can be cheaper than conventional education, but only in the long run. There must always be heavy investment initially. The question then is 'How willing are government and institutions providing open and distance learning to invest in these programmes?' True, the government has been heavily involved in the NITEP and TDMS programmes but this seems to have been a result of heavy external funding. It is dubious how much government revenue is directly invested in distance education and open learning. Therefore as Uganda struggles to meet its enormous education demands, the question of the sustainability of distance education and open learning programmes needs to be critically given attention.

10
Adult Literacy Efforts

Anthony Okech

Introduction

This chapter reviews adult literacy efforts in Uganda and assesses their contribution to literacy practice in the country. No attempt will be made to isolate the contribution of adult literacy efforts from other literacy education, since they play only a remedial role: literacy is normally acquired in primary school. Here, we only assess the extent to which adult literacy efforts have enabled adults to acquire and make use of literacy and what factors have been favourable or constraining in the process.

The chapter begins by explaining the way the term 'literacy' is understood in this review and highlighting some of the recent and current debates on literacy. This is followed by a historical overview tracing the development of literacy in Uganda, with particular emphasis on adult literacy efforts. The chapter then discusses various aspects of the adult literacy efforts in order to establish the factors that may have been favourable or adverse towards their effectiveness.

Since literacy can only be meaningfully conceived of and discussed in its social context, the chapter also examines the context of literacy practices in Uganda. This should bring out the contextual factors that affect the potential of literacy efforts to result in the beneficial use of literacy and the creation of a literate society.

Understanding literacy and its role

In its literal sense, literacy is the ability to read and write. A literate person is one who can do that, an illiterate person is one who cannot. Recent studies and debates have, however, emphasised that literacy should not be understood as merely possessing these basic skills but rather as the use of those skills to read or write a text in a given context to achieve a purpose. Here, literacy is used to mean applying the knowledge of reading and writing a particular script. As the authors

who first advocated for this 'practice model' of literacy put it:
> Literacy is not simply knowing how to read and write a particular script but applying this knowledge for specific purposes in specific contexts of use. (Scribner and Cole 1981: 236)

Like other words in a language, literacy has many extended meanings. One extension, referring to 'the 3Rs', includes 'numeracy' as part of literacy. Other extensions, developing from the distinction between basic and functional literacy, use the term to refer to the various other areas of knowledge that people learn in adult literacy programmes, covering, for example, health knowledge, agricultural skills or carpentry and qualifying them as 'functional literacy'.

The term literacy is, in fact, sometimes used as a synonym for knowledge or skill, as in 'computer literacy' or 'legal literacy'. In this sense, at times even those who cannot read and write are said to have literacy, for example, the environmental literacy manifested in traditional society. This can lead to the kind of paradoxical or rather confusing statement quoted by Alan Rogers as having been made, 'quite seriously', by someone at a workshop in Nepal: 'Illiterate people are literate' (Rogers 2001a: 3).

Talking about making use of literacy brings to mind the various claims that have been made about the crucial role played by literacy. Some writers, for example, Goody (1968; 1986), Havelock (1982), Eisenstein (1979) and Olson (1994), examined the various roles that literacy has played in the development of the various institutions of the West, including religion, law, economics, politics and science. These authors explained how literacy lead to the development of a kind of rationality, giving rise to the idea that illiterate people lack the powers of logical reasoning. Literacy was thus seen to bring about the development, not only of institutions but also of human individuals. Other studies brought out the correlation between illiteracy and underdevelopment as shown, for example, in a low gross national product in countries with high rates of illiteracy (see for example Phillips (1970)). The conclusion drawn from these studies and observations was that development and logical thinking were consequences of literacy.

Many recent writers on literacy have questioned the validity of that conclusion . Since Scribner and Cole advanced the 'practice model', a trend that came to be known as the 'New Literacy Studies' (Gee 1990) has focused more on the uses of literacy in different contexts. These studies have made it increasingly clear that literacy is meaningful only when it is used to produce some result. The mere knowledge or skills of literacy do not by themselves bring about change. One should therefore distinguish between causal and instrumental conceptions of literacy:

> What our new understanding requires is that we move away from causal talk about what literacy does to people and towards the instrumental talk about what people do or can do with literacy (Olson, 2001: 4).

Taking this line of thought further, Alan Rogers has stated emphatically that the economic and social benefits of literacy do not come from learning literacy skills but from using literacy skills: 'I would argue that virtually no one has benefited from learning literacy skills; people only benefit from using their literacy skills to achieve some purpose.' (Rogers, 2001b: 21)

Literacy education has therefore to be 'contextualised, (that is, associated with personal realities)' (Mezirow 1996). Rogers argues that seeking to promote a common literacy learning programme may in fact hinder the learning of literacy skills, not help it (Rogers 2001a, p.8). The 'New Literacy Studies' have identified different kinds of literacy as differentiated by the context of use and the purpose for which it is used. They refer to them as different literacies (e.g. Barton, 1994). This raises the question of which literacy to teach.

Writing in the context of Uganda, Parry (2000: 61) gives the following factors, which differentiate the literacies:
- They may be associated with different speech communities and textual traditions.
- They may involve different ways of approaching written text and using it in relation to oral language, hence result in radically different reading behaviour on the part of individuals.

- They may have totally different social functions and equally different ideological implications.

Parry identified the following dominant literacies in Uganda: schooled literacy, the literacy first encountered in primary school and then developed through the years of education; bureaucratic literacy, the literacy of government offices and other administrative institutions; commercial literacy, practised especially through the use of invoices, receipts and commercial accounts; technical literacy, practised especially through the use of technical plans and instructions and other communicative practices in technical work; religious literacy, practised in different ways by the three main religious groups represented in Uganda; and creative literacy, practised through creative writing (and reading) and expository writing, e.g. scholarly works or memoirs.

Recent studies have added another dimension to the discussion of literacy within its social context. They have shown that there can be beneficial use of literacy only where literacy is supported by the social institutions of the given social system. For example, works by Barton (1994) and Street (1993; 1995), studies in the Philippines by Doronila (1996) and Bernardo (1998) and studies in South Africa by a team of researchers (Prinsloo and Breier ed. 1996) have made it increasingly clear that literacy is best understood when it is seen as embedded in the social practices of the different communities. Indeed, these studies seem to establish that adult literacy efforts are only effective and sustainable when they develop and maintain literate practice to the point where it becomes part of community practices and community life. The effort should therefore be to make not just literate people (individuals) but literate societies (Olson and Torrance ed. 2001). What have adult literacy efforts in Uganda done towards achieving this?

An overview of adult literacy provision

This section presents a very brief history of the provision of adult literacy in Uganda. A slightly more detailed overview can be found in the 1999 evaluation of adult literacy in Uganda, published by the World Bank (Okech et al 2001). A fairly detailed review of on-going adult literacy programmes can be found in a study by the author of this chapter, published through restricted circulation by the Uganda office of the Netherlands Development Organisation (SNV) (Okech 1994).

The beginnings of adult literacy education
The introduction of literacy was initially a by-product of business ventures and religious missionary work, which brought first Arabs then Europeans to Uganda from the mid-nineteenth century. These taught literacy first to adults. Ssekamwa (2000) traces the introduction and development of western education in Uganda from the arrival in 1844 of the Arab Sheik Ahmad bin Ibrahim with a few other Arabs and Swahilis at the court of Kabaka Ssuuna II of Buganda. Although the Arabs and Swahilis came as traders, they also taught Islam and soon started teaching some of their adult followers to read the Koran.

Church Missionary Society (CMS) volunteers reached Uganda in 1877, among them Alexander Mackay. This was in response to a letter published in the Daily Telegraph of England in November 1875, written by Henry Morton Stanley, who had come to Kabaka Mutesa's palace earlier that year. Kabaka Mutesa had asked Stanley to write home to ask for teachers to come and teach in his kingdom. Two years after the arrival of the CMS volunteers, missionaries of a French Catholic missionary society, the White Fathers, arrived, among them Simon Lourdel. Both Mackay and Lourdel are remembered for playing important roles in establishing their respective Churches in Uganda. However, both sets of missionaries started teaching not only the Christian religion but also reading, writing and numeracy. Later they introduced also agriculture and some technical skills.

Initially, teaching was in the missionaries' homes, compounds, churches or mosques. They had not yet had time to set up proper schools. But that soon changed, as Oliver relates. As the Christian community increased, 'Education began to outgrow its avowedly evangelistic beginnings. The first schools at the central stations of both Catholic and Protestant missions had been designed to train catechists' (Oliver 1965: 212). The education activities of the missionaries soon extended to children as well and they started establishing proper schools by 1898 (Ssekamwa 2000: 39).

The colonial government did not at the beginning involve itself in establishing, financing or administering schools. Thus the Phelps-Stokes Commission (1924-1925) could say,:

> The missionaries, both Protestant and Roman Catholic, who have played so large a part in the history of Uganda, have up to the present had practically the whole education of the country in their hand ... An education system which branches out into the whole protectorate has been brought into being in co-operation with the native chiefs (Quoted by Ssekamwa 2000: 44).

In view of the way literacy was introduced in Uganda, and the fact that religious missions provided education almost exclusively for almost half a century, it is not surprising that religious literacy 'may be the most deeply embedded form of literacy in this country' (Parry 2000: 63). Kate Parry explains that this literacy is complicated by the different ways in which the three major religious groups have used the written text. For Muslims the sacred text, in Arabic, should be recited rather than read and 'serves mainly, then, as a mnemonic'. For Catholics, the sacred text is made accessible through oral means but there is less emphasis on learning the text by heart. 'The Protestant tradition, on the other hand, lays particular emphasis on individuals reading the text for themselves' (ibid: 63).

This Protestant tradition seems to have been a very significant factor in the development of literacy in Uganda, as confirmed by the following observation: 'At the end of 1893 the Protestant community at the capital experienced a typical manifestation of evangelical "revivalism" but associated in this case with one of the most remarkable and spontaneous movements for literacy and new knowledge which the world has ever seen' (Oliver 1965: 184). The Anglican missionaries made the ability to read a precondition for baptism. The Catholic missionaries only required a good mastery of the abridged catechism and prayers by heart, although they also taught literacy.

The Protestant approach accelerated the development of literacy in several ways. First, there were translations of New Testament texts and soon the whole Bible. In 1902 Bishop Tucker found that the complete Bible translated by George Pilkington had sold 1100 copies in the year of publication, together with 4000 New Testaments and 13,500 single Gospels (Oliver 1965: 186). Secondly, there was an exponential growth of 'reading rooms' and teachers. The 'readers' not only developed the practice of reading for themselves but were also very curious to understand all that they read. The missionaries, embarrassed by their questions, 'had to write home to headquarters for reference books and commentaries' (Oliver 1965: 185).

There was no similar explosion of enthusiasm for reading among the followers of the Catholic missionaries. It would be interesting to examine the extent to which the Protestant approach promoted a better acquisition of literacy among their followers than the Catholic one. Could this be part of the explanation for the prominence the Protestants have enjoyed in the leadership of Uganda?

The rise and fall of the 'reader' class
The spread of these new religions, together with literacy and the type of education brought in by the foreigners, gradually developed a new class that came to be known in the local language as *abasomi* or *abaasoma*: 'the readers'. It is significant to note that the root of these words okusoma has continued to be used in many Ugandan languages to mean both 'to read' and 'to pray'. In the first sense, the abasomi meant those who were under instruction (mainly religious) or were adherents of the new religions. In the second sense, the abaasoma were the class of those who had read, and were therefore 'educated'. These words and concepts persist to distinguish the 'educated' (lettered) from the 'uneducated' (unlettered) in Uganda up to the present. To be a 'reader', especially in the second sense, was an achievement and privilege. As Parry explained while commenting on schooled literacy:

> This literacy has a powerful social function, for through the mechanism of exams, it controls access to the metropolitan

social structure and hence modern international culture. In short, it plays a significant role in class formation and, incidentally, in siphoning off successful individuals from the rural areas (Parry 2000: 62).

The colonial government joined in gradually but it was only after the Second World War that the government programme became somewhat systematic, mainly to occupy the demobilised indigenous soldiers who had fought in the war and so keep them from any mischief they might have been tempted into. The Department of Public Welfare was established and a number of ex-service men were deployed there as welfare assistants. This was the forerunner of the Department of Community Development which has for long been in charge of adult and non-formal education.

After Independence in 1962, the Government of Uganda joined other African governments in determined efforts to promote the acquisition of literacy by all their populations for the purpose of enhancing socio-economic development, a goal to which the OAU Heads of State had committed themselves at a meeting in 1961 in Addis Ababa.

It was in this context that in 1964 the Government of Uganda launched a national mass literacy campaign, built upon the traditional literacy approach: teaching reading, writing and simple numerical skills. The campaign was in twenty-two languages with a primer and follow-up reader in each of those languages. Although the notion of functional literacy was introduced into the campaign in 1966 it could not make much impact since the primers and follow-up readers in use had adopted the traditional approach.

The campaign soon lost its initial momentum, reaching a very low point in 1971 when Idi Amin came to power. However, in his erratic ways, Amin gave the campaign a temporary boost when he revived the literacy teaching activities. This temporary boost soon died out and by the time Amin's government was overthrown in 1979 there was very little government provision of literacy programmes, a situation which continued until the early nineties. During this period there was what one could describe as 'the fall of the reader' in Uganda. The *abaasoma* lost their privileged position as Amin and his rather poorly educated army shared what they had looted from the fleeing Asians. The polished educated class could not compete with the ruthless unschooled at the looting game.

The revival of literacy efforts
Some efforts were made to revive adult literacy provision during the 1980s, in line with the 1982 Harare Declaration, in which African governments reaffirmed their commitment of 1961. Workshops held in 1983, 1987 and 1989, co-financed by the Government of Uganda and UNESCO, produced an informative document on the state of literacy in the country and a plan of action for the eradication of illiteracy. This was in the context of the Africa Regional Programme for the Eradication of Illiteracy by the year 2000, an outcome of the 1982 Harare meeting. A structure known as the National Intersectoral Committee for the Eradication of Illiteracy was put in place, composed of 25 members, comprising 15 government ministries, 6 local NGOs and religious organisations, 1 national political organisation, 1 international NGO representative and 1 representative of influential and interested persons. It was chaired by the department in charge of adult literacy, the Department of Community Development.

This committee was set up to work together in initiating, planning and implementing adult literacy programmes, in the realisation that meaningful adult literacy programmes cannot be provided in isolation by one department alone but need a joint effort. The committee was to be replicated at district level. An evaluation of adult literacy programmes in Uganda carried out in 1999 found that the committee was no longer effective at national level and, except in one or two cases, the situation was no better in the districts (Okech et al 1999; 2001).

There was also a series of training workshops in preparation for a needs assessment for Functional Adult Literacy, which was to be carried out in the whole country. At least six workshops were held between 1985 and 1988 but, because the government could not provide funding, no needs assessment survey could be carried out until 1992 when UNICEF and the German Adult Education Association (DVV) were able to assist.

It was also during this period of revival that a number of indigenous voluntary organisations sprung up to address the gap in adult education provision. First was the Kiira Adult Education Association, which operated from 1976 mainly in the four districts in Eastern Uganda. The National Adult Education Association started operating in 1979 and slowly spread to many parts of Uganda. Some time later, the Multipurpose Training and Employment Association was formed in a part of the area where the Kiira association was operating. These earlier associations in the field of adult education were later joined by many more in the various regions of Uganda. They are discussed further in Chapter 5.

Although considering adult literacy to be very important for people's participation in the democratic process and in development, the government that came to power in Uganda in 1986 found so many pressing problems to deal with that it could not include adult literacy programmes on the priority list of its plans until the 1991/92 financial year. This partly explains why external assistance was also not available for adult literacy before that time. The same situation applied to some extent to the field of education as a whole. However, as the decade developed, there was a veritable rebirth of education and learning in general, and reading promotion in particular.

The re-launch of government adult literacy provision in Uganda, accordingly dates to 1992 when, with technical assistance from UNESCO for the design phase, and financial assistance from UNICEF and the German Adult Education Association, the Government started a pilot adult literacy project in parts of the eight districts representing the four regions of Uganda. The success of the pilot phase and its expansion into a national programme is well documented in the 1999 evaluation (Okech et al. 1999, p.11-17; 2001, p.5-7). The evaluation also documents adult literacy education provision by some NGOs in Uganda: Action Aid, Women's Empowerment Programme, Save the Children (UK), Soroti Catholic Diocese Integrated Development Organisation (SOCADIDO) and Literacy and Adult Basic Education (LABE).

The National Adult Literacy Strategic Investment Plan
Since 1999, the Government Adult Literacy Programme has continued to expand and by 2001 was operating in parts of each of the districts of Uganda. That year, the programme received a significant funding boost when the government included functional adult literacy among the priority programmes in its Poverty Eradication Action Plan funded by a special privileged Poverty Action Fund, which cannot be diverted to other purposes. During the same year, a five-year National Adult Literacy Strategic Investment Plan (NALSIP) 2002/2003-2006/2007 was drawn up to ensure optimal expansion and development of the programme. It is intended to reach, by June 2007, at least 50% of the adult population who were non-literate in June 2002.

The NALSIP incorporated a framework for collaboration between government and civil society in the provision of adult literacy education, implemented through memoranda of understanding signed between the government and various organisations. There are, however, a number of organisations offering adult literacy autonomously without such formal agreements. In addition to the organisations documented in the 1999 evaluation, a number of others have joined in the effort. Notable among these is the Adventist Development and Relief Agency (ADRA), whose activities were documented in the study on literacy and livelihoods by the World Bank and DVV, in which Uganda was one of the case studies (Oxenham et al. 2001).

With the NALSIP, therefore, the adult literacy programme in Uganda is set to expand rapidly, without adopting a mass campaign approach. The NALSIP document acknowledged that the task had barely begun when it stated:

> However, the provision of adult literacy in Uganda still falls far short of the need, and even demand. Both the Government and the NGOs/CBOs efforts reach only 4.3% of the 6.9 million non-literate adults'(Republic of Uganda 2002: 2).

The conviction that there is demand for adult literacy among the population is strong in both government and NGO circles. The NALSIP document mentions demand in the quotation above and the process review of 1995 had also reported overwhelming demand for the programme (Cottingham et al. 1995). This demand seems to be supported by the various needs assessment surveys for adult literacy that have been carried out since 1992 (Okech 1992; 1999; 2000; 2002).

The SOCADIDO Literacy Promoter is cited in the 1999 evaluation as having stated:

> There is a lot of demand out there but SOCADIDO, and all NGOs, cannot meet the demand. It is a challenge for the Government to take on this area more seriously. Churches, NGOs have tested the waters and proved that they can be sailed (Okech et al. 1999: 26).

Programme effectiveness and factors affecting it

This section looks at the extent to which adult literacy efforts have been effective and what factors may have affected their performance and effectiveness. Three points are considered to assess the effectiveness of the efforts:

1. The size of coverage, that is how much of the need the provision has been able to meet in quantitative terms.
2. The internal efficiency of the programmes, that is, how successful the programmes have been in completion rates and minimising 'waste'.
3. The learning that has taken place.

Several aspects of the programmes will then be examined to see what factors affected their effectiveness.

Coverage

The early adult literacy efforts by the missionaries produced, in those areas where they were operating, a significant number of people who could read and to some extent write. Christian missionary work spread quite fast to several parts of Uganda. Since for the Church Missionary Society literacy was a precondition for baptism, the growth in the number of Christians meant growth in the number of literate people, mostly adults during the first few years. The number of Bibles, New Testaments and single gospels sold by 1902 is an indicator of the impressive reach of the missionary literacy efforts. As the missionaries gradually shifted their focus to children, their contribution to making adults literate lessened, but did not stop completely. The extent of their coverage was significant while it lasted.

Adult literacy provision by the colonial government was limited. The establishment of the Department of Public Welfare and its involvement in adult education work was, as already explained, mainly to keep the ex-servicemen out of mischief. There was very little coverage of adult literacy through this department during the colonial period.

The mass literacy campaign which started in 1964 was the most widespread adult literacy education effort in Uganda's history but there was no systematic evaluation of the effort after it came to an end during the nineteen-seventies. The confusion of the late seventies and early eighties led to the disappearance of much of the documentation from which any evaluation could be done later. However, the needs assessment survey for adult non-formal basic education carried out in eight districts of Uganda in 1992 interviewed some people who had taken part in that mass literacy campaign as administrators, teachers and learners. Some of the findings from those interviews were:

1. A number of individuals benefited from the campaign by acquiring basic literacy, that is, a rudimentary ability to read and write their names and some simple statements, including very simple arithmetic statements. This must have contributed something to the reduction of the illiteracy rate which is estimated to have fallen by at least 10% during the sixties and seventies.
2. The campaign might have made greater contribution if it had been better conceived and better planned. The campaign does not seem to have had clear, realistic objectives, to have been properly designed or to have had a systematic curriculum or implementation plan. The materials were, apparently, as a result prepared in a rather ad hoc manner which could only accidentally respond to the needs of the learners.

3. The campaign also suffered from the use of untrained and uncommitted adult literacy teachers. The use of school children to teach adults was particularly unsuitable. It was felt that the situation would have been better if the teachers had received some training for teaching adult literacy and had been paid some honorarium which would have increased their commitment to the task.
4. Eventually, however, the upheavals that severely affected Uganda's social and economic life during the same period played a big role in bringing the campaign to an abortive end.

There is really no way of measuring how much of the estimated 10% increase in literacy during the sixties and seventies was the result of the adult literacy campaign. All one can say is that those who participated in it felt that it had contributed something.

Since the government re-launched adult literacy provision in 1992, it has used a selective approach that covered only parts of selected districts. During the first four years the provision was limited, on a pilot basis, to eight districts only, with an average of only two sub-counties per district. The Process Review of the project in 1995 calculated that the project had cumulatively reached only 15,700 learners. Even after the pilot phase was assessed as successful and was recommended for expansion, the expansion was to be 'in a controlled manner', responding to demand and to the readiness by districts to take ownership of the programme. The result of the approach was that by the time the programme was evaluated in 1999 the total enrolment was given as only 137,022. In 2001, the National Adult Literacy Strategic Investment Plan estimated that only about 4.3% of the 6.9 million non-literate adults were being reached.

In summary, the situation in 2002 was that there seemed to be a lot of demand for adult literacy education, of which only a very small percentage was being met. However, the government is firmly committed to responding to this demand and to reaching 50% of the non-literate adults by 2007. This is extremely ambitious. According to UNESCO Institute for Statistics, Uganda is one of 28 states that 'could possibly improve their literacy rates by between 30 and 40 percent' by 2015 (UNESCO Press Release No. 2002-55). The government has set aside a certain amount of money in the budget for the task, although there are funding gaps when the budget is compared to the task at hand.

Internal efficiency
Low completion rates and wastage have often been cited as common features of all adult literacy programmes. There is the paradox between the people's desire for adult literacy programmes, usually expressed during needs assessment studies, and actual enrolment and participation in the programmes. To some extent this is true of the Ugandan situation. It was, however, surprising that in the 1999 evaluation, the calculated completion rate was over 70%. Responses by the facilitators yielded an average attendance rate of 80%. The evaluation report itself raised doubts about the figures made available by the programme managers, in view of the weak monitoring system in place. However, the fact that a considerable number (over 80%) of those who had completed the first nine months and successfully taken the proficiency test were still participating in the programme was an indicator that the figures may have some validity. In terms of completion and attendance, therefore, the internal efficiency of the adult literacy provision in Uganda has not been bad in recent years.

Internal efficiency is also measured in terms of cost-effectiveness, the value of the outputs and outcomes compared to the inputs. The 1999 evaluation also undertook a cost-effectiveness analysis of the adult literacy provision. The test that had been administered to children who were in the fourth year of primary education and adults who had completed at least nine months of literacy learning had yielded better results among the adults. It seemed that four years of primary schooling was required for acquisition of a similar level of literacy. The evaluators, therefore, compared the cost of the nine-month programme and that of four years of primary education.

The cost of enabling adults to acquire literacy through the government nine-month programme was found to be about $5 per learner, whereas the cost of the required four years of primary education was calculated at $80. Of course these figures do not give the whole picture because primary schooling gives much more than just the ability to read, write and do simple mathematical operations. It should also be kept in mind that the government programme was operating through unpaid volunteer facilitators. Nevertheless the figures are still a very interesting indicator of the cost-effectiveness of the adult literacy programme.

Acquisition and retention of literacy
The 1999 evaluation of adult literacy programmes in Uganda revealed that the programmes were largely effective in enabling the learners to acquire the basic skills of reading and writing as well as some functional knowledge in numeric manipulation, health and sanitation, agriculture, environmental education and civic education. Although to some extent satisfied with this achievement, most of the learners felt that it was inadequate and they wanted to learn more. Some of them stayed on in the programme although they kept repeating what they had already learned.

The evaluation went further to investigate the use of the newly acquired literacy and other functional skills and found that there was some use of all the skills and knowledge but on a limited scale. Reading and writing skills were in many cases not used because of lack of reading materials and in some cases writing materials. A small percentage of the sample, however, reported that they did not use reading and writing because they did not have enough skills. There was, therefore, little evidence to show that learners were able to appreciate and enjoy the benefits and opportunities they had acquired; which is one of the objectives of the government programme.

The use of the functional knowledge, although observable to some extent, was limited both by contextual factors and by the rather inadequate knowledge that had been acquired. The large percentage of the learners who had passed the proficiency test and were still attending classes shows that the learners felt they had not had enough and they needed more. Overall, the evaluation concluded that, although the literacy programmes were achieving something, the quality and levels of achievement were still low and needed to be enhanced.

Measuring the retention of literacy skills is made very difficult by the high percentage of 'literacy graduates' who continue to attend the classes, in most cases merely repeating what they have already covered. The evaluation was not designed to cater for this phenomenon and could not, therefore, meaningfully measure retention. If what is happening among school leavers is a good indicator, one could assume that the rather rudimentary literacy acquired in adult literacy programmes may also be fading away fairly fast, in view of the limited opportunities for use.

Literacy programme participants
The most important of the factors that account for the success or not of the literacy programme is the human factor, including the participants or learners themselves. In recognition of this, all programme providers set out to make their programmes respond to the needs and desires of the prospective learners and to cater for their characteristics in the programme design. It is accordingly almost routine for all programmes to start with a situation analysis and needs assessment survey for literacy before designing and implementing the programme.

The majority of participants in all adult literacy programmes in Uganda are women, which to some extent reflects the higher illiteracy rate among women. The 1999 evaluation found that they formed over 80% of the participants. Since girls have been and are still to a great extent disadvantaged in formal education, their greater participation in adult literacy activities works to redress the imbalance. However, the ratio of women to men in the literacy classes is usually much higher than the ratio of illiterate women to illiterate men in the area. It is reported in most cases that illiterate men are not interested in attending the classes. Some of the reasons have to do with mixed classes of men and women where men feel uncomfortable. This has raised the debate about the desirability of segregated classes for men and women.

Another striking feature among the participants is that the majority are people who already had some formal education, some even up to the upper levels of primary education. The 1999 evaluation found that 70% of the participants had had school education. The question this raises is whether the adult literacy programmes are missing their true targets. This situation seems to arise both from the way the programmes are designed and the way they are implemented.

All the needs assessment studies for literacy in Uganda have indicated that there are large numbers of people with some primary education who demand adult literacy classes. Not taking full account of this, the programmes have so far been designed at only one level. They usually admit people, whether they have ever been to school or not, and all the learners are put together in the same class. Many people without prior formal education have been intimidated by this situation and have either dropped out or never joined in the first place.

A third important characteristic of the participants is that they are usually from among the very poor, although, it seems, not the very poorest of the community. The fact that the programme is attracting the poor gives it the potential to play a useful role in poverty reduction. Indeed, most of the participants join the programme in the hope of finding a solution to their poverty. Practically all the needs assessment surveys for adult literacy in Uganda have come out with poverty as the problem about which the people are most concerned and for which they want a solution. For some participants, the programme has made a positive difference in their struggle against poverty, as many reported to the evaluators in 1999, but not for the majority. In any case the difference reported by many of the women is really minimal. The evaluation in fact concluded that the programmes needed to do much more to make a really meaningful difference in alleviating the poverty of the people.

The completion rate in the Uganda programmes, as already discussed, was amazingly high. However, several studies have found irregularity in attendance to be also quite high. Most of the participation problems are related to the problems faced by women, arising from their roles and the workloads assigned to them by the culture of their society. This is shown by most of the difficulties listed by the learners.

It is clear from this that adult literacy programmes in Uganda must be designed with special consideration for women's problems and that therefore women must be adequately consulted during the designing process. This calls for a special effort because most of the forums where consultations take place are dominated by men and the women's case may not be effectively articulated. However, all programmes seem to have made it a routine to decide together with the learners on the key issues about the programme. This may partly explain the high completion rates.

Objectives and approach
Recognising that the need to learn to read and write is in most cases not as urgent as the need to find urgent solutions to the problems of poverty, all the literacy programmes in Uganda make a link between literacy and activities geared towards poverty reduction. Practically all the programmes mention development among their objectives.

The government approach has since 1992 emphasised the functional aspects of literacy and was designed to:
- Help people to be sensitised and aware of the true nature and reasons for their situation and problems, and how their conditions can be improved.
- Enable people to acquire practical knowledge and skills and the proper attitudes to use these to improve their living conditions.

(National Plan for Functional Literacy, May 1996).

To achieve this two-fold task the methodology selected was described as 'integrated' and it was explained that the integration covers these three dimensions:

Integration of subject matter: This approach brings the knowledge from different subjects, or 'programme areas' to bear upon a problem or an effort. Such integration has been found necessary because, in anyone's life, one problem may arise from a number of different things and it is usually not possible to solve a problem or promote an effort by looking at one aspect only.

Integration among service providers: This approach is also integrated because it makes use of different professionals or sectoral workers in the field to address the learning or development issue at hand. It is often not possible for the literacy facilitator alone to cover adequately the different subject areas the learners need. They are therefore encouraged to bring in extension workers from agriculture, health, co-operatives and so on to strengthen the learning process.

Integration of learning and life: This approach keeps learning and life together by tying the learning to those things that the learners are already doing, helping them to do them better before enabling them to start on new activities. To ensure this link to life, the approach aims at immediate application of what is learnt in real life situations. Follow-up activities are therefore designed to take the facilitators and learners from the classrooms to the learners' work, which, for the vast majority of the learners, is in their homes and surrounding fields.

The differences in approach observable among the different programmes arise more out of the way the link between literacy and the other developmental activities are forged in practice than in their core content. While some programmes make an effort to integrate literacy training with training for the other developmental activities, in others literacy is handled side by side with the other programme areas, hoping that the literacy will contribute to them. In some cases the need for literacy had been realised because its absence had adversely affected activities that were already in place.

There has recently been much international debate as to which of these approaches is most effective. A study sponsored by the World Bank and DVV (Oxenham 2001) seems to reinforce the conclusion by Alan Rogers: 'Start with development projects and fit literacy learning into development projects. "Literacy comes second" model' (Rogers 2001a: 24). The main approach in Uganda, that used by government, does not reflect this model.

An exciting and significant addition to adult literacy provision in Uganda is the REFLECT approach, introduced by ActionAid, a British-based international NGO. The architects of REFLECT explain that the approach seeks to build on the theoretical framework developed by the Brazilian Paulo Freire, but provides a practical methodology by drawing on Participatory Rural Appraisal (PRA) techniques. An important characteristic is that in REFLECT there is no textbook, no literacy 'primer', no pre-printed materials other than a guide for facilitators that is produced locally, preferably with the input of the facilitators themselves. The 'REFLECT Mother Manual' states:

> If most literacy programmes have failed then perhaps abolishing the primer may be one of the keys to success (Archer and Cottingham 1996).

In 1995 the pilot phase of REFLECT was evaluated in the three countries where it was being piloted: Uganda, Bangladesh and El Salvador. The findings were published in the British Overseas Development Administration (ODA) Education Paper, Number 17, 1996. The Paper concluded that REFLECT was more effective than the literacy approaches using primers.

Some NGOs in Uganda and also the government programme in some districts have adopted REFLECT or some of its aspects. However, the 1999 evaluation of literacy programmes in Uganda did not find any significant difference in effectiveness between the REFLECT and the government approach.

Programme providers: a pluralistic approach

The historical overview has shown how adult literacy education was at the beginning for quite a period of time provided almost exclusively by religious missionaries and their followers. The colonial government had only a limited involvement in education, leaving religious bodies to be much in charge of their various provisions.

After Independence, the government of the newly independent state immediately took full charge of education. Religious bodies were pushed aside and gradually withdrew from secular education, limiting themselves to religious instruction. Recently some of them have showed renewed interest in providing secular education and are providing some, but very little, adult literacy education. Considering, as Parry wrote, that religious literacy is perhaps the most deeply embedded form of literacy in Uganda, the discontinued involvement by the religious bodies was most likely a significant lost opportunity.

Apart from government, there is a variety of other agencies

providing adult literacy in Uganda, including international or foreign NGOs, local NGOs, and individual initiatives, some of them set up as commercial enterprises, referred to as 'the private sector'. This is in line with the atmosphere of pluralism in educational and developmental efforts which is actively encouraged by government. The encouragement by government has given rise to many initiatives, all operating autonomously, in most cases without reference to each other.

This pluralism allows the providers to invest in their programme according to their different beliefs and approaches. It therefore also enables the beneficiaries to have choices according to their needs and beliefs. This freedom of choice and action is motivating to the providers because people and agencies have a certain degree of confidence that they can undertake a literacy programme of their own liking and carry it through without being interfered with.

However, in spite of the considerable number of NGOs and CBOs that claim to be providing adult literacy, their input still adds very little to the efforts by government. Some of them operate in several districts while others may cover only several villages. Some of them have concentrated with intensive programmes in a selected area while others have a sprinkling of provision in different parts of the country. The common characteristic of their adult literacy activities, however, is that they are often small-scale efforts with very limited coverage.

In effect, the scattered sprinkle of interventions have not been able to make much of an impact. Not only do most of them have rather limited coverage, but often their planned duration is fairly short, in line with their project approach. In spite of this limited coverage and short duration, practically all the interventions have gone ahead to create an autonomous structure for their programme, a structure which comes and goes with the project, leaving nothing behind to continue with what they have started. Perhaps the impact would be greater if there was more joining of efforts to strengthen a common provision structure.

One way in which some literacy providers have tried to ensure sustainability is by basing their provision on the people themselves. For example, the Bundibugyo ActionAid Project, where REFLECT was piloted, first encouraged the formation of a people's council to be in charge of the programme. The literacy programme would then be stimulated as a people-driven initiative that should be sustained by the people themselves even after the end of external intervention and the departure of outside agencies. The Bundibugyo project was interfered with by the invasion of an anti-government rebel group, which destabilised the area for some time, so the community-based initiative could not come to the desired maturation. However, ActionAid has since handed over its adult literacy activities in Mubende District to community-based management committees. Save the Children (UK) has done the same in Arua Municipality and so has the Women's Empowerment Programme in several districts of north-western Uganda. The sustainability of these initiatives is yet to be evaluated.

It would seem that people's movements initiated for developmental work in Uganda have problems taking root. The co-operative movement has, for example, faced many crippling organisational problems in spite of great institution-building efforts by the Uganda Co-operative Alliance and the Government Co-operative Department. Many local NGOs or CBOs operating in Uganda today quickly come to be controlled by and depend on one person or a few individuals whose accountability to the people keeps dwindling. There is also a strong dependency syndrome which makes these provisions so highly dependent on government or other providing agencies that it becomes practically impossible to wean them off.

This does not of course mean that this situation is unavoidable. With the awareness created through adult literacy and education programmes it may be possible to strengthen the community enough for them to take charge of their programmes effectively. So, the option of establishing a people-driven adult literacy and education provision, which will rely for its sustainability on the people themselves, remains open. However, there is no doubt, as stated in the CONFINTEA V Hamburg Declaration, that , 'The state remains the essential vehicle for ensuring the right to education for all, particularly for the most vulnerable...' (UNESCO 1997: 3)

Literacy facilitators and supervisors

The name facilitator is used here to refer to anyone who instructs others in literacy. However, in general, it is only in REFLECT and a few non-government programmes that these are called facilitators. In the government programme they are known as instructors.

Most adult literacy facilitators in Uganda work on a volunteer basis without any remuneration. Both the 1994 study by Okech and the 1999 evaluation looked into what motivates such facilitators and also at the level of their motivation. The findings were that, working within their communities, many of them felt they were doing something good to help the less fortunate. They were happy to share their educational privileges with the rest of the community. Their satisfaction was to enable their village mates to change for the better. That is why they were able to produce results even without pay.

However, practically all of them stated they would be happier if they were remunerated. The high turnover and inadequate commitment among facilitators is to a great extent the result of working without pay. Both studies observed that the volunteer spirit seemed to be waning and that it was risky for the programmes to hope to continue running purely on the good will of unpaid volunteers.

With or without remuneration, the work of an adult literacy facilitator requires a person with special dispositions. Functional literacy of one type or another, which is the aim of most of the programmes, requires a certain degree of selflessness, a willingness to help others improve outside the adult literacy classroom. From the point of view of the community, it requires a person they can trust, one they can identify with. It is in recognition of all this that most adult literacy programmes in Uganda lay emphasis on selecting facilitators according to certain guidelines and in close consultation with the community.

While that procedure has to a great extent ensured the selection of facilitators acceptable to the learners and the community, it would seem that the facilitators' ability to handle the learning experience with the learners in the manner required by the functional literacy approach has not been so satisfactory. In some cases even the literacy level of the facilitator has been so low that they can only teach the most elementary levels of reading, writing and arithmetic.

Another weak point, especially in the government programme, is the very inadequate training received by these facilitators, in most cases between three and five days duration, once only. This is an even greater problem because of the very low education level of most facilitators. Although most facilitators have been effective in helping the adult learners acquire a basic level of literacy, the quality and level of provision needs to be enhanced: without better quality facilitators, it will be difficult to improve it.

There is everywhere the awkward situation of the learners being very predominantly female while the facilitators are predominantly male. Even with the very special efforts that some of the programmes have exerted, it has still not been possible to improve on the female to male ratio. There are far fewer educated women around in the rural areas where adult literacy programmes mainly operate, and those who do exist are hampered by the many other burdens thrown upon them by the culture of their society. Although many of the female learners indicated when they were asked that they did not have any problems with having a male facilitator, there were a number of cases where the learners would have preferred a female facilitator, partly to allay the suspicions of their husbands who sometimes prevented them from participating in classes run by a male facilitator.

Supervision and monitoring are very deficient in most of the programmes, especially in the government programmes. Some centres are not visited by supervisors for many months and some remain inactive for months without the knowledge of the supervisor. Both the 1994 study and the 1999 evaluation have some very revealing anecdotes to illustrate the deficiency. With the classes, facilitators and learners facing the many difficulties which have been listed, the programmes stand very little chance of success unless they are supported by constant supervision. This supervision should play two major roles: ensuring that things are being done according to plan and providing technical support to ensure and maintain quality. In view of the small amount of training the facilitators have received in all cases, this technical support is really essential.

Monitoring data are still rather inadequate. There are cases when there were signs that even the number of learners given was more guesswork than fact. Visits to the field seemed to indicate something else. Monitoring of the regularity of attendance and of the drop outs and the reasons for both does not seem to be given much attention. As a result there is plenty of useful information missing, making it difficult to assess the performance of the programmes and to see how they can be improved where necessary.

Facilities and materials
In the traditional approach it was considered all right to use school classrooms for adult literacy classes. The practical problem was that, since almost all schools use their classrooms until evening they were not usually available at times when adult literacy classes required them.

Today, growing professionalism in adult education has brought about the realisation that school classrooms are neither physically nor psychologically suitable for adult learners. Both for practical reasons and as a matter of principle, classrooms are now rarely used as venues for adult literacy classes in Uganda. The problem is finding suitable alternatives.

Among the solutions tried were the community centres which were built in the 60s by the government at every sub-county headquarters to serve various purposes, including adult literacy. Although these centres served as adult literacy centres in the 1964 Literacy Campaign, they were far from being adequate, with only one available per sub-county. Secondly, their location at the sub-county headquarters was unsuitable because they were too far from many learners, were too much the centre of public focus and would therefore expose the learners too much. Many people also found it safer to keep away from administrative headquarters associated with taxation and other law enforcement activities. Later, during the seventies, the community centres were diverted to other uses and since then many new sub-counties have been established without such centres.

Other alternatives used have been churches or mosques, village halls in the very few places where they exist and in a few cases even private houses. The programme providers have encouraged the communities to construct simple shelters for the classes on their own, but this has been done in very few places. Some well-funded projects have assisted the learners and their communities by meeting some of the costs of the learning shelters. However, a very large number of the classes, both in the government and NGO programmes, just meet under trees, exposed to wind and rain. Surprisingly, many learners, as reported in the 1999 evaluation, did not seem to be particularly dissatisfied with having to learn under trees.

As regards seating, the participants either bring along something to sit on or sit on whatever is available at the meeting place: logs, stones, leaves or even the bare ground. Trying to write in an exercise book placed on the ground or on one's lap is not very conducive to learning the skill of writing.

Practically all class centres are provided with a blackboard, but there is often a shortage of chalk, except in the well-funded NGO projects. The recently increased government funding should hopefully improve this situation. The government programme provides at least a few primers and in most cases a teacher's guide to every class centre. In some languages there is also a follow-up reader with its teacher's guide. Several studies have found weaknesses in the materials and recommended their revision. The 1999 evaluation reported that there was a demand for instructional materials in programmes which did not provide them.

The provision of materials for adult education provides a big challenge in Uganda: the multiplicity of languages in the face of inadequate resources. The people of Uganda speak over thirty distinct languages as their mother tongues (Ladefoged 1971). Although about 20% of Ugandans are at least bilingual in local languages, this bilingualism or multilingualism has many combinations and does not therefore lead to one common language (Okech et al. 1999: 55). In any case there is a strong belief today, as endorsed by UNESCO, that all people should first learn literacy in their mother tongues. The lack of materials in many languages is a great hindrance not only to mother tongue literacy but also to the development of a literate society.

The context of literacy practice in Uganda

The framework briefly presented at the beginning of this chapter highlighted the recent trends which emphasise the need to consider literacy as a practice rather that just a skill. The view is that literacy education should be associated with the personal and social realities of the participants and that there can only be beneficial use of literacy where literacy is supported by the social institutions of the given social system. A quotation from a study done in the Philippines a few years ago seems to be very relevant here:

> There is no money in this world that can be found to sustain and indefinitely maintain literacy campaigns or even non-formal literacy programs for each and every adult who drops out of school at an early age. Therefore the problem for development is precisely on the maintenance and expansion of literate practice to the point where it becomes part of community practices and community life, a literate tradition, as it were. (Doronila 1996: 18)

Although, as explained above, there is a shortage of reading materials in many languages, literacy is already part of some community practices in Uganda. Prof. M. Reh and her team from the Research Centre on Multilingualism, University of Hamburg, Germany, are documenting this through the ongoing research on 'Literacy Practices in Cross-cultural Perspectives, Bolivia and Uganda'. The 1999 evaluation of the adult literacy programmes in Uganda also found out that there was much use of literacy skills by the adult literacy 'graduates' through 'circumstantial reading, e.g. reading of posters, notices, and labels on doors and drugs'. To that extent, therefore, adult literacy efforts are contributing to the expansion of literate practice in Uganda.

The practice of adult literacy education providers in Uganda to promote a common literacy learning programme for all their participants raises questions about the genuine likelihood of their contributing to the different literacy practices or literacies, as emphasised by recent studies. There does not seem to be enough attention being paid to maintaining and expanding literacy activity in the varied community activities and practices. The programmes all seem to promote a single basic literacy rather than varied literacy practices.

However, within the single literacy perspective, several efforts are working towards making Uganda a more literate society. Apart from the efforts aimed at enabling all Ugandans to acquire literacy (universal primary education and functional adult literacy), there are those aimed at increasing access to relevant books and other reading materials and those intended to develop among all Ugandans the desire and practice of reading into a well-established culture.

One characteristic of Uganda at the end of its decade-and-a-half of turmoil was the serious lack of books and other reading materials for all purposes. This was most acutely felt in schools, where books are essential tools. Over the past decade the situation has steadily improved. At first there was concentration on school textbooks, which came from foreign or international publishers. Gradually, locally published materials increased, starting with newspapers but then developing also in the area of book publishing. Currently, there is a healthy sign of growth in all aspects of the process.

There is a steady growth of writing by local authors, both for the formal education system and for the general readership. Almost every week the newspapers carry a review of a newly published book written by a Ugandan and some Ugandans seem to be going into book writing as a full-time career.

One important area where little has been done is that of writing in the local languages. Although the education policy is that in the rural areas the language of instruction in the first four years of primary education should be the local language, no language has the required books for satisfactory implementation of that policy. Most languages do not, in fact, have any books at all for use in those classes. However, writing in local languages is receiving a strong boost from adult literacy programmes. The Government Functional Adult Literacy programme has produced two or four books each in about 20 of the over 30 Ugandan languages.

Several languages and districts have revived local language committees and their activities will, hopefully, start to make a change in this situation. Another source of hope for local languages is that a number of writers have recently had their local language books published and that some publishing houses are putting special emphasis on producing local language books. This is an encouragement to those who would like to write in the local languages.

One of the constraints faced by writers in Uganda during the seventies and eighties was the lack of local publishing outlets. Today, not only are the international publishers back (Oxford, Longmans, MacMillan) but there are also quite a handful of local publishers some of whom, like Fountain Publishers, with over 300 titles carrying their label, are growing into really big-time publishers. Local publishing is steadily increasing the availability of up-to-date relevant reading materials and so making reading more relevant and worthwhile for Ugandans.

An important category of publishing, which has increasingly provided Ugandans with worthwhile reading, is the newspaper industry. Not only are there more regular newspapers on the market, but also the quality of much of the writing is quite good. This reflects the increased opportunities for professional training in journalism and communication. Although the newspapers still have a very limited readership, they have a language coverage giving them the potential to be read by perhaps as many as 70% of the population. That potential is, however, still very far from being fully realised, because of a combination of factors including the low income levels of the majority of the population, the limited distribution network of some of the papers and the low priority accorded by many people to expenditure on reading materials.

To work together to strengthen the publishing industry and the book trade, the Uganda Publishers' Association was formed in 1992. Among the activities to the credit of this association are: organising book exhibitions and children's book days; organising training workshops to impart professional skills; participation in book policy formulation; recognising distinguished book professionals; promoting literacy campaigns; and organising National Book Weeks.

Working with the Uganda Publishers' Association in those activities is the National Book Trust of Uganda (NABOTU), which brings together all stakeholders in the book industry, government, NGOs and international development support organisations, to promote books and reading. The National Book Week Festivals organised by NABOTU have become a regular annual event.

In book distribution and book selling, too, Uganda has come a long way. Kampala has bookshops, which are not only very well stocked, but are also able to supply the titles they do not have within a reasonably short time. Moreover, the liberalised economy and the ready availability of foreign exchange make it easy for one to pay for a book from any part of the world whenever one wants. Up-country towns are not so well served. People there have in some cases to take the trouble to look for books from Kampala.

The last category of efforts to be considered are those aimed at developing the desire and practice of reading into a well-established culture among Ugandans. It would seem that not much specific action has been taken in this line. The Reading Association of Uganda, founded in 1998, is running several projects to promote reading through sensitisation seminars, readers clubs in and outside schools, and advocacy with central and local government authorities. The Reading Association of Uganda regularly participates in the National Book Week festival through its 'Reading Tent' and other sensitisation activities. As a member of the International Reading Association, the Reading Association of Uganda hosted in 2003 the third Pan African Conference on Reading. Another example of an effort to promote the reading culture is a programme named, 'Back to Books: Plan of Action for Masaka Area' launched in 1995 by Rev. Father Peter Bakka, Diocesan Archivist and Librarian, Masaka Diocese (Bakka 2001).

Conclusion

Adult literacy was the earliest provision of literacy education in Uganda, started by the missionaries. Through this provision, adult literacy made a significant contribution to the development of literacy practice in Uganda. However, as focus shifted to children's education, the contribution of adult literacy efforts diminished. Even the mass literacy campaign of the sixties made only a limited contribution before coming to an abortive end. The revival of adult literacy efforts during the last decade and especially the government's five year strategic investment plan for adult literacy are very promising as a way of enabling seven million non-literate Ugandans to make use of literacy. With contextual factors also becoming more favourable, the future of adult literacy in Uganda should be bright. But, finally, to use the words of the Director General of UNESCO:

> We must draw upon the lessons of experience. We know, for example, that one size does not fit all: instead of standardised programmes, more customised approaches are needed.
> Koichiro Matsuura, International Literacy Day Message, 2002)

11
Meeting the Needs of the Marginalised in Uganda

Alice N. Ndidde

Introduction
This chapter examines the extent to which adult education has contributed to the empowerment of marginalised groups in Uganda. Adult education here includes but also goes beyond the notion of imparting knowledge and skills to adult men and women for day-to-day survival, to include a transformative process that enables the marginalised to understand, analyse and respond to their environment in a proactive manner. It also refers to a process that can lead to the changes in social power relations that are vital in bringing about empowerment. For the marginalised, this means having access to knowledge and skills (both mental and physical) and self-awareness that leads to greater decision-making power and control.

The need for empowerment
Marginalisation means being on the periphery or margins of society. The concept as used by Ellen Gumede, (1997), and John Mary Waliggo (1999) denotes a situation where people as individuals, or a particular section of society, are not at the centre of their society's decision making. They are discriminated against, oppressed, exploited both politically and economically and excluded from enjoying the benefits and opportunities enjoyed by others.

In marginalised groups we include those marginalised by the social, cultural, economic and political environment, especially rural and the urban poor, women, people with disabilities and internally displaced persons/refugees. These categories and others not mentioned here share common characteristics which include: low levels of literacy and general education, poor health, unemployment, lack of access to and control over productive resources like land and low income levels. They have limited engagement with national programmes targeting social, economic and political transformation and fit well Gumede and Waliggo's description of stigmatised, oppressed and exploited groups who do not actively take part in decision-making processes in the country.

These marginalised groups suffer neglect, isolation and hopelessness. They do not have self-confidence and esteem. They lack legal advice and protection. Many lack the capacity to demonstrate their potential. Women with disabilities are doubly disadvantaged, both as women and as disabled people. The negative attitude of the general public towards them has led to self-pity, dependency and a culture of silence among the marginalised.

The situation of internally displaced persons deserves special mention. Generally the internally displaced persons and refugees living in camps are characterised by high levels of poverty, overcrowding in poor housing, inadequate health and education services, malnutrition, food insecurity, family disintegration and psychological trauma. The women and children among them are most affected. They have limited access to income generating activities and cannot defend themselves against rape and defilement, often resulting in unwanted pregnancies, sexually transmitted infections and HIV/AIDS. The children are abducted and denied the right to enjoy normal early childhood development in terms of education, access to health, good nutrition, recreation; instead they are exposed to early violence and war. In parts of Uganda, some have been 'temporarily' displaced for over a decade so that children spend their entire childhood in camps.

The policy context

Alleviation of the conditions of the marginalised groups in Uganda is reflected in both constitutional and policy objectives. Uganda as a member of the United Nations is bound by the UN Charter to respect human rights for all. Uganda also signed the UN Convention on the elimination of all forms of discrimination against women. This requires that all signatory governments take the necessary action to ensure that women are not marginalised and oppressed. In addition, Uganda ratified the UN Standard Rules on Equalisation of Rights and Opportunities for People with Disabilities. The main goal was that all nations must expand the participation of people with disabilities in the economic, social, and political development of their countries. Uganda also endorsed the Jomtien (1990) Declaration and the Dakar Framework for Action (2000), which set targets for the achievement of education for all children, youth and adults.

The 1995 Constitution of the Republic of Uganda adequately identifies the marginalised groups both in the national objectives and in Chapter Four of the fundamental and other human rights, where it gives emphasis to the rights of the marginalised. It also gives sufficient empowering principles for their eventual liberation. Principle VI states:

> The State shall ensure gender balance and fair representation of marginalised groups on all constitutional and other bodies.

Article 21 affirms equality and freedom from discrimination when it states:

> All persons are equal before and under the law...a person shall not be discriminated against on the grounds of sex, race, colour, ethnic origin, tribe, birth, creed or religion, or social or economic standing, political opinion or disability.

Article 32 assures affirmative action in favour of the marginalised groups. It states:

> Notwithstanding anything in this constitution, the state shall take affirmative action in favour of groups marginalised on the basis of gender, age, disability or any other reason created by history, tradition or custom for the purpose of redressing the imbalances which exist against them.

Article 35 stipulates that:

> Persons with disabilities have a right to respect and human dignity and the state and society shall take appropriate measures to ensure that they realise their full mental and physical

potential. Parliament shall enact laws appropriate for the protection of persons with disabilities.

In this context, the Government of Uganda, together with non-governmental organisations and other development partners have committed themselves to a number of obligations including major social, economic and political policy frameworks and strategies geared towards removing inequality and marginalisation. These focus on key concerns like reduced poverty, improved access to resources, improved literacy levels, fair representation at decision-making levels, and meeting basic needs of all people, including the marginalised groups. (Vision 2025; PEAP 1998; PMA 2000; Local Government Act 1997, National Gender Policy 1998, the Education White Paper 1992, ESIP 1998, NALSIP 2002)

The policies and strategies have been translated into affirmative action and many programmes targeting the marginalised groups are being implemented. Among these are adult education programmes.

Current efforts in adult education to meet the needs of the marginalised

The recognition that adult education is an indispensable agency in the process of women's empowerment and that of other marginalised groups is evident in the objectives of most of the adult education programmes offered by both the government and non-governmental organisations in Uganda. Through adult education programmes, it is envisaged that these marginalised groups can acquire knowledge and skills which will enable them to better understand their situation, increase their productivity and competitiveness, leading to increased income, and ultimately improve their social and economic well-being. The programmes are designed to enable participants to acquire practical knowledge and skills and to use these effectively to improve their living conditions. They aim at building the capacity of the marginalised groups to challenge their subordinate position, increase their self-confidence and self-respect, and gain more control over their lives and circumstances. The ultimate goal is achievement of the national goal of sustainable development. Examples of such programmes are: Government's FAL Programme, Women's Empowerment Programme – West Nile, ActionAid's REFLECT Programme, Save the Children's UK Literacy Programme in Arua, National Plan for Functional Literacy, May 1996, (Okech et al. 1999, NALSIP 2002)

In order to achieve these objectives, the curriculum focus is quite broad, comprising adult literacy and other programmes including tailoring, cookery, carpentry, agriculture, crafts, health, income generation and community education. It also includes other educational activities aimed at changing the status quo such as human rights and legal education, and leadership skills training. In addition, deliberate strategies have been put in place by different adult education agencies involved in policy making and implementation to try and address the specific needs of the marginalised groups. For example, employment of gender and special needs education specialists, training of programme staff at all levels in gender analysis skills, integrating gender concerns in training and instructional materials and using participatory methodologies that build on learners' existing knowledge, experience and skills.

Adult education and persons with disabilities
As regards women with disabilities, the National Union of Disabled Persons of Uganda (NUDIPU) has gender programmes directed at addressing the imbalances that exist, for example between disabled women and men and between disabled and able-bodied women. NUDIPU trains gender trainers at the national level through non-formal education. It has also organised workshops to sensitise members of the public and people with disabilities themselves on issues that affect them. This is gradually leading to the recognition of gender imbalance and a change in society's attitude towards people with disabilities especially the women. (ACFODE 1995, Mazima E.1994)

Vocational education and training has been one of the major interventions available for persons with disability. According to Twimukye, M. (2000) the majority of people with disabilities are currently engaged in the informal sector such as dressmaking, craftwork and leather work, skills which they learn at vocational centres and through apprenticeship. These adult education programmes recognise that persons with disability are usually among the poorest of the poor and the most marginalised and uphold the concept of their inclusion into education and development.

Adult education and those affected by war
Akite (2002) found that vocational skills training was one of the strategies used by NGOs operating in northern Uganda to reintegrate former abducted persons into the community. The bulk of adult education programmes for internally displaced peoples and refugees are aimed at meeting their welfare and security needs in respect of food security, health education, water and sanitation, income generation and small loans management skills for small-scale enterprise, extension education and proper marketing. Adult education is also used as a tool to facilitate resettlement and restore security in the war-torn areas (Nakayenga 2000).

Evaluation of adult educational programmes
Evaluation studies undertaken so far (Okech et al. 1999; Bown and G. Mayatsa 1998; WEP 1999; Kisira, Mwesigwa et al 1999; Twimukye 2000; Akite 2002) reveal that to a certain extent adult education programmes are making a difference in the lives of the beneficiaries. Studies indicated improved economic productivity, better family health care, nutrition and many other benefits. For example women and other marginalised groups who have actively participated in functional adult literacy programmes have acquired literacy skills which they are using effectively in income generation, home management and food production. Other indicators of women's empowerment have been shown to include: participation in decision making at household and community levels; involvement in civic activities, especially the governance of their communities and the election of leaders of their choice without manipulation; the ability to earn and utilise their own income. Self-confidence and self-esteem, awareness of their civic, legal and political rights and assertiveness are some of the social and psychological outcomes of adult literacy.

As regards persons with disabilities, adult education has generally enabled them to achieve increased economic skills, increased self-awareness and confidence, the ability to involve themselves and be accepted, advocacy, and political involvement. All these are critical issues in their empowerment. (Mazima. E. 1994, Okia R. 1995)

Access and participation

In spite of these encouraging results, adult education programmes in Uganda still have inherent weaknesses and face many challenges as they work towards the empowerment of marginalised groups. Studies indicate that the majority of the marginalised groups do not enrol in adult education programmes. The few who enrol exhibit high levels of irregular attendance, absenteeism and drop out. For example, the National Adult Literacy Strategic Investment Plan (NALSIP 2002) pointed out that in spite of previous attempts to deliver adult literacy services, all government and NGO efforts currently reach only 4.3% of the 6.9 million non-literate adults. The majority of the non-literate are women, especially those in rural areas and war ravaged districts, persons with disabilities, internally displaced persons and the pastoral communities. The National Household Survey (2000) revealed that 5.5 million women and about 1.4 million men in Uganda are non-literate. According to the analysis of the 1991 population census it was discovered that 55.8 % of persons with disability have not attained any formal education. Their literacy rate is currently estimated at 37%. That of pastoral communities of Karamoja is estimated at 6% (NALSIP 2002).

During the past two decades, wars, insurgencies and cattle rustling have resulted in mass displacement of people in every part of the country. According to Nakayenga, (2000), in her study of the education needs of the internally displaced persons in Banda Parish, Kampala District, Uganda had by 1998 over 400,000 internally displaced persons from the northern and eastern regions alone, excluding those of western and central regions. There is also a sustained influx of refugees from Sudan, Democratic Republic of Congo, Rwanda, Burundi, Ethiopia and Somalia. Many of the internally displaced persons and refugees are resource poor, non-literate, and unskilled and are often cheated and exploited. There is evidence that adult education and other development programmes have not yet reached these poor and vulnerable groups and according to Ministry of Finance and Economic Planning Discussion Paper 5 (2002), the major government and private interventions aimed at empowerment do not adequately reach them.

Karamoja Region in North Eastern Uganda registers the lowest attendance rates in both formal and non-formal education. The main problem that hinders participation in education programmes there is the shortage of food. In many cases people have no choice but to leave their homes and (or) learning centres to look for food. Women, in particular, have benefited very little from education in Karamoja, with a literacy rate of 6% as compared to 20% for men (Okech 2000).

In spite of that dismal situation, there have been practically no specific adult education programmes aimed at empowering women. With support from the World Food Programme, the government functional adult literacy programme was extended to Karamoja in 2001, with a special focus on women. The Alternative Basic Education for Karamoja (ABEK) was started in 1997 to meet the special educational needs of the region. It targets children but adults may follow their children to attend. They are not allowed to register but they are allowed to learn and a number do take advantage of this opportunity.

Low levels of participation in educational programmes are detrimental to the empowering process of the marginalised groups. A high literacy rate among women is not only empowering but also an important factor in sustaining the rising trend of involvement, persistence and performance of children in the Universal Primary Education (UPE) system. Adult education empowers women to provide financial, material and moral support to their children, to be able to participate in monitoring their children's learning and to take an active role in the management of schools. It also brings about attitudinal changes that result in long term psychosocial and economic benefits such as the capacity to analyse and solve problems, increased participation in local settings and community decision making, better self image, increased independent thought and many other aspects of personal development (Oxhenam et. al 2001, Okech et al 1999, Cottingham et al 1995, WEP 1999).

Barriers to access and participation
Barriers to access and participation include the absence of a comprehensive adult education policy that focuses on creating inclusive cultures and practices at all levels of the educational system. The educational inclusion of the marginalised groups cannot proceed very far without developing the capacity of learning centres to respond to learner diversity. For example, Twimukye (2000) reported that adult education programmes being implemented by organisations of able-bodied people are still not sensitive to the needs of people with disabilities; their organisation, teaching methods and even physical environments fail to cater for their special needs. Furthermore, society, including those people delivering education to people with disabilities, are still prejudiced against them. The learning environment is equally insensitive to the special needs of female learners.

There is also a big challenge arising from lack of funds. Lack of resources implies the absence of adult education activities for adults within the marginalised groups and this contributes to their further exclusion and marginalisation. In the absence of government resources, it has been a common practice for NGOs and private institutions to take on the challenge of providing education to children within the marginalised groups, i.e. the girl-child, children with disabilities, etc. but little is done for marginalised adults.

Other barriers are social and cultural, such as the division of labour and resources by gender at all levels, negative attitudes towards the marginalised groups and inadequate capacity among planners and programme designers to design relevant and accessible programmes.

Programme content stereotyping

Vocational training programmes are widespread in Uganda, mainly targeting women especially those who have dropped out of the formal education system; male and female persons with disabilities; refugees and internally displaced persons. These programmes aim at equipping learners with knowledge and skills for employment in both the formal and informal employment sectors. The education and training provided meets an important practical need allowing the marginalised access to employment. However, the majority of these programmes continue to maintain the 'traditional' content stereotyping. In other words, certain educational activities/courses have been designated to a particular category of persons on the basis of preconceived opinions.

Kwesiga J.C. (1994) analysed the educational activities of 340 women groups and found that the shift from the traditional forms of curriculum content focusing on the traditional roles of women was proceeding very slowly. Some of the predominant vocational courses for younger girls and women she identified included tailoring, cookery and domestic sciences, handicrafts, nursery teaching and typing although in urban areas some women had gone into training in metalwork, shoemaking, leather tanning and carpentry.

Limiting adult education and training to areas traditionally identified as 'women's work' does not challenge the gender division of labour and participation in decision-making. It consequently maintains low-income women in their marginal positions. The training of women in areas traditionally identified as 'men's work' may not only widen employment opportunities but may also break down the existing occupation segregation. It may help to abolish the traditional gender division of labour and allow both horizontal and vertical mobility in employment.

Improvement-oriented focus at the expense of transformative focus

Adult education in Uganda aims at improving the welfare of the marginalised groups but to a large extent ignores the basic causes of their marginalisation and oppression. In other words, it is improvement oriented and not aimed at transforming social/power relations. It focuses on meeting practical needs for survival such as food, water, fuel and income, nutrition education, and imparting the knowledge and skills needed to access these. Of course these are relevant to the marginalised groups because neglecting practical needs leads to poor health and reduced quality of life. However, focusing on them in isolation from strategic ones reinforces people's marginality in society. Addressing the strategic needs of the marginalised groups requires a fundamental re-examination of social structures and institutions; and of how resources are allocated and benefits shared. This should lead to attitudinal and structural changes and shifts in power relations (Moser 1993, Mbilinyi 1993, Babikwa 2003)

Programme focus for women
Programmes that concentrate on equipping women with the knowledge and skills to perform better their traditional roles (health education, home management, crafts making, domestic science, improved methods in agriculture production, etc.) unconsciously reinforce the subordinate position of women. Programme planners and curriculum designers need to design educational programmes that will also enable women to challenge the oppressive systems and change their power relations. For example, nutrition education programmes targeting rural mothers always focus on teaching them how to prepare and feed both themselves and their children a balanced diet. Significant results would occur if the curriculum were broadened to address such issues as gender bias in allocation of food at household level and eating habits. Studies have shown that gender relations in food allocation and eating habits militate against women and girls eating nutritious and adequate food especially in areas where food insecurity is prevalent (Jitta & Ndidde 1995).

Working with micro-finance programmes run by Action for Development (ACFODE) revealed that it is one thing for a woman to acquire knowledge and skills in income generation and indeed increase her income but quite another to have control over it (ACFODE, 2002). Many other productive oriented education programmes are also limited in content. Much as their aim is to achieve economic independence they do not address contextual issues such as control over resources, gender, specific individual and group interests which are critical in influencing access to and management of key resources. They tend to perpetuate a welfare orientation by leaving out the other entrepreneurial skills required to manage a successful business enterprise, like simple market research, marketing, management skills, book-keeping, negotiation skills, etc. Such programmes need to diversify their curriculum to address the strategic issues that impede the marginalised from achieving economic independence.

Uganda Women's Finance Trust (UWFT) is one of the few organisations that have encouraged training that empowers women to become economically independent. Besides training women in business management skills like record keeping, marketing, loan and group management, it trains women in specific areas like bee keeping, poultry, dairy, piggery and food processing. The training also offers a wide variety of information to enhance the competitiveness of women in business.

A recent study by Babikwa (2003) found out that despite the high degree of women's participation in community-based environmental educational programmes, existing gender relations at community and household level have continued to militate against women's ability to implement the skills they have acquired. For example, access and control over land, the main resource among most of the farming communities in Uganda, continues to be skewed in favour of men. Because the land usually belongs to men, the family or the clan, many women lack the power to decide when and where to apply their newly acquired skills in land management. In situations where women have access, men still largely have control over farm products, including the marketing and sharing of accrued benefits. Some women have as a consequence deliberately refused to apply the recommended sustainable land use practices. This has in turn kept women on the periphery of socio-economic empowerment and development, with multiple negative consequences for their well-being, that of their children and that of society as a whole.

As regards functional adult literacy programmes that target women, it is one thing to acquire literacy skills and another to retain and continually utilise them. A relatively high number of women who graduate from literacy programmes relapse into illiteracy over the years. Reasons given include: lack of reading materials and that the few materials that exist do not meet women's needs and interests. Even if reading materials are available, the traditional division of household labour makes it impossible for the women to find time to read. Other factors that constrain retention and utilisation include: lack of a literate environment, lack of relevant and gender sensitive continuing literacy programmes and unequal access and control over productive resources, e.g. capital, land and strategic information.

Programme focus for internally displaced persons
While most adult education programmes for the internally displaced persons are targeted toward alleviating their economic and physical needs, which are immediate and practical, they lack a holistic approach that would take into account the various dimensions of needs such as human rights, decision-making and leadership, resettlement, peace education, gender concerns, coping with change and community integration. In addition they need education that will equip them with skills to meet their welfare needs and build their capacity to challenge the conditions that marginalise them.

Some progress in this direction is being made by working through improvement-oriented programmes to confront oppressive systems, structures and practices, using bottom-up approaches; but the pace is slow. (Refer to REFLECT programme, VEDCO sustainable agriculture programme, and CEFORD women empowerment programme, etc.) There is a need to consolidate the gains so far made and to scale up such programmes until the marginalised are strong and articulate enough to collectively challenge and question their subordination.

The methodologies used in adult education work

Most adult education programmes in Uganda today encourage the use of participatory methodologies for both facilitation and learning. Their use is premised on democratic perspectives aimed at creating conditions for emancipation. The approaches and methods encourage creative and active involvement of the participants and building on their knowledge and experiences (ActionAid 1998, Nandago 1998, MoGLSD 1997, LABE 2000). However, while there is a genuine intent to use participatory methods, it has been observed that adult education instructors or facilitators tend to fall back on more familiar and less challenging methods. The language, concepts, illustrations and other pedagogical techniques they use tend to reinforce learners' dependence on the instructor or facilitator. They do not encourage the active participation of the learners in the learning process and more especially in decision-making. They usually do not alter existing roles and unequal relationships. Such methods are not transformative and empowering.

In order to bring about empowerment, the methods and techniques used in the learning process should be aimed at developing learners' capacity to be creative and analytical.

This calls for a departure from the 'orientation' type of training to more systematically conceptualised, organised and regular training and follow-up of instructors/facilitators. The training should also endeavour to clarify the theoretical aspects surrounding participatory methods and their practical implications for learning outcomes. The current practice indicates that many adult educators use their experience as primary school teachers while yet others learn on the job through trial and error. 'Training' is ad hoc and usually short. For example, Okech et al (1999) found that in the government functional adult literacy programmes many of the instructors had been trained for just three days and had never had any refresher training. This was also true of the supervisors, most of whom had themselves no orientation in adult education and literacy methodology. In addition to the limited duration of training, Babikwa (2003) found out that educators of educators do not emphasise the relationship between the learning goals, the learning methods used and the theoretical implications of that relationship. This omission leads trained educators to use participatory methods in a technocratic manner. To them, methods seem to be tools to be picked up freely and used without any consideration of their theoretical and philosophical orientations. And in case wrong outcomes emerge, the blame is put on the learners who are accused of being 'laggards'.

Conclusion

This chapter has shown that alleviation of the social and economic conditions of the marginalised groups and their personal and political empowerment are the main objectives of adult education in Uganda. However, due to inherent weaknesses in the adult education policy and the implementation process, the transformative educational needs of the marginalised groups are not yet adequately met. Many of adult education programmes have not greatly changed the peripheral position of the majority of the marginalised groups, especially that of women. Programmes should begin to look beyond basic economic needs and to address the deeper causes of marginalisation if adult education is to have positive and sustainable results.

12
The Afrikan University Adult Educator and the Challenge of Language, Education, Development and Empowerment

Paulo Wangoola

Introduction

It is generally agreed among adult educators that the raison d'être of adult education is development and empowerment. In this cross-cutting article, key issues, interpretation, understanding and orientation are outlined to challenge adult educators, in Uganda and Afrika as a whole, whatever their area, level or media of engagement, to reflect on the extent to which their intervention may be on course.

As a social engagement, at its core development action can only be about the pooling together and mobilisation of resources by a people. People are a people because they share a memory, history, language, culture, worldview, destiny and homeland. In the global community of peoples, the Ugandan adult educator can only operate from the Afrikan base. Against the background of apparently mutually exclusive identities, a case is made for the unity of Afrikan peoples. The chapter then proceeds to unpack key concepts: knowledge, language and development and comes to the conclusion that there is no knowledge without language, no language without knowledge, and no knowledge outside culture. Further, no community can exist or survive, let alone prosper in a sustainable manner, or have a future, without a homegrown knowledge base of its own, and the means to maintain, deepen and upgrade that knowledge.

Development, then, is a people's mobilisation of their own knowledge and other resources for sustainable individual and collective well-being. In other words development is cultural action, with language at the centre. As knowledge is culturally generated, it is also culturally encoded, in symbols that can be verbalised. A speech community hides away its knowledge in its language so that it is only fully available to members of the speech community who have been brought up inside the speech community's culture. It follows that Afrikans approach the body of knowledge generated by the Anglo-Saxons (the creators and owners of the English language as based in Europe, USA, with satellites in Canada, Australia and New Zealand) with overwhelming disadvantage. The chapter argues that the white man's knowledge and language can only be the basis for the disempowerment and stunting of the Afrikan's development potential. In this regard, the way forward for liberation and empowerment lies in mother tongue education; the real missing link in Afrika's development endeavours.

The chapter argues that as a product of an education system that outlaws the use of the mother tongue, the Afrikan university adult educator, intellectual and scholar cannot be an empowered adult educator. Consequently s/he cannot empower others in a systematic and sustainable manner. But then, the university adult educator is not the only one who is disempowered. The chapter identifies three knowledge sites which are disempowered: the Western-trained intellectual and scholar; the NGOs, CBOs and CSO sector; and mother-tongue organic intellectuals and scholars, who are also custodians of indigenous knowledge. As these three knowledge and truth sites are disadvantaged together, only united and co-ordinated action can empower them, severally and collectively. The chapter then challenges the university adult educator to spearhead a collaborative partnership for the three knowledge sites to articulate a new knowledge paradigm rooted in Afrikan indigenous knowledge, ways of knowing and language. This can be the only hope for education as cultural action, and therefore development and empowerment.

This chapter does not focus narrowly on the Uganda situation but discusses issues affecting Afrika as a whole. This is because the issues raised have their full meaning only in the context of Afrika as a whole. This is, however, not meant to deny their specific applications in the Ugandan context.

A historical moment
It is quite self-evident that today one finds oneself in an expired Old

World. This Old World is heavily pregnant with a new one. The stakes are high!

The globalising, predatory white supremacist capitalism has mutated into fascism; that is a social order that has outlived its social usefulness. It is a social order which is an impediment to the further progress of countries, nations and peoples of the world as a whole; but especially the countries, nations and peoples in the South. It can no longer enjoy the overwhelming support of the people, and can only be maintained by undisguised force. Between countries the gap between the haves and have-nots has never been so wide; and it continues to grow. Within countries the rich become fewer and richer, while the poor, in ever-growing numbers, are forced into deeper poverty.

It seems that the resource and power divide between the masters of globalisation and their collaborators on the one hand, and on the other, the people, is so wide that it is not bridgeable by peaceful means. Nor can it be maintained by peaceful means; indeed the chasm itself is an ever-present act of war against the people and the environment. It is not surprising, therefore, that military expenditure has increased globally and in Uganda. Heightened militarism has entailed the devaluation of the lives of the oppressed, in order to justify or prepare the ground for attacks against them, and to kill them on a mass scale. What is more, this level of militarisation makes democratic politics and the politics of accountability impossible.

Militarism also affects the quality of education, and removes from its goals key concepts like that of an inquiring mind, critical intelligence and emancipatory education. Instead, premium is given to education for robotisation to meet the needs of the 'market' i.e. capital. In the case of Uganda, and Afrika as a whole, this means foreign capital, itself a continuation of war. Adult education has, in Uganda and Afrika in general, found itself caught up in this, rather than developing critical consciousness as its practitioners often claim.

Two broad schools of thought have emerged to make sense of the post-cold war moment, and the opportunities and challenges it presents. According to Huntingford, for example, this is a time of the 'clash of civilizations' for 'the strong' to conquer and subdue 'the weak'. This is the logic which drives the bellicose policies of George W. Bush of the US and his little brother Tony Blair of Britain in their war against 'terrorism'. On his part Kofi Annan, Secretary General of the UN, has said that the century is a century of dialogue between all the civilisations of the world, in which even those civilisations that were said to have died will resurrect for inclusion and recognition.

The two schools are about war and peace; the culture of war and the culture of peace. In fact this generation is witnessing a historical conjecture which privileges it with the possibility to seize the moment to become the worthy midwife to a New Humane World Order; an order with inter-civilisation dialogue and liberative governance as an essential part of its hallmark. It is an order in which everybody has a role to play, if it is to be achieved. Intellectuals, scholars and educators have a special role in this endeavour. Just as education is central to the imposition of the culture of war, it is equally critical for the building of the culture of peace, dialogue and liberative governance. As Nyerere taught, if education was used to enslave, it can as well be used to liberate. To be liberative education must be emancipatory, catalyse and engage critical thought, precipitate critical intelligence, engage with the masses of the people, be participatory, stimulate social progress and be empowering. And herein lies the challenge to the Afrikan University adult educator.

The Afrikan university adult educator will be relevant to the twenty-first century to the extent s/he engages with these strategic challenges, and participates in the preparation of the Afrikan nation for inter-civilisation dialogue.

Inter-civilisation dialogue: some basic assumptions and questions

Within the word dialogue are embedded two Greek roots and concepts: *di* meaning two, and *logue*, meaning talk or reason. Dialogue therefore is about two or more people or parties talking and reasoning together. Dialogue therefore assumes comparability and a measure of equality or claim to equality.

For the Afrikan university adult educator, scholar and intellectual to effectively participate in the preparation of the Afrikan peoples for inter-civilisation dialogue, several key assumptions and questions have to be clarified and cleared. Of particular importance are: Who is an Afrikan? Are Afrikans a people – I suppose the way Europeans, Asiatics, Chinese and Arabs, for example, are a people? Have Afrikans authored a civilisation or civilisations, contemporary or past?

Who is an Afrikan? Are Afrikans a people?
The popular reasons given for denying the Afrikan peoples and continent their eloquent unity, is the vastness and diversity of its peoples and cultures. It is a continent of about 12 million square miles, peopled by about 700 million: black, yellow and white, and all manner of shades between black and white. The continent is peopled by Afrikans, Arabs, Asians, Chinese and Europeans. These peoples embrace a broad spectrum of spirituality and religions: Afrikan spirituality, Christianity, Judaism, Islam, Hindu, Confucius, Rastafaria, and their denominations. In their immediate mass consciousness these people belong to thousands of nationalities and ethnic categories; speak an equal number of languages and dialects; belong to different cultures and practise different traditions. Millions are steeped in Afrikan spirituality, while others are Arabised, Jews or westernised.

In such a setting, how can anything be Afrikan? And how can anybody be Afrikan? Some people, particularly Europeans, 'having fallen in love with Afrika', solve the problem by declaring everybody who 'resides on the Afrikan continent' to be Afrikan. Others restrict the Afrikan club to 'holders of passports' issued by any country on the continent, etc, etc.

The view taken here is that the Afrikan peoples are like a tropical rainforest. It is the existence of thousands of species in the flora of a tropical rainforest that define this type of forest. The apparent diversity among Afrikan peoples is built on bedrock of unity. They are like the trees in the rainforest. The canopies may not touch, but beneath the surface the roots freely and closely intermingle. This is how.

Language
A leading Afrikan philosopher and scholar, Prof. T. Obenga, has demonstrated that contemporary Afrikan languages share the same

structure with the language which was spoken by pharoanic Egypt. Indo-European languages do not share this similarity and linkage. Moreover, many words used in ancient Egypt are still easily recognisable in Afrikan languages. Some words continue to carry the same, similar or recognisable meaning in contemporary Afrikan languages. Considering the centrality of language in a people's history and identity, the definition of who an Afrikan is must include the ancient Egyptian linguistic connection. Afrikans are peoples who share a linguistic unity with the ancient language of Kemet (Egypt).

Moreover, another leading Afrikan scholar and linguist, Prof. K.K. Prah, has established that the criteria used to classify Afrikan languages were intended to depict Afrika as the Tower of Babel. If the same criteria were used to classify European languages, Europe would have more than 350 languages; and The Netherlands at least 15! The point being that Afrika is not any more divided by language than Europe is. In fact what are classified as thousands of languages are dialects which can be harmonised and standardised into about ten of what Prah has called core languages.

Music and dance
Afrikans tend to have a digitally clear sense of rhythm. Whatever their language, dialect, cultural category or geographical location, when singing, Afrikans invariably move their bodies to the rhythm of the music. Indeed the two are so interlinked that in many Afrikan languages/dialects, Runyakitara of Uganda for one, the word for music is the same as the word for dance.

The oiginal human cast
Fortunately, it is an established fact the world has come to live with that Afrika, in particular the Great Lakes Region, is the cradle of humankind. The only way a mammal without fur could have survived the tropical ultraviolet rays was by developing melanin under the skin. The original human was therefore black, pitch black. Other colours emerged later as a result of mutation, with varying levels of melanin deficiency. It is a characteristic of the Afrikan to be full-melanited. Indeed it is the Afrikan who gives colour to the peoples of the world.

Common history, common destiny

The common history of Afrikans is attested to by the continent's linguistic and cultural unity. In more recent history, the Afrikan peoples are the world's only people who over hundreds of successive years, have suffered enslavement at the hands of the Arabs; and massive kidnappings of tens of millions into cross-Atlantic slavery in the Americas and the Caribbean, at the hands of Europeans. Today Afrikans are a people who are the most marginalised and the most oppressed at home, abroad and everywhere. They hold the key to a Free World; for the world can only be free to the extent the most oppressed are free.

Shared worldview

Afrikan peoples share a worldview centred on being and doing good to all around you, people and nature. The health and well-being of the individual is irrevocably tied up with what surrounds him/her and what s/he interacts with. This is because each individual is considered to be an extension of everything that surrounds her/him; and everything that surrounds you is an extension into you. This worldview is summed up in the Ubuntu philosophy. Ubuntu philosophy holds that 'I am because we are; and because we are, therefore I am'. A useful aid to understanding Ubuntu philosophy is the European counter philosophy of human existence. According to Descartes, you do not have to go beyond yourself to explain your existence! Hence, 'I think therefore I am'.

Afrika's contribution to civilisation

The world, particularly the Western world, has had to come to terms with the fact that Afrika is the cradle of humankind. It is as yet to concede Afrika's contribution to world development and civilisation. Indeed miseducation and amnesia on this subject explains why many Afrikan intellectuals believe and peddle the fallacy that Afrika has made no contribution to world development and civilisation. Many believe foreign domination and humiliation is a fair price for Afrikans to pay, in return for 'development'; after all 'we cannot make even a needle'! Adult educators in Uganda and Afrika in general have a big challenge to counter this fallacy.

Afrika is not only the cradle of humankind; it is as well the cradle of civilisation. This civilisation centred on the Nile Valley, culminating in the glorious Egyptian civilisation. It was a civilisation authored by Afrikans; if you prefer, black people. In the murals by Egyptians in the pyramids they built, they depicted themselves as black. The Egyptians sculpted their great leaders in huge stone, some of which still exists, five thousand years and more later. The great leaders have typical Afrikan features. Moreover, the ancient Egyptians called their land Kemet. It is the Greeks who called it 'Egyptos', meaning 'land of the black people'. And, as already observed, recent studies have revealed a close link between phaoronic Egyptian and contemporary Afrikan languages.

Once again, who is an Afrikan?

An Afrikan is a historical product. S/he is the product of humanity in its earliest history, and subsequently shaped by interaction, competition and struggles with other peoples. In the more recent past, Afrikans are the product of the struggles with Arabs and Europeans. Important landmarks in this struggle have included enslavement at the hands of the Arabs and Europeans; conquest, occupation and the stealing of land from the north by Arabs and from the south by the Europeans; as well as cultural degradation through Arabisation and Europeanisation. As a result of all this, while Afrika is the homeland of Afrikans, millions have been dispersed in the Diaspora, particularly in South and North America and the Caribbean. The question of the Afrikan nation is not a question of residence on the Afrikan continent; nor of the colonial-neo-colonial immigration question of passports. In fact passports/citizenship around artificial colonial state creations is an additional mechanism to legitimise European/Arab land grabbing and continued domination.

Afrikans are a people whose ancestors have authored civilisations in Ethiopia, Egypt, Mali, Ghana, Songhay, Bunyoro-Kitara, Monomotapa, etc. They are a people whose freedom and progress has been impeded by their struggles with Arab and European peoples, and who now seek new relationships based on equality, justice and co-existence informed by Ubuntu philosophy.

Afrika is now the home of all peoples of the world: Arabs, Asians, Chinese, and Europeans. You do not have to be Afrikan to have the right to live on the Afrikan continent. It is important, therefore, for Afrikan peoples and all the other peoples living in Afrika to have and be true to their identity, and from their identities, to negotiate a humane order of peaceful co-existence, which recognises this land as an Afrikan homeland. Afrikans can only negotiate a new humane order on the Afrikan continent informed by Ubuntu philosophy. By this philosophy for example, it is not Ubuntu for about 4500 white farmers in Zimbabwe, about 0.03% of the total population, to own more than 70% of the land, moreover including the very best! This type of order can only be possible under conditions of war, in fact genocide, against the Afrikan peoples.

Development is like a mirror

Europeans are eager to lay claim to Greece as the cradle of their civilisation. Greece inspires them to greater achievements, in the footsteps of their founding ancestors. Indeed it is difficult to imagine European advancement without the linkage with Greece.

It is difficult to imagine Afrikans forging ahead on the road to progress without historical unifying point(s) of reference, any more than one can imagine the Baganda without Kintu; the Kikuyu without Mumbi; the Zulu without Shaka; the Basotho without Moeshoeshoe, etc. Development is like a mirror. An object is as far behind the mirror as it is in front of it. Thus a people can forge as far ahead as they can source back for inspiration in their history. Many people have to invent myths and half-truths to provide historical points of reference which will enable them to surge forward. In the case of Afrikans truth is magic! In fact stranger than fiction!

Any Afrikan adult educator, intellectual and scholar who wishes to be relevant in the twenty-first century, and to empower communities, peoples and the Afrikan nation into inter-civilisational dialogue has to be able to reclaim Egypt as Afrika's historical reference point. Afrikan communities, peoples and nation can then say, 'we have done it before; we can do it again – in fact do it better'!

Knowledge is power; is the university adult educator empowered?

Adult education is considered to be an empowering force because of the assumed link between knowledge and power. Under the circumstances it becomes necessary to closely examine knowledge and education. What is knowledge? What is education? What is the source of power in knowledge, and in education?

Quite clearly, to empower, one needs to be empowered. The most important basis for a claim to empowerment by a university adult educator is the knowledge they have acquired through the education system they have gone through, and are part of. Can the university adult educator be said to be truly empowered?

Knowledge and language

A community is moulded out of a group of people who over time live in close physical proximity to one another, in a given ecological space. Driven by the survival instinct, these people engage in activities to avoid danger and to procure the material needs for their sustenance: love, food, shelter, happiness and clothing. Out of trial and error our early ancestors died and survived the hard and precarious way. In the process they came to understand nature and themselves better. Over time they learned nature was systematic, and therefore predictable. They also noticed that certain human action on nature tended to maximise benefits for human survival. Thus, in the course of the procurement of the material requirements for their sustenance, groups of men, women and their children created knowledge. Knowledge in the sense of what helped them to understand their environment better, and the skills to enable them survive better therein.

Knowledge then grows out of the soil of shared experience, over time and space; in a particular ecological setting. Knowledge is concrete and specific, to solve concrete and specific problems, to the specific and peculiar advantage of the creators and owners of that knowledge.

To ensure that both positive and negative lessons acquired during the production process were not lost, to avoid having to reinvent the wheel over and over again, and to avoid the limitations of individual memory, groups devised the means to carefully and safely store group knowledge in group memory. The principal reason for the emergence of human speech was to facilitate the orderly human action on and interaction with nature, and the need to accumulate and store group knowledge and experience generated in the process. The group stores its knowledge in verbalisable symbols called words, as well as non-verbalisable body movements. A coherent set of words developed by a group is what is called language.

As a social product, knowledge is produced by a speech group for that group's specific and peculiar interest of self-preservation, in interaction, co-operation, competition and rivalry with other groups. Over time the group classifies its knowledge into junior, intermediate, advanced, general and classified. Group members are able to access group knowledge and information consistent with their physical and spiritual growth and development; the breadth, depth and subtlety of their education and training, socialisation, role and responsibility.

On the basis of the shared joy of surviving together, and solidarity in the face of common threats, the group develops a feeling of connectedness and a collaboration in which an attack on one becomes an attack on all. Precisely because in this there is advantage to the individual, as the whole becomes greater than the sum of its parts. When and as this occurs, the group becomes a community. As a community it generates a knowledge base consistent with its own experience of joys in survival and solidarity under threat, extolling what has worked for them, and condemning or cautioning on what has not worked out well for them. This community experience, in coded form, is stored in the speech community's language; in words, phrases, idioms, parables, jokes, songs, dances, taboos, etc.

Thus although knowledge may have a global dimension, it always bears the local stamp of its creators. Indeed knowledge takes on a global dimension on the basis of local excellence. It is therefore critical to recognise, as reality, black knowledge for the black people; yellow knowledge for yellow people; and white knowledge for the white people. Universal knowledge is the point of intersection between all these knowledges.

Quite clearly then, collective knowledge production for collective good transforms people into human beings, and hence a community.

The less a people engage in collective endeavours of knowledge production for their collective good, the less human they become, and the less community they become! The more they wither away.

Knowledge as culture

In order to ensure that women, men and their children organised themselves in the most effective and sustainable way for their individual and collective well-being and in a manner which, as well, preserved nature's wholesome health, rules and regulations were developed to govern the different relationships. These include self with self; self with and among others, with nature, the departed, the yet unborn; and with the gods. Like the community's experience, these rules were recorded and preserved in the community language, in idioms, proverbs, parables, stories, history, traditions, taboos, ceremonies, etc. These rules defined a people's way of life; that is a people's culture, with language as the central feature. The anthem of *Ekibiina ky'Olulimi Oluganda* (the Luganda Society) sums up the centrality of language when it declares *'Olulimi lye ggwanga'*, that is, 'a nation is its language'.

Quite clearly, the act and process of a people acting on nature generates knowledge and language; and ultimately defines the culture within which knowledge continues to be generated, stored, transferred, applied, updated and upgraded. Knowledge creation therefore is realised through cultural action.

Education and empowerment

No community can possibly exist or survive, let alone sustainably prosper, or have a future, without a home-grown knowledge base of its own and the means to maintain, deepen and upgrade that knowledge. Education is the deliberate system and process devised by a community to incrementally expose and pass on its knowledge and skills to its children, boys and girls, men and women, elders (male and female), and leaders on an on-going basis. In its entirety, education is about a community replicating and improving on itself, in its own image. Some of the education takes place informally and in non-formal situations; while some of it occurs in designated places.

Though not linear, a number of stages in educational development and responsibility can be discerned: the stage of imbibing; the stage of being a doer and a teacher to others; the stage of being a defender of knowledge; and the stage of questioning established knowledge, and expanding the frontiers of knowledge, through dialogue, studies and research.

Since knowledge creation, transfer and application is cultural action, it means that there is no knowledge without language; no language without knowledge; no knowledge outside culture; and there is no culture outside a people's experience. Moreover, the culture of a speech community provides to those who have been raised and socialised from the inside of the community, the keys, passwords, indexes, explanatory notes and order within which the meaning encoded in the words of that community bursts into full blossom. It follows therefore, that the bottom line of education is that it is cultural action. As language is central to knowledge as culture in motion and in action, mother tongue education is the key to knowledge creation, access and transfer. Mother tongue alone can, with minimum effort, open the doors to the inner meaning of words.

On the basis of this logic, a person can only be said to be educated and empowered when he/she is not only fluent but deep in his/her people's language and culture, which in turn opens the doors for them to be deep in the knowledge of their people. Being deep in one's people's language and knowledge, in addition, opens cross-cultural doors for one to make sense of other speech communities' language and knowledge, and to use them to enrich their own knowledge and mother tongue. Above all, an educated person has confidence in their people's heritage to be the only viable and sustainable basis for their advancement.

Development as cultural action, starting where you are!

Development is about a people harnessing the knowledge they are masters of; that is, their own home-grown knowledge, supplemented by knowledge adaptations from other peoples, and applying it for that people to be more and better of itself. Development is cultural action, starting from where you are. It helps a people position themselves better to interact, co-operate and compete with other peoples. As cultural action development is a people's collective activity, whose action is harmonised and synergised by a shared memory, history, identity, language, homeland and future.

As can be imagined, knowledge transfer from one generation to the next is central to development. Even then, it should be pointed out that no individual or a people have the monopoly of knowledge. For that matter therefore, *amagezi si goomu; ndi mugezi n'omukobere;* and moreover, *n'omugezi yeena awubwa*. These are Ganda and Soga sayings meaning, 'nobody has a monopoly of knowledge'; 'the learned learn from others', 'even the wisest makes mistakes'. Thus, just as individuals learn from one another all the time, so do communities. However, even where knowledge is imported, it needs to be translated into cultural and linguistic forms that harmonise with the overall system of knowledge as understood by members of the receiving speech community. The alternative is to introduce separate, parallel and conflicting thought processes, language systems, values and assumptions. This makes learning immensely painful and superficial – round pegs in square holes; probably comparable with a goat being fitted with the memory of a dog!

The environment, history, worldview, value system, language structure and psyche of Afrikans and Europeans are materially different. For Ugandans, for instance, to make the English language and English knowledge as the basis for modernisation is to make the Ugandan development project so inefficient that in the global community of nations Uganda cannot be competitive or record sustainable levels of development, science and technology.

Uganda's education system: the real stumbling block to empowerment

In 1987 the NRM Government appointed an Education Review Commission under the Chairmanship of Professor Ssenteza Kajubi to 'inquire into the policies governing education in Uganda'. Five years later a White Paper was issued, detailing government acceptance of the Ssenteza Kajubi Report, and its implementation intent. According to the Minister of Education then, Amanya Mushega, the White Paper constituted NRM Government overall policy 'to establish the highest quality of education possible as the basis for fundamental change and revolution'. Yet when it came to the fundamental question of language, government could not embrace revolution.

The NRM Government language policy remained the same as had been instituted by the colonialists: in the rural areas the medium of instruction from P.1 to P.4 will be the relevant mother tongue; with the rest of the primary education cycle in English. In urban areas the medium of instruction will be in English throughout the primary cycle. Then Kiswahili and English are made compulsory subjects to be taught to all children throughout the primary cycle, without distinction between urban and rural. These two languages (Kiswahili and English) continue to be compulsory subjects for all secondary school students and examinable at PLE, and 'O' levels; while in addition, from S.1 English takes over as the only medium of instruction. And in an examinations-driven education system, Uganda's five officially designated mother tongues (Luo, Runyakitara, Luganda, Ateso/Akarimojong and Lugbara) will be taught as a subject in primary schools but only those who wish may offer to be examined in them for the Primary Leaving Examination!

It is Government policy therefore not to give any meaningful chance to any Ugandan or Afrikan mother tongue beyond the elementary primary education level; although even then, no policy instrument has been drawn or any practical action instituted, to make this token recognition of mother tongues a reality! This simple, yet brazen act of promoting the foreign language of a former colonial, but now neo-colonial master, makes it impossible for the education system in Uganda to be the basis of 'fundamental change, revolution and development'. In fact it makes education the central problem rather than the prime solution to Uganda's endeavours for empowerment and development.

The government policy for adult literacy programmes is that literacy must be learned in the mother tongue. This positive orientation is, however, greatly disadvantaged in practice. Adult literacy programmes are not given anywhere near the priority that primary education is given, are seriously under-financed and depend on ill-trained unpaid volunteer teachers. Adult education therefore stands little chance of mitigating the disempowering effect of the formal school system.

Through the use of English as the official language of government, colonial education was designed to create an elite divorced from the masses of the people; and to whet their appetite to become English, with room to be upgraded into American; itself a cultural impossibility! Secondly, after, and in the course of, disconnecting the Afrikan elite from their mother tongue and knowledge base, they are trained to accept Western knowledge to be the basis of the development of the Afrikan continent.

Language is so central to identity and culture that no one can immerse themselves in another people's language without corresponding cultural degradation. Thus out of the colonial-neo-colonial education system emerge half-baked Afrikans; less than quarter-baked Englishmen/women; with the rest uncooked! They cannot fluently speak or understand English; they miss out on subtleties and nuances. In the end they have to make do with varying levels and degrees of 'pidgin' English. Armed with Pidgin English the Afrikan elite can only approach the body of knowledge developed, coded and stored in the English language with severe handicap. Compared to an English mother tongue speaker, Afrikan elite may suffer a 30%, 40%, 50% handicap; who knows? Thus out of the colonial education mill, as perpetuated and intensified in Uganda today, Afrikan elites emerge as 'pidgin scholars' and 'pidgin scientists'. They can excel in their pidgin environment, but in the global community of scholars and scientists they cannot consistently be part of the cutting edge in the generation of knowledge in the English language. This is particularly the case in adult education.

In October 2001 this author met Prof. Peter Jarvis, a prolific British adult educator, at the University of Georgia, Atlanta, U.S. Professor Jarvis expressed the concern that since the demise of the Afrikan Association for Literacy and Adult Education (AALAE) Journal of Adult Education, he was not aware of any journal of adult education coming out of Afrika. What is more, as editor of an international journal of adult education, he received many articles, mainly from Nigeria. However, it was rare to receive an article of publishable quality. Because of the need to have some articles by Afrikan adult educators, so as to enhance the international image of the journal, Prof. Jarvis was working on a proposal to train Afrikan professors and Ph.D. holders on how to write good-quality journal articles! This project is a clear wake-up call to the Afrikan adult educator; even their top-notch scholars cannot write good quality articles in the English language!

The North American and European adult educators are usually ahead of their Afrikan colleagues for other reasons as well. For example, they have better library facilities, and most of the literature is by Euro-Americans. In addition, a lot of material by Afrikan adult educators is more easily available and accessible in the North than on the Afrikan continent. Thus while adult educators in the North read what the North, Afrika, Asia and Latin America write, the Afrikan adult educator has very limited access to what the North writes, and virtually nothing written by Afrika, Asia and Latin America!

Pidgin scholars are weighed down by a debilitating dependence. Even white American scholars before independence from Britain, and long after their independence, felt severely handicapped by British imperialism! It can only be left to the imagination as to how much more handicapped Afrikan scholars would be today! Referring to that time, this is how Kathryn Van Spanckeren expressed what American scholars felt about British domination:

> Dependence is a state of degradation fraught with disgrace, and to be dependent on a foreign mind for what we can ourselves produce is to add to the crime of indolence the weakness of stupidity. (Van Spanckeren 1994:14)

Indeed even when pidgin scholars excel it is usually by out-dated imitation. This is what Kathryn Van Spanckeren writes again about the American experience:

> American awareness of literary fashion still lagged behind the English, and this time lag intensified American imitation. Fifty

years after their fame in England English neo-classic writers such as Joseph Addison, Richard Steele, Jonathan Swift, Alexander Pope, Oliver Goldsmith and Samuel Johnson were still eagerly imitated in America. (Van Spanckeren 1994:14)

The extremely brilliant and courageous scholars and scientists who attempt to break out of the pidgin mould, like Prof. Charles Ssali of Uganda or Dr Obel of Kenya, are ruthlessly beaten back into line by their mediocre and spineless colleagues. The spineless scholars and intellectuals are driven by their exaggerated respect for white power, and the eagerness to ingratiate themselves with white supremacy. The rest of the way, the 'pidgin economy' and 'pidgin democracy' that Uganda is takes over!

The discrimination against Afrikan languages (and with it Afrikan indigenous knowledge, its bearers and people as a whole) knows no bounds. For example, by law (The Universities and Other Tertiary Institutions Act of 2001) and Constitution (clause (2) article 6), Uganda prohibits the use of any Ugandan or Afrikan language in higher education. English has the monopoly, because it is 'the official language' of government! The preference of the mother tongue of the Anglo-Saxons over Afrikan mother tongues is based on the silent myth that the latter cannot serve as the medium of intellectual and scholarly discourse of complex ideas and concepts. In fact the use of Afrikan languages in formal higher education is banned precisely because of their potential for this role.

By training and by law Uganda's elites (including university adult educators) have to work in an alien language. This ensures that in their scholarly work and intellectual discourse the elite cannot engage the masses of the people and their culture. The elite scholars are impoverished as they miss out on popular mass nourishment by way of informed debate, feedback and sounding board. The elite's scholarly work and discourse therefore cannot be the basis of the intellectualisation of the population, which would otherwise raise the threshold of public debate and challenge to scholars, to create a dynamic that would raise the quality of intellectual discourse at all levels and points of the national knowledge chain.

After systemically undermining Afrikan languages and culture the scene is set for the idle fallacy that Afrikan languages cannot be the medium of intellectual discourse or discourse in science and technology. But the ancient Egyptians, Ghana, Mali, Songhay, Monomotapa or Maya did not speak English. Nor do the Japanese or the Chinese today! The Europeans fully understand the importance of language in a people's development and place in history. For this reason every European country conducts its education, from kindergarten to university, in their mother tongue, upon which other languages are learned as tools of communication. Even the smallest European country, Iceland, with a population of 230,000 and one university, conducts its education in the Icelandic language; a language not spoken anywhere else in the world. Yet this did not stop Halldor Laxness from winning the 1955 Nobel Prize for Literature for his works in his mother tongue. In fact, today the Asian countries which are reputed to have made impressive progress in development, science and technology are also the countries which conduct their education, from kindergarten to university, in their mother tongue, and take their culture seriously; for example China, Japan, Korea, Thailand.

Language is a tool capable of rising to any challenge assigned to it by its owners and creators.

From a global and political perspective Uganda's education system is in reality a 'Bantu Education' (the education developed in apartheid white South Afrika, as inferior, low cost education, designed to turn Afrikans into admirers of white supremacy, and the willing and happy drawers of water and hewers of wood). In essence it is miseducation; that is the removal of good education out of the Ugandan public, school children, students, teachers and professors, and its replacement with junk education. The problem is compounded further by the fact that positions of leadership in the county are entrusted to the miseducated; in fact the more miseducated, the more strategic the position of leadership, the more the power and authority. Compare this with China, where nobody can be appointed to a position of power and authority unless they have gone through the Chinese education system.

Above all, development is about mobilising and unleashing the entire people's genius. Yet after pidgnisation, the Afrikan elite cannot engage mass society and its culture. Indeed it is the task of the elite, as eloquently exemplified by Gen. Museveni to shut off mass society and its culture and to condemn it to 'backwardness' – to ensure that development cannot be a mass phenomenon, and part of mass culture.

As Kwesi Kwaa Prah has pointed out:

> It is in the language of the masses that social transformation in its most far-reaching sense makes an impact. A society cannot develop if language is the monopoly of a small and restricted minority whose orientation is directed outside, towards cultures that have had an imperial or colonial relationship with the society that is endeavouring to develop. Education for the masses must be done in the languages of the masses so that development becomes a mass phenomenon, which is part of mass culture. (Prah 2002)

A people whose language is oppressed is an oppressed people. Indeed a people without a language soon lose their culture, religion and land! For Afrikans therefore to conduct their education in the European languages of the oppressor is to engage themselves not in modernisation but pidginisation, obscurity and eventually extinction. Equally, the Afrikan elite cannot spearhead 'nation-building' based on the English language; for oppression cannot be the basis of unity. Nation-building can only take root and blossom if centred on the languages of the masses. This is the only way nation-building becomes a mass phenomenon, and part of mass culture.

Intellectual viability: the mother of all power and empowerment

Up to this point a case has been made that intellectual sovereignty and viability is the source and foundation of power and empowerment. Central to intellectual sovereignty and viability is the generation of knowledge by a people with a shared memory, history, identity, language, homeland and future. Such knowledge generation must be in the mother tongue or, in modern challenge to the Afrikan peoples, in an Afrikan language or languages/dialects. Moreover such knowledge generation must engage society in its entirety, in a dynamic knowledge chain, that is the general public, school children, students and out of school children and youth, intellectuals and scholars. It is this sort of knowledge chain which has the capacity of generating knowledge which does not move ahead of the people, but rather, moves ahead with the people – thereby strengthening and empowering every point and segment of the knowledge chain.

As matters stand today, three sites of knowledge and truth can be identified in Uganda: the university; the NGOs; and Afrikan indigenous knowledge. As has been demonstrated, the university adult educator, intellectual and scholar have been disempowered by the system of 'Bantu education'. He/She cannot plug into the energies of the Ugandan mass population; and has no hope of engaging the mass society of communities for whom English is the mother tongue.

The NGOs, CBOs, etc, through engagement with sections of the population, activism and research, as well as through their engagement with donors and the state, constitute a clear knowledge and truth site. Yet most of the NGOs and CBOs have to comply with donor requirements to access funding packages designed to disempower and compromise them, together with the populations they work with. As a result, therefore, NGOs and CBOs become a disempowered truth site.

The third truth site consists of the organic mother tongue intellectuals and scholars, and custodians of Afrikan indigenous knowledge system. It is not particularly difficult to imagine that this is a truth site, which is, as well, disempowered. The disempowerment of this knowledge and truth site has been through church, mosque, school and state propaganda, persecution, criminalisation, banning and burning centres of education, training and research.

The disempowerment of the three truth sites emanates from one source: the notion that the way forward for Afrika is modernisation. And that modernisation is about Afrikans abandoning their 'backward' knowledge base, ways of knowing and culture and the adoption of the white man's knowledge, language and culture. The challenge to intellectuals and scholars in the three truth sites who seek empowerment is to come together in unity, learn from one another's weaknesses and strengths, identify opportunities and threats, and determine the way forward. The way forward will inevitably include the articulation of a new dynamic knowledge and truth chain, which enables the three sites to share, collaborate and engage with mass society, severally and together. It will entail learning and unlearning, and the mobilisation of the university and NGO truth sites to support and energise Afrikan indigenous knowledge into the viable and sustainable resource base for the sustainable advancement of Afrikan peoples. As the most exposed of the three sites after 50 years of experience, the university adult educator has the challenge and obligation to initiate a collaborative partnership between the three truth sites.

Conclusion

At the end of the day, Uganda, like Afrika, has to choose between education for liberation, in which case they choose mother tongue education; or else education for enslavement, in which case continue the colonial agenda with English, French, Portuguese, etc. But either choice calls for struggle and sacrifice; even the choice of education for enslavement. This is because not only Uganda, for example, will choose the slave route to 'progress'; many other countries and peoples will make the same choice. But the master only wants and takes the most competitive slave. At the end of the day the question of language policy for the entire broad spectrum of education, formal, informal and non-formal; elementary, intermediate and advanced, is a question of struggle. But what is better: to struggle to be the best slave on the market; or to struggle to be free?

13
International Partnership and Co-operation in Adult Education

Anthony Okech

Introduction

Adult education in Uganda has benefited from co-operation with various external agencies in bilateral and international arrangements. The word co-operation is used here to cover various forms of working together, sometimes also referred to as collaboration or as partnership. This chapter reviews direct co-operation involving international adult education agencies, programmes or activities in Uganda. This excludes indirect co-operation that comes, for example, through budgetary or technical support to government, which indirectly supports adult education.

Co-operation between any two parties raises issues regarding the relationship between the two sides. This is particularly so because there is almost always some sort of inequality between any two parties. Inequality may arise, for example, from physical endowments, economic status, intellectual capacity or overall development status. Inequality from any of these various sources may lead to unequal power balance in co-operation. This influences the nature and results of co-operation, affecting the extent to which it is beneficial to either party.

International co-operation in various aspects of education was one of the main reasons for the creation of the United Nations Educational Scientific and Cultural Organisation (UNESCO). The United Nations Charter had been signed in San Francisco on 26th June 1945. Five months later the United Nations Conference met in London and signed the Act creating UNESCO on 16th November 1945.

The main preoccupation of the founders is to promote and organise international co-operation through the communication of knowledge, the confrontation of different experiences and the discussions of ideas; these objectives could be achieved in collaboration with national organisations and international non-governmental federations. The new Organisation must undertake a crusade against illiteracy, considered by various delegates to be incompatible with dignity. (UNESCO Institute for Education 1997a: 6)

Among the most significant forums through which co-operation focusing on adult education has been promoted have been the UNESCO International Conferences on Adult Education in Elsinore (1949), Montreal (1960), Tokyo (1972), Paris (1985) and Hamburg (1997) popularly referred to as CONFINTEA V, the abbreviation for the French for Fifth International Conference on Adult Education. The UNESCO General Conference in Nairobi (1976) also made significant contributions in the area of adult education and is therefore often quoted together with the five International Conferences on Adult Education.

Each of the five conferences addressed the issue of international co-operation in the field of adult education. Three sets of recommendations are quoted here to serve as a framework for analysing the international co-operation in which Ugandan adult education has been involved. The first conference in Elsinore set down certain principles to guide the establishment of 'permanent international co-operation' as follows:
- Adult education should try to develop a spirit of tolerance.
- It should work towards reconciling east and west.
- It should bring the people closer together and not just governments.
- It should recognise the need to improve the living conditions of the masses and to create situations of peace and understanding. (UNESCO Institute for Education 1997a: 14)

The Tokyo conference had the following admonition among its 'conceptual bases of international co-operation':

Co-operation was not to be confused with a process of

> 'westernising' the whole of mankind; the developing countries, in trying to find a means of projecting their own historical identity, must offer alternative ways of life and new scales of values (UNESCO 1972: 26)

The Nairobi recommendation on the development of adult education had this advice:

> Care should be taken to ensure that international co-operation does not take the form of a mere transfer of structures, curricula, methods and techniques which have originated elsewhere, but consists rather in promoting and stimulating development within the countries concerned, through the establishment of appropriate institutions and well co-ordinated structures adapted to the particular circumstances of those countries. (UNESCO 1976, Recommendation 62)

In the context of the above quotations, this chapter seeks to answer the following questions:
- In which ways and to what extent has adult education in Uganda benefited from international co-operation?
- In which ways and to what extent has adult education in Uganda contributed to international co-operation?
- To what extent, in particular, has international co-operation stimulated and promoted the establishment of appropriate institutions and structures for adult education in Uganda?
- To what extent has adult education in Uganda been able, through international co-operation, to project Uganda's historical identity and offer alternative ways of life and new scales of values?
- How much has the co-operation contributed in bringing peoples closer together, promoting tolerance, peace and understanding and helping to improve the living conditions of the masses?

The chapter is not a detailed record of all the co-operation activities that have taken place, but a review of examples of co-operation that addressed the various aspects of adult education. These aspects have been identified as:

- Professional development of adult education providers and their institutions
- Provision of physical infrastructure and equipment
- Curriculum and materials development
- Implementation of adult education with final beneficiaries
- Research and publication
- Development of an enabling environment for adult education.

Professional development of adult education providers and their institutions

Co-operation in this category has covered training activities within the country, scholarships for training and participating in forums outside the country, funding for the organisational and managerial development of adult education institutions and organisations and provision of personnel for technical assistance to develop and support the institutions. Adult education in Uganda has mostly been at the recipient or beneficiary end, but has to some extent also contributed to the professional development of providers in other countries.

Professional training for educators

In international co-operation, the German Adult Education Association (DVV) has perhaps played the most significant role in the professional development of adult education providers in Uganda. The DVV had as its objective to:

> Work with Ugandan partners to promote an adult education system geared to helping people learn how to more effectively satisfy their basic needs, acquire job skills, and improve their income (IIZ/DVV 2001: 33).

It has had a steady programme of co-operation with selected adult education agencies in Uganda since January 1986, although there had been sporadic co-operation activities before that. The main objectives of the co-operation in the early stages were:
- Rehabilitation of adult education infrastructure
- Training

- Materials development and provision.

The Institute of Adult and Continuing Education (IACE), then known as the Centre for Continuing Education (CCE) was strategically targeted to develop capacity for training in adult education so that this could have a multiplier effect. For this reason IACE annually received about 30% of the funds provided by the DVV. This enabled IACE to undertake needs assessment studies, develop training programmes, try them out on a pilot basis and refine them for implementation as full-time long-duration programmes.

Some of the pilot programmes in the form of short courses also performed the function of producing the first adult educators locally trained in Uganda. This was the case with the series of ten-week courses for trainers in Adult Education and Development (1983-1989) and the annual cycles of the course in the Evaluation of Adult Education and Development Programmes (1990-1995). The short courses had in a few cases an immediate multiplier effect through the development of organisations like the National Adult Education Association and the Adult Education Centre in Nyenga, Mukono District. The founders of the Uganda Rural Development Training Programme (URDT) also sharpened their ideas and skills through participation in these courses.

Academic staff of IACE and other Ugandan partners of the DVV also built their capacity through participation in various international forums, made possible through DVV support. Some of the highlights of such participation were the world assemblies of the International Council for Adult Education: Buenos Aires (1985), Bangkok (1990), Cairo (1994) and Ocho Rios, Jamaica (200); the general assemblies and other activities of the African Association for Literacy and Adult Education (AALAE) and other adult education forums such as the UNESCO International Conference on Adult Education, the latest being CONFINTEA V in Hamburg. There have also been a few meetings, workshops, or conferences organised specifically by DVV to bring together representatives of their partners from different countries to focus on specific tasks. Ugandan educators have attended and contributed to these. One of the current tasks is the project to develop a series of adult education textbooks with an African perspective.

A number of other international partners have also provided opportunities for in-country training in adult education and participation in forums outside the country. UNESCO has in a number of cases sent experts and funding for training activities, for example in information supports for Adult Education (1983), in developing a national plan for adult literacy (1987) and in curriculum development for adult education (1994). UNESCO has also provided some fellowships for adult educators from Uganda to go on study visits to various countries in and outside Africa and to participate in forums organised by UNESCO or one of its institutes, in particular the UNESCO Institute for Education in Hamburg.

In-country training and participation in international forums have also been promoted by ActionAid, a UK based international NGO, through its Uganda office, ActionAid Uganda.

Considerable professional capacity has also been built at the Literacy and Adult Basic Education (LABE) through collaboration with World University Services (WUS), the British Department for International Development (DFID), the Netherlands Development Organisation (NOVIB) and the European Union (EU) and COMIC Relief. LABE has as a result today been able to support civil society organisations, the government department in charge of adult education and local governments in various aspects of literacy. A sign of LABE's developed capacity is that in 2002 it won the UNESCO NOMA Literacy award.

A number of Ugandan adult educators have also benefited from scholarships through international co-operation. Here, too, the DVV has been the leading partner. Initially the focus of the scholarships was at the certificate and diploma level, because that is the level that was likely to be dealing directly with the communities, the DVV's main concern. Later, there has been some shift in the practice and a number of adult educators have undertaken both first degree and advanced degree studies through DVV scholarships. Scholarships for study and training in adult education have also come from other sources, in particular the British Council and the ODA; through these over ten academic members of staff of IACE were able to pursue higher degrees or other postgraduate courses in Adult Education in the UK, especially during the period 1984-1989. The British Council has also supported a link between IACE and the University of Cardiff School of Social Sciences.

Professional capacity has further been developed through the provision of books to support the training programmes. Here again, the strategy of the DVV was mainly to equip IACE as a training institution. The short courses and the full time diploma and degree programmes in adult education have benefited greatly from the books DVV has provided. Book development co-operation is dealt with in another section, as are also the efforts to establish resource centres for adult education.

Funding and technical assistance
Another aspect of international co-operation has been in the area of funding and technical assistance for organisational and managerial development of institutions. While technical assistance in adult education has been more for specific tasks like training and curriculum and materials development, there have also been a few cases of technical assistance in organisational and managerial development.

Some of the technical assistance was provided through short-term consultancies, like, for example, that provided by Dr Ampene, who was sent by UNESCO, and Dr Oxenham and Professor Bown sent by the British Council and Overseas Development Agency. The latter two worked specifically with IACE. Others have been through longer-term arrangements, for example, the establishment of a DVV Liaison Office in Kampala from 1991 to 1996 and the provision of technical support to LABE by WUS. As LABE developed, volunteers who come to work with, while also learning from LABE, have replaced the arrangement.

Networks
International co-operation also helped to build capacity for adult education in Uganda by enabling Ugandan adult educators to establish contacts and network with colleagues in other countries. In this aspect co-operation through the African Association for Literacy and Adult Education (AALAE) was particularly significant. Many useful

exchanges of experiences and ideas took place in AALAE. The thematic networks established in AALAE contributed to enriching knowledge and strengthening skills in several areas of specialisation among adult educators in Africa. The contacts and networking spread worldwide through the International Council for Adult Education (ICAE).

Provision of physical infrastructure and equipment

Many of the external partners who supported adult education in Uganda were not eager to invest in infrastructure development. More were willing to co-operate in the provision of equipment. However, there were a few instances of support for the development of infrastructure for adult education.

The most significant has, perhaps, been the building donated by DANIDA, the Danish International Development Agency. This is a big building comprising two blocks, one housing administrative offices, classrooms and media studios, the other a two-hundred room residential wing. The residential wing was taken over as a university hall of residence for female undergraduate students but there are moves now to have it restored to its rightful function of adult education. When the administrative and classroom wing developed serious leakage through the flat roof and some war damage, DVV contributed to the repairs.

DVV also contributed to some building construction, which they categorised as 'investment'. This was particularly in connection with investment in income-generating activities to generate resources to sustain adult education work among the partner organisations. Support by DVV for construction of office and classroom space was minimal, as this was not in line with their policy.

DVV and most other international partners have been willing to support their Ugandan partners by paying rent for office and classroom accommodation, even over long periods, but have been very reluctant to invest any money in construction or purchase of buildings. It has been rather difficult for the Ugandan partners to understand this policy, since they feel construction or purchase of buildings is a more sustainable option. In the case of DVV, the explanation was that investment in infrastructure development was not in their mandate. It also seems that, generally, the international partners who were willing to invest in large-scale infrastructure development were those that worked with the Uganda Government. A few national and local non-governmental organisations have been able to make rental arrangements in such a way that they were eventually able to acquire the premises.

There have, however, been a few cases where non-governmental organisations have been supported by international partners in constructing significant administrative and learning space. Notable examples are the Uganda Rural Development Training (URDT) Programme in Kagadi, Kibale District and The AIDS Support Organisation (TASO) that operates all over Uganda. Tororo Community Initiated Development Association (TOCIDA) has put together various inputs from both local and international sources to develop a useful rural training centre about twelve kilometres west of Tororo Municipality. There are others that have benefited in a similar manner.

Curriculum and materials development

Co-operation with UNESCO has played a significant role in promoting the development of ideas and curricula for adult education in Uganda. The earliest example, the Namutamba Project, was mainly based on a teacher training college and formal primary schools. However, it is relevant to adult education because it treated the school as a nucleus for educational activities in the community. The project developed a curriculum that was relevant to rural development and provided for the involvement of adult community members as resources in the school, while ensuring that the adult community could also benefit from the school as a resource for learning and development. The project therefore came to be known as Basic Education Integrated into Rural Development (BEIRD). It infused agriculture and appropriate technology into the curricula of teacher colleges and primary schools. The main period of the project ran from 1971 to 1979, but it was revitalised in 1986 and was recommended by the Policy Review Commission (1989) to be further developed into the Basic Education for National Development (BEND), which is provided for in the White Paper on Education (1992).

In 1982 a senior lecturer at the then Centre for Continuing Education, Makerere University participated, under UNESCO sponsorship, in a UNESCO sub-regional workshop on 'Information Supports for Adult Education'. Upon his return, he started, with support from the Uganda National Commission for UNESCO, a series of training and planning activities for the development of information supports for adult education in Uganda. An international workshop on 'Illustrations for Development' held at Kyambogo, Kampala, in September 1982, was the first in a series of activities. A national workshop on 'Information Supports for Adult Education' followed at the same venue in 1983.

The 1982 workshop enabled participants to reflect on the visuals they used in communicating their messages and to plan for better development and use of these. Co-operation with UNESCO made it possible for communicators from different sectors in various countries in Africa to meet, share experiences and learn from one another and from experts in development communication. It also strengthened the co-operation in this field between Uganda practitioners and Afrolit, the African Society for Literacy, which had experience in research and practical work in the design and use of illustrations in communicating development messages.

The series of follow-up activities triggered by the 1983 national workshop on Information Supports for Adult Education began a process of reflection in the areas of health education, agricultural extension and other forms of adult education. Message designers and visual artists started reflecting on their work and the need for study and training in communication was recognised. Makerere University Centre for Continuing Education started designing short courses in various aspects of communication. These contributed to the development of the degree programme in mass communication that Makerere University started offering some years later.

The discussion of the role of co-operation with DVV in capacity development for adult education in Uganda has already indicated the contribution this partnership made in the development of curricula and materials. The development of the professional adult education study and training curriculum at the university benefited greatly from the experimentation possible in short courses, leading to the development of the full diploma and degree programmes.

Co-operation with DVV also contributed very significantly to the development of the curriculum and the materials in different languages for the national government functional adult literacy programme. This exercise also received support from UNICEF (Uganda office) in co-operation with the relevant government ministry and IACE. As the initiative moved from a pilot project in eight districts to become a national programme covering increasingly more districts, UNICEF specialised more and more on supporting the training of instructors while DVV concentrated more on materials development. Curriculum and materials development for the literacy programme later benefited from co-operation with other international partners with special focus on specific areas of the country. The World Food Programme (WFP) in 2000 supported needs assessment and curriculum and materials development for the pastoralist Karamoja region in north-eastern Uganda, while the Icelandic International Development Agency (ICEIDA) did the same for the mainly fishing islands of Kalangala District in Lake Victoria.

The other DVV Ugandan partners were able to use the co-operation to develop training curricula and materials in their different areas of focus. The following are some examples.

The National Adult Education Association designed a training programme for its branches in adult education for sustainable development, developed and published some primers and readers to support literacy among adults, developed a distance education training programme for literacy instructors and has established environmental training programmes, with a national demonstration farm near Kampala.

The Kiira Adult Education Association has used the co-operation with DVV to support the development of literacy among adults through literacy education, the publication of readers and newsletters, training of instructors and running literacy education activities for adults. In more recent years, the association has focused on working to improve its members' living standards by organising savings co-operatives and training in various entrepreneurial skills.

Tororo Community Initiated Development Association co-operated with DVV and other external partners, especially in developing and implementing programmes in organic farming and appropriate technology for more efficient and productive work. This included the acquisition and training in the use and care of donkeys as beasts of burden. TOCIDA also developed theatre as a medium of development communication and made a significant contribution to the promotion of literacy education for adults by developing primers, instructors' guides and follow-up readers in languages of Tororo District that did not yet have such materials.

The National Women's Association for Social and Educational Advancement (NWASEA) focused on programmes dealing with health care, family planning, child-raising and uplifting women's situation, especially through well-managed savings and credit activities. So apart from literacy programmes, NWASEA had programmes on management of income-generating projects, self-reliance, capacity building and leadership.

REFLECT is one of the most interesting contributions to programme development in adult education in Uganda in recent years has been the REFLECT innovation developed by ActionAid Uganda, and spread to many programmes in Uganda through co-operation with other national and local organisations. REFLECT stands for Regenerated Freirean Literacy through Community Empowering Techniques, and is a method of promoting not only literacy but also community education and community development in general. It is described elsewhere in this book (Chapter 10) and is being increasingly applied in Ugandan adult education programmes.

Implementation of adult education: final beneficiaries

International partners in adult education in Uganda have practised varying degrees of involvement in the final implementation of adult education programmes. Some have used personnel from their countries of origin, or external experts, practically all the time in various aspects of the development and implementation of the programmes, and in a few cases have worked directly with the rural communities. Others have involved themselves only in the preparation of the general operational framework, in some cases with some degree of joint planning or approval of the programmes, but not in the actual implementation. DVV normally worked in this way, except in the few cases when the liaison officer participated in the implementation of some activities. Other partners have been satisfied with coming to an initial agreement on the goals and design of the programme over a given period of time but have limited their role to monitoring through reports from their Ugandan partners.

Some external partners see their participation in the implementation of programmes as a short-term measure to build capacity among the local partners and then let them get on with it. Others, it would seem, see their participation as ensuring proper use of the resources they have provided.

Research and publication

One significant outcome of the co-operation with UNESCO was the publication, in 1984, of the *Directory of Adult Education in Uganda* by Anthony Okech, published at Makerere University, in collaboration with UNESCO. It was one of the earliest publications on adult education in Uganda and has served as a source for many later studies and writings on adult education in Uganda. Another piece of writing on adult education from about the same time in the context of co-operation with UNESCO was the work on the *History of Adult Education in Uganda* by Julius Odurkene and Margaret Okello.

In the co-operation between the DVV and Ugandan adult education, IACE was to play the leading role in research but the nature and quantity of the research activities were to a certain extent determined by the situation. It is important in this regard to note that the earlier work of IACE (formerly Department of Extra-Mural Studies and CCE) had not been addressing adult education as a discipline and profession. When attention was turned towards the discipline and profession of adult education during the seventies and eighties, the immediate demands were the development of appropriate programmes, trying them out and assessing how well they worked. That is why needs assessment surveys, programme reviews and evaluation were the dominant types of research activities.

Programme development and implementation also demanded so much time from the few professionals trained in adult education that they did not have much left to dedicate to other forms of research. This to a great extent explains the rather small amount of research and publications not directly related to programme development and implementation.

Some of the research was related to IACE's own programmes, especially studies done in preparation for full academic and professional programmes in adult education. The first such study was carried out in 1982 to determine the training needs for extension officers and development workers. Another survey was carried out in 1987 to determine adult training needs that could be met through distance education. In 1992 a smaller study was carried out focusing on needs related to labour and trade union issues. The most comprehensive study to determine the training needs of adult learners in Uganda was carried out in 1994/95 with financial support from the DVV and the Danish Volunteer Service (Rutangye 1995). All these studies played significant roles in informing the development of programmes at IACE and to a lesser extent in other faculties of the university and other institutions of tertiary education.

IACE members of staff have also undertaken a number of studies related to other adult education activities in Uganda. A serious limitation is that very few have been published and are not therefore easily accessible. The following studies, which the author of this chapter carried out over the years, illustrate the kind of studies that have dominated IACE staff members' research activities. He has carried out or led a considerable number of programme-oriented studies for both government and non-government agencies, national and international. The list includes:

- Study of People's Knowledge, Attitude and Practices related to the Health Education Programmes of the Ministry of Health (1990)
- Review of Adult Literacy Programme of ActionAid Uganda (1991)
- Survey for Adult Literacy in Uganda (1992)
- Study of Innovative Approaches to Adult Literacy/Education Currently Used in Uganda (1994)
- Evaluation of the Kenya Adult Education Project Implemented by the Kenya Adult Learners' Association (1997)
- Study to Formulate the National Non-Formal Environment Education and Community Training Strategy for the National Environment Management Authority (1997)
- Training Needs Assessment for the East African Cross-Border Biodiversity Project (1998/1999)
- Evaluation of the Functional Adult Literacy Programmes in Uganda (1999, published by the World Bank in 2001)
- Baseline Study for the Church of Uganda Community Education Programme in Karamoja (1999)
- Needs Assessment Survey for Functional Adult Literacy in Karamoja (2000)
- Needs Assessment Survey for Functional Adult Literacy in Kalangala (2002)

Research and publication must also be assessed in the context of what was happening in Uganda during the seventies and eighties. The socio-economic conditions were in various ways hostile to research and publication. There was insecurity that restricted movement. There was also lack of freedom, making research in certain fields a politically dangerous undertaking. Then there was the dire economic need, forcing lecturers and other potential researchers to undertake menial jobs to supplement their income in order to provide for themselves and their families. And, of course, there was no money for research.

Perhaps the most widely known published work on adult education in Uganda is the 1999 World Bank sponsored evaluation of adult literacy programmes in Uganda published in 2001 by the World Bank

Publications as *Adult Literacy Programs in Uganda* (Okech et al 2001). A member of the team that carried out that evaluation, Anne Katahoire, contributed to another World Bank publication, *Strengthening Livelihoods with Literacy* (Oxenham et al 2002). The DVV journal, Adult Education and Development, has also been a channel for publications by Anne Katahoire (Vol. 44, 1995) and Anthony Okech (Vol. 58 and 59, 2002).

Anne Katahoire is also one of the authors of a book on *The Psychology of Adult Learning* to be published in 2004 by the UNESCO Institute for Education (UIE) and Pearson South Africa. This is one of the series of books under the textbook programme 'African Perspectives in Adult Learning' (APAL) sponsored by UIE and DVV to produce adult education books relevant to the African context. Anthony Okech of IACE is a member of the series editorial board.

In recent years IACE has published a significant number of study materials for distance education, especially for the External Degree programmes. IACE developed its capacity for publishing distance education materials through co-operation with the Commonwealth of Learning, the University of Nairobi and the German Foundation for International Development. However, there is still an acute shortage of publications on adult education in Uganda.

Development of an enabling environment

A significant area of co-operation between UNESCO and adult education in Uganda was the development of plans and proposals for the revival of adult literacy programmes. This started in the mid-eighties as a follow-up to the commitment made by African ministers of education at a meeting in Harare in 1982 which recommended a Regional Programme for the Eradication of Illiteracy in Africa (by 2000). The UNESCO regional office in Africa (BREDA) in Dakar undertook to support African member states in developing plans for adult literacy programmes. Officials from BREDA and experts they provided were therefore able to come and hold workshops in Uganda and support Uganda to develop the plans. In 1991, UNESCO was able to send a consultant to refine the final proposal and this led to the launch of a pilot project in 1992 to revive the government provision of adult literacy, which had almost died out during the difficult years of the seventies and eighties.

An assessment of the results of international co-operation on adult education in Uganda

Guided by the recommendations on international co-operation in adult education cited in the introduction to this chapter, this assessment looks at the extent to which adult education in Uganda has benefited from international co-operation; how adult education in Uganda has contributed to international co-operation; the extent to which international co-operation stimulated and promoted the establishment of appropriate institutions and structures for adult education in Uganda; and how the co-operation contributed in bringing peoples closer together, promoting tolerance, peace and understanding and helping to improve the living conditions of the masses.

From the review in this chapter, it seems that international co-operation has benefited adult education in Uganda in various ways and to a great extent. International co-operation gave impetus to the professional development of adult education, which was an important prerequisite for its further development. It also enabled the government to re-launch its adult literacy programme, which has now expanded to cover most of the country. It is also through international co-operation that civil society organisations in adult education have been able to develop their capacity and are now playing an important role.

It may be more difficult to assess the extent to which Ugandan adult education has contributed to international co-operation, since this contribution is most likely spread to many different countries. One can, however, mention some examples of inputs that are likely to have made some contribution. Ugandans have been active participants in various international forums. They, for example, played some leadership roles in AALAE and its networks. Adult education activities in Uganda have also in a number of instances served as interesting case studies that have attracted study visits from other countries. The National and Kiira Adult Education associations, for example, have hosted several such study visits.

There have been several exemplary activities in Uganda that have attracted international attention and admiration and stimulated similar efforts elsewhere. Uganda was one of the three countries where the REFLECT approach in adult literacy was first experimented. Not only was the experiment successful, but Uganda has developed as the home of REFLECT in Africa, spreading its use to many other countries in Africa through training and other technical assistance. Uganda has also been the model in public education in the struggle to control HIV/AIDS and manage its consequences. This has served as an example to many other countries, especially in Africa. Another exemplary activity has been LABE whose work, in addition to receiving a Noma prize, has been since cited as an example of best practices in adult literacy.

Ugandan adult education professionals have also started contributing academically in adult education. The evaluation of adult literacy programmes in Uganda published by the World Bank has been used as reference by many other researchers and writers from different parts of the world. The other publications on adult education by Ugandans referred to in this chapter are also making contributions to the body of knowledge in this field.

The fact that Ugandan adult education is now able to contribute in these various ways is to a great extent evidence that international co-operation has stimulated and promoted the establishment of appropriate institutions and structures for adult education in Uganda, and has not just taken the form of a mere transfer of structures, curricula, methods and techniques which originated elsewhere.

There was, indeed, a fear of such a transfer taking place when the DVV first proposed to open a liaison office in Kampala in 1991, after six years of successful co-operation. Inspired by the debates then taking place in AALAE, some adult educators objected to the setting up of such an office. Since DVV was providing the funding for much of the adult education activity going on, it was feared that the presence of a DVV official in the country would leave the Ugandan partners no freedom to plan and execute their programmes in a manner appropriate to the Ugandan situation. DVV, they feared, would impose its agenda, interests and worldview on adult education in Uganda. In the face of this debate, DVV made it clear that it would open a liaison office only if it received an explicit consent from the Ugandan partners.

The argument continued. Other Ugandan adult educators supported the setting up of a DVV liaison office in Uganda. These argued that co-operation with DVV had from the start taken the form of a professional partnership. The AALAE secretariat then argued that this was not possible, comparing it to a cat asking a rat to be its partner. Those who supported the partnership maintained that they were not that vulnerable and could successfully stand their ground in the face of any possible imposition of a foreign agenda. In any case, they felt, the only way to reduce the hostility between the two agendas was to bring their authors closer together for better mutual understanding.

In the end, Ugandan adult educators accepted that the DVV could open a liaison office in Kampala. The office was there for six years but it is not easy to say what real difference it made. One thing that can be said for certain is that it promoted a closer understanding between at least one German family and people in Uganda, especially those in adult education. Some follow-up activities at individual level are evidence of this.

International co-operation in adult education has also in various other ways promoted better understanding among people by enabling Ugandans to work together with people from different countries of Africa and the rest of the world. Long-lasting friendships and collaboration have resulted from some of the co-operation activities.

Finally, an important recommendation among those cited in the introduction is that international co-operation should help improve the living conditions of the masses. This chapter has shown how the support obtained through co-operation activities has often been used for income-generating and other livelihood skills development. This is because adult education in Uganda has focused mainly on the problem that the people express as the most serious in their lives: poverty. The extent to which adult education has contributed to better livelihood is yet to be comprehensively evaluated. The evaluation of adult literacy programmes in Uganda (Okech et al. 2001) gave some indication of the participants' conviction that their participation in adult literacy programmes had indeed improved their lives. Many reports from adult education providers say something similar.

The lament is that adult education programmes still reach a very small percentage of those in need of them. Recent commitments (Jomtien 1990, Hamburg 1997, Dakar 2000) for increased international co-operation have not produced significant practical results. The challenge to adult education in Uganda is how to attract more international co-operation to enable it to reach many more of the millions who are in need and would benefit from adult education for better living conditions.

14
Challenges and Prospects of Adult Education in Uganda

David K. Atim and Anthony Okech

Introduction

A dynamic and complex phenomenon such as adult education, normally meets challenges on the way to achievement. Amidst the challenges, it is important to discern the prospects for progress. Challenges, in this context, are difficult or undesirable situations that call for action in order to achieve a goal, while prospects are the opportunities or possibilities of achieving success. In this chapter, the discussion of the challenges and prospects of adult education in Uganda takes account of past experience, the current status and the future. In Chapter 1, it was quite evident that the evolution of adult education in Uganda has not been smooth. Several challenges were encountered.

Four decades after Uganda's independence, adult education still suffers from a number of limitations. These include: low appreciation of the role of adult education in social and economic development; lack of clear and comprehensive government policy and directives; no co-ordination of existing adult education activities; inadequate funding for programmes; shortage of suitable educational equipment and materials and of trained and committed personnel for adult education work. Several factors also hinder effective mobilisation of the people for participation in adult education programmes. This situation has imposed serious limitations to the extent to which adult education can successfully be used as an instrument of social and economic development.

This discussion of challenges and prospects of adult education in Uganda is based on a comprehensive view of adult education as comprising a variety of components. In Uganda, these components have tended to operate in isolation from one another. Different chapters of this book have expressed the view that it would be beneficial for all adult education agencies to co-ordinate their efforts through a national network. This approach has been applied in countries such as Tanzania, Zambia and Kenya with considerable success (Atim, 1982).

Challenges

The challenges of adult education in Uganda are discussed under the following aspects:
- Understanding adult education
- Demand for adult education
- Policy, legislation and national commitment
- Planning, networking and co-ordination
- Resources and financing
- Language
- Research and professional development
- External relationships

Developing a common understanding of adult education
Chapter 1 and several other chapters have indicated that adult education is understood differently by different people in Uganda. The range of understanding stretches from those to whom adult education is synonymous with basic literacy training to those who consider any form of learning by adults as adult education. Equating adult education with basic literacy training for adults, some people in key decision-making roles relegate adult education to a marginal activity through which 'illiterate' people acquire the rudiments of reading and writing. It is not surprising that they do not see this as something worth serious investment.

The poor understanding of adult education and its role often arises from the restrictive view that seems to see education as something one goes through in childhood and youth in preparation for adult life. Education in adulthood is seen more as a second chance for those who did not go through education at the right time or as an unnecessary luxury. Undertaken at the wrong time, therefore, such education is not seen as having much potential to be effective or much time to be fruitful.

A big challenge which adult educators face in Uganda is to develop an understanding of adult education that demarcates the field clearly and makes it be seen as a set of activities that have a significant role to play. However, as discussed in Chapter 1, defining adult education has continued to be problematic. The clientele, scope and methodologies involved in adult learning delivery complicate the task of defining adult education. The guidance coming from key organisations like UNESCO sometimes seems to make the matter even more confusing.

The 1976 UNESCO General Conference limited adult education to 'the entire body of organised educational processes…', while UNESCO's Fifth International Conference on Adult education (CONFITEA V), in 1997 opened it up to 'the entire body of on-going learning processes…'. The CONFITEA V definition matches the growing emphasis on lifelong learning of which adult learning is a component. It is also more in line with the view of learning as a life-wide activity in which individuals and communities participate in a wide variety of contexts.

As adult educators in Uganda become increasingly aware of these trends, they face the challenge of establishing a focus in such a diverse field. As they strive to advocate for clear policy, political will and national commitment in adult education, they need to be able to demarcate clearly the field for which they are advocating, to explain its scope and demonstrate its role. They need to present a common front of those who are involved in and profess that field. One important requirement for such a front is for the different individuals involved to develop a common understanding of their mission.

There is growing emphasis in Uganda on adult education as an area of specialisation and professionalism. It is important to be able to show who is and who is not an adult education professional, to explain what the professionals profess. Adult educators/educationists in Uganda need to identify themselves, agree on the specialty of their professionalism and make this clear to the rest of society, especially those in decision-making positions.

Demand for adult education
Concern for adult education has meaning only if there is a demand for it and this is often taken for granted. Demand for adult education arises when prospective participants have a felt need or a desire to which adult education is perceived as an appropriate response. Perhaps the clearest indicator of demand in adult education is the level of participation in programmes offered. Various types of adult education provision in Uganda have had varying responses at the different levels.

Adult literacy, for some time now offered as functional adult literacy, has had quite a good response, but still leaves much room for concern. Adult literacy programmes in Uganda have targeted the non-literate population, with the aim of eradicating illiteracy. However, the evaluation of adult literacy programmes in Uganda carried out in 1999 (Okech et al. 2001) found that over 70% of the participants in adult literacy programmes had attended school, with a significant proportion having completed more than four years of primary education. This raised the question whether the programme was missing its target, which in turn led to the more basic question whether there was demand from the non-literate population in the first place or whether it was the nature of the programme that failed to attract or drove away participants. The fact that this situation was similar in programmes offered by the government and non-governmental agencies poses a challenge to all adult education providers.

The second challenge is posed by the drop out from adult literacy classes. Although the 1999 evaluation revealed a surprising basic level completion rate of about 80% in the adult literacy programmes, there has also been evidence of planned adult literacy classes failing to take off or surviving for only a short period due to non-enrolment, poor enrolment or massive drop out. These may be only a few cases, but they are also worth the concern of adult education providers because they have occurred in areas with significant numbers of non-literate people. What is more puzzling is that such classes are often planned after consultation with the communities. The answer has to some extent been provided by studies that show that people sometimes have a real interest in participating in literacy classes but are hindered by various factors. One factor is frequent or seasonal movements, especially by men, in search of livelihood. Another factor is domestic work for women and in some cases objection from their husbands. The challenge is to find appropriate responses to these situations.

Studies and reports from practitioners in the field have also shown that there is much demand for continuing education programmes from people who have completed the basic level of the literacy programme. Some of the demand is for specific knowledge, for example to learn English, while some is for programmes to enable them to obtain recognised qualifications that they can use to find employment. Many adults in fact aspire to obtain the qualifications obtained in the formal education system. The challenge for adult education in Uganda is to develop a programme suitable for adults but leading to awards that are comparable to those of the formal education system, perhaps enabling them to re-enter the formal system at an appropriate level, for example the tertiary education level.

In recent years there has been a significant increase in the demand by adults for education at higher (post-secondary) levels. Although the greater part of this demand is from younger adults (up to 30 years old), a significant number of adults in their forties and fifties have also been taking advantage of the increasing opportunities. The external degree programme at the Institute of Adult and Continuing Education, for example, accounts for more than one-quarter of Makerere University's student population, although it still consists of only three degree programmes and has been running for just over ten years. Most of these external degree students are adults already working or who have been out of school for some time. This is also true of students on the university's evening programmes.

Other programmes leading to diplomas and certificates at the post-secondary level are also drawing significant enrolment. These are usually in practical skills like accountancy, business management, computer technology or applications, project planning and management and public administration. Many private commercial institutions have come up to respond to this demand. There has as a result been a proliferation of diplomas and certificates, some of doubtful value. There is a challenge in this respect to establish a qualifications authority and develop a qualifications framework that will enable the Education Standards Agency to ensure quality in all the different education programmes offered in the country.

On the whole, therefore, it can be said that there is among adults in Uganda an abundant desire to learn at all levels. What is important is for adult education provision to ensure that programmes offered respond to the needs, aspirations and desires of the potential participants. Needs assessments, which have become a fairly common practice especially in adult literacy programmes, should be thoroughly carried out using methodology that enables the voice of adults to be correctly heard and so produces programmes that respond to the real felt needs and interests of the adults.

Policy, legislation and national commitment
Chapter 4 reviewed government policy and strategies for adult education in Uganda. In recent years, Uganda has come up with several policy documents, usually the result of consultations among the various stakeholders. Some of those policy documents were discussed in Chapter 4. However, as explained in that chapter, the policy position with regard to adult education is still inadequate in Uganda, mainly because policy statements relating to various aspects of adult education are scattered and therefore not effective in supporting the practice.

The clearest policy statement on adult education in an official government document was in the White Paper on Education adopted by the National Resistance Council (then the Parliament) in 1992. Other relevant statements are found in the various policies addressing specific concerns such as health, agriculture, water, poverty, formal education, children and women. Adult literacy has of late received increasing attention culminating in the development of the National Adult Literacy Strategic Investment Plan (NALSIP). The feeling among practitioners and analysts is that NALSIP would have been more meaningful if backed by a comprehensive policy on adult literacy and adult education in general. There is obviously a need to have the policy consolidated, backed by legislation and brought to life through national commitment.

The prospects seem to be good because various stakeholders have started working together towards the development of such a consolidated policy. For this to be systematically taken forward, the stakeholders need to look at different aspects:

The providers: Policy issues may include resources, management structures, staff training, curricular development, monitoring and evaluation capacities research and development required to inform effective field work, technology utilisation, and so on.

The participants: Issues in this aspect may include policies in other sectors that create a demand for learning and training, measures to enhance learner participation in the design, delivery and management of the programmes, measures to ensure productive use of the new knowledge and skills that participants acquire, e.g. provisions for post-literacy programming, bridges to formal education and so on.

Partnership and collaboration: Provision for improved intersectoral collaboration between adult education and formal schools, agricultural development, public health, local government institutions, donor agencies, the private sector and the different civil society institutions. Widespread consultations will have to be a part of the whole process of the policy development because, perhaps more than any other activity, the success of adult education hinges on policies adopted in sectors other than adult education itself. A major concern will have to be adequate provision for local capacity building, not only through knowledge and skills but also by making the required resources available for local level activity.

Legislation is essential in order to expand and delineate the framework within which adult education can operate. By means of legislation, adult or non-formal education needs to be provided with a role in national development, particularly with under-privileged groups in the rural areas and poor urban communities. The significance of government legislation in strengthening the adult education movement in a country is very apparent in the provision of adult education in Kenya, Tanzania and Zambia as well as in overseas countries such as Sweden and India (Atim, ibid). In these countries, legislation provides specific administrative regulations covering the practice of adult education. One impact of such legislation would be to ensure that appropriate facilities of educational institutions, e.g., schools, colleges, universities and libraries are made freely available to adult education.

In addition to policies and legislation there is a need for national commitment to ensure that these do not remain lifeless statements on paper. However, the existence of adequate policy and legislation provides the essential base upon which it is easier to build the national commitment.

Planning, networking and co-ordination
It has come out clearly in the various chapters of this book that the Government of Uganda follows a pluralistic approach in the provision of adult education, without a strong systematic strategy or structure to promote co-ordinated action or mutual support. Various aspects of adult education are carried out in different government ministries or agencies within the same ministry. In the districts, different directorates or departments carry out the various aspects.

Chapter 5 also showed that there are a number of NGOs and CBOs that focus on the different aspects of adult education. They, too, have largely operated without much systematic co-ordination or even networking for mutual support. In recent years there have been efforts to promote networking among civil society organisations through networks that they have set up. These have not yet had much success but the efforts continue and more will be said about them later in this section.

Adult education has usually been an insignificant component of government ministry and district planning. In some districts, it has sometimes been difficult to identify the adult education components in the plans. As a result, there has often been no clear budget-line for adult education activities. With the advent of the National Adult Literacy Strategic Investment Plan (NALSIP) the situation has changed somewhat for adult literacy education. Being funded under the Government's Poverty Action Fund (PAF), adult literacy activities have now to be systematically planned for at both national and district levels, in implementation of the five-year NALSIP. The plans are required both annually and quarterly. This demand should, hopefully, improve the quality of planning for adult literacy and influence the planning in other aspects of adult education as well.

Adult education planning by government is also constrained by the lack of systematic government policy, as already discussed. The development of such a policy would therefore contribute significantly to improving planning. A policy that takes a more integrative view of adult education would further promote more co-ordinated planning, with the accompanying advantage of more efficient use of resources, mutual support and programmes that are not wasteful of community participants' time.

Adult education planning is further constrained by inadequate capacity for planning in the districts and lack of reliable data, which affect planning in general. To contribute towards overcoming this weakness, LABE, one of the national NGOs engaged in adult education has for a few years tried to work with a few selected districts to prepare district adult literacy plans. Partly because of the lack of co-ordinated planning among adult education providers, but also other reasons, LABE does not seem to have had much success in this effort.

As stated above, in recent years there have been several efforts at co-ordination among the different adult education providers, promoted mainly by civil society organisations. The main aim of these networking efforts has been to enable civil society organisations to speak with one voice while lobbying the government and advocating for better provision of adult education. Other objectives have been to share information and ideas and to support one another in the effort.

Networking efforts have given birth to Uganda Joint Action for Adult Education (UJAFAE), Literacy Network for Uganda (LitNet) and Uganda Adult Education Network (UGAADEN). Of late, these organisations have developed a certain amount of collaboration with the relevant Government Ministry of Gender, Labour and Social Development and relevant government institutions. One fruit of this was that civil society organisations made a significant contribution in the development of NALSIP and continue to play a role in its further elaboration for implementation. However, a proper collaboration mechanism has not yet been elaborated and adopted.

The education policy adopted by Parliament in the 1992 Government White Paper on the Education Policy Review Commission Report provided for an overall co-ordination mechanism for adult and non-formal education through a National Council for Non-formal and Adult Education with district committees to work with the local communities. Although many aspects of the White Paper have been implemented, nothing has been done about this provision, more than ten years later.

Because of the multiplicity of agencies, the need for co-ordination machinery is clearly apparent. The means of co-ordination can be both formal and informal. Examples of formal co-ordination are offered by the Tanzania Directorate of Adult Education, which operates under the National Advisory Committee in the Ministry of National Education, and the Statutory Board of Adult Education in Kenya. Less formal co-ordination is effected by non-statutory organisations such as the Zambian Adult Education Advisory Board which co-ordinates much of the work of voluntary agencies (Atim, 1982). It is important that co-ordination operates at regional and local levels as well as at the national level. It is at the local level that programmes are implemented.

In recommending a co-ordinating body for adult education in Uganda, it is believed that it would:
1. Encourage more agencies to become involved in adult education.
2. Minimise the chances of duplication of activities by agencies.
3. Lead to programmes being more focused in specific needs.
4. Encourage research in adult education by various agencies.
5. Facilitate flows of information in adult education.

Adult education needs to be co-ordinated not only between the obvious providers, but also with other agencies concerned with different aspects of development. The system of ward adult education committees in Tanzania, local district committees in Kenya and regional representatives in Zambia are good examples.

Resources and funding

The chapter on the economics and financing of adult education revealed that, in general, adult education is poorly financed in Uganda. The discussion showed that the inadequate funding leads to the use of poorly trained educators or trainers, many of whom are unpaid volunteers with only limited commitment to the tasks. It also leads to lack of facilities, equipment, and educational materials. The result is not only insufficient provision to meet the needs and demands, but also poor quality in the provision, limiting the learning output.

The exact amount of funding that goes into adult education in Uganda is difficult to assess, as was pointed out in Chapter 8. The two main reasons given for this were the diverse nature of the provision undertaken without much co-ordination and the secrecy surrounding information on finances. Moreover, there has been no comprehensive study of the financing of adult education in Uganda. The only systematic analysis that has been undertaken was limited to financing of adult literacy in the 1999 evaluation of adult literacy programmes in Uganda (Okech et al 2001).

The sources of funding discussed in Chapter 8, namely, government, individuals, donors, NGOs and the private sector, all have their limitations. The government and NGOs are mainly engaged in functional adult literacy and adult basic education, including health, civic and agricultural extension education. Donor funding supports both government and NGO activities. At the adult literacy and basic education level individual financing is low. There has been some change in this situation with private enterprises starting to offer adult literacy, basic and continuing education for a fee, especially in the urban areas. The response has been good although such provision is still very little.

Financing by individual adults for their own education has increased significantly in recent years at the further higher education levels. Many adults have enrolled for both general and specialised programmes at post-primary, post-secondary and university levels. The opening up of university education in Uganda to non-government sponsored students during the last decade has resulted in thousands of adults re-entering the education field, through both the face-to-face and the distance learning modes.

In spite of the financial boost that functional adult literacy has received from government since 2001 as a result of its being included as a key strategy under the Poverty Eradication Action Plan, the funding still remains inadequate. There is still a big gap in the funding to be filled if the programmes are to provide all the necessary resources for adequate access and quality. The availability of adequate resources is linked to the putting in place of appropriate policies and legislation and the development of a strong national commitment. These will institute and support fundraising strategies from both within and outside government revenue to include levies from the private sector and more donor support.

Adult non-formal education and the formal education system
Many aspects of adult education are dependent on the formal system of education, relying on it for personnel, physical facilities and teaching and learning materials. The relationship between formal education institutions and non-formal adult education can be systematically enhanced for more efficient use of personnel and non-human resources. For example, in Tanzania, integrated teacher-training programmes meet the needs of both the formal schoolteachers and adult educators. In Zambia, there is an integrated curriculum development service; while in Kenya students form community formal institutions actively participate together with the out-of-school members of the community in such activities as extra-mural air-drama programmes.

In Uganda, the Namutamba Integrated Rural Development Project was largely based on the interactions between schools and non-formal education in the community. (See Chapter 13) The project was later expanded and left open to spread to all parts of the country as Basic Education for Integrated Rural Development. The 1989 Education Policy Review Commission Report and the ensuing 1992 White Paper on Education sought to turn this integrated educational approach into national policy and practice emphasising it with the subtitle: Education for Integrated National Development. However, in the implementation the integrated approach is not visible. The provisions on paper need to be put into practice through various measures.

The link between formal education institutions and non-formal adult education is also there, through institutions that engage in some form of outreach or extension programmes. The most prominent in Uganda has been the Makerere University Institute of Adult and Continuing Education (see Chapter 6). For a period of time it was the only such institution in Uganda. Today more institutions have joined in and thousands of adults are able to pursue further studies at all ages through a variety of delivery modes. There is, however, still room for a relationship of mutual assistance to be further developed between the formal and non-formal systems of education networks in order to strengthen the positive impact of each sector to the development of the society.

Language

Chapter 12 discusses the issue of language in education in Uganda. Reliance on English as the language of formal education and official communication no doubt inhibits education. Language has been a big challenge in Uganda in a number of aspects. Several efforts to adopt a common national language have all been fruitless because of the failure to reach a consensus. The policy of using the different Ugandan languages in education has not effectively been translated into practice by developing the required syllabuses and materials and training the personnel. As discussed in Chapter 12, the policy itself has been defective, seriously marginalising the Ugandan languages in relation to English.

In adult literacy programmes a greater effort has been made to use Ugandan languages. However, even there only the very basic instructional materials have been available. Outside the learning environment there is often nothing written in the local language and the only written materials are in English. As a result, participants in adult literacy programmes usually demand to acquire literacy in English since they have no opportunity to put to use the literacy acquired in the local language.

In spite of the stated policy to develop the use of Ugandan

languages in education, the actual trend seems to be that the importance of local languages in education is receding rather than increasing. A large percentage, possibly the majority, of formal education graduates is more literate in English than in their mother tongue. In this situation, many languages are becoming marginalised and those who speak only those languages are as a result also being increasingly marginalised in education and in life.

Research and professional development
The study of adult education as a discipline and the professional training for adult education are fairly new in Uganda. The number of adult educational professionals in Uganda is, therefore, still very small. As explained in Chapter 6, even though the relevant university department has existed for fifty years, its focus was for most of that time on doing university extension work and meeting the further education needs of adults outside the formal school system, not in professional training and the study of adult education. There was in addition no other institution providing for any adult education professional study or training.

Since the professional study of adult education is new, there has also been very little quality research on adult education in Uganda. The Institute of Adult and Continuing Education has several hundred reports of research carried out by students of the Diploma in Adult Education (since 1987) and the Bachelor of Adult and Community Education (since 1997). These are, however, more learning exercises in research with very little new information or insights. Members of staff have carried out only a few research projects, most of them on a rather small scale, due to shortage of time and finances. A team from the Department of Adult Education and Communication Studies, led by Anthony Okech carried out an evaluation of adult literacy programmes in Uganda, which was commissioned, published and widely publicised by the World Bank (Okech et al 2001). Anne Katahoire of the same Department contributed to a World Bank study on literacy and livelihoods (Oxenham et al 2002). To boost its research capacity IACE may borrow a leaf from the Institute of Adult Education in Tanzania where there is a well established Research and Planning

Department headed by a senior research fellow and staffed by several research fellows specialised in various disciplines.

The growth of the professional training and academic study of adult education at Makerere University and more recently at a few other institutions at a lower level will hopefully improve both the availability of professionally trained personnel for adult education and of researched information to strengthen adult education in Uganda. The IACE at Makerere University is still constrained by a number of factors in its effort to contribute to both aspects, as discussed in Chapters 5 and 6. These factors, marginalisation within the university, inadequate staffing, inadequate financial allocations and poor facilities, need to be addressed to enable IACE to play its role effectively. The adoption of policies and legislation that strengthen the position of adult and non-formal education at national level could also strengthen the position of institutions such as IACE.

There have also been suggestions that the IACE would fare better with some autonomy from Makerere University and that this would enable it to render its full service to the national adult education network. This suggestion seems to be supported by a number of observations. Adult education organisations generally tend to assume the structure and orientation of a service agency. The character of such organisations is defined by an unrestricted responsiveness to clientele. Indeed, very often responses replace purpose, in the sense that clientele pressures and demands take precedence over goals set from within. An adult educational organisation, it seems, must adapt its aims, roles and functions to the wishes and needs of its various interest groups. A university like Makerere is an organisation that has a tendency to maintain its traditions and hence is often seen to be operating on an old set of goals and regulations. The operational tendency of adult educational institutions such as the IACE would seem to render its location within a university inappropriate.

In Tanzania, because of this lack of general agreement between the roles and functions of the adult education unit, on the one hand, and those of the university, on the other, the government decided to separate the Institute of Adult Education from the University of Dar-es-Salaam and make it an independent, parastatal organisation funded directly by the government. This way, the Institute has been able to expand its role as part of a wider government sponsored campaign to raise the educational levels of Tanzanian society through adult and non-formal education.

In Uganda, there has been a strong resistance to this arrangement on the ground that IACE, as a part of the university, plays a role that is different from that played by an autonomous institution. A better solution could be to strengthen another institution outside the university and maintain IACE within the university. Such an institution would take on the role played by the Institute of Adult Education in Tanzania. After all, in Tanzania, the academic study and professional training in adult education has continued to develop within the University of Dar es Salaam after the Institute obtained autonomy.

External relations and partnerships
Chapter 13 reviewed the relationships and partnerships that adult education in Uganda has enjoyed with various external organisations and agencies, both bilateral and multilateral. Some of these relationships, for example with AFROLIT, AALAE, and ICAE, have been of a professional nature through which Ugandan adult education has enjoyed professional support, while also making some professional contribution. Others have been relationships in which Ugandan adult education has benefited from financial and other material support, for example with DANIDA and UNICEF. Others again have been relationships with both financial and professional support. The most outstanding in this category has been the relationship with the German Adult Education Association (DVV), as discussed in Chapter 13. UNESCO, British Council, and the British ODA/DFID could also fall into this category.

The term 'partnership' has often been broadly used to refer to all these different types of relationships, especially in more recent times with the growing trend of referring to all donors as development partners. The attention of adult educators in Africa was drawn to this term through the exciting exchange of views between AALAE and DVV which in some way marked the beginning of the demise of AALAE. While the ideal would be a true partnership relation instead of the unequal donor-recipient relation, the truth is that often it is a fairly one-way affair, with the donor giving the funds and setting the terms, while adult education in Uganda merely receives both.

It is important that adequate capacity is developed to enable Ugandan adult education to play its role in relevant international activities. Uganda has much to contribute and much to benefit through greater international exchange in the field of adult education. Avenues for sharing ideas and experiences through publications, participation in conferences and other forums should be proactively and vigorously explored. Not enough is being currently done in that direction.

Prospects

Any consideration of the prospects of adult education in Uganda must take account of the present situation in the country and the opportunities that exist to the practice of adult education. The discussion here will be focused on:
- Intellectual leadership
- Poverty eradication and redressing imbalances
- Decentralisation and rural development
- Civil society and community participation

Intellectual leadership
The discussion of challenges earlier in this chapter shows that adult education in Uganda could benefit greatly from greater intellectual leadership. Some of the benefits of intellectual leadership would be: a shared understanding of adult education; researched information and insights for better planning, programming and facilitation; a greater contribution in the national arena; and increased participation in international exchanges.

The prospects here depend on the continued growth of the professional development and research in the specialised institutions. The Institute of Adult and Continuing Education can play a leading leadership and facilitation role in the country's adult education campaign. It already has the experience of 50 years of extra-mural adult education, over 36 years of distance education for adults and 20 years of professional training and research in adult education. At this time of reflection, IACE should be able to learn from the mistakes of the past and carry through its achievements to its future, more expanded roles.

The changing mode of operation at Makerere University, which is devolving more decision-making and management functions to the different units of the university, should increasingly enable IACE to perform its roles with the flexibility often required in adult education. The university is currently making efforts to make itself more relevant to the needs of society, as a contribution to strengthening decentralisation in Uganda. This is an opportunity of which IACE can make much use. The steady improvement of communication in the country also offers greater opportunities for the institute to reach more people throughout the country than it could before.

In addition to the IACE, there are other government institutions that are developing in the area of adult education. Examples of these are Nsamizi Training Institute for Social Development and Uganda National Institute for Special Education (UNISE). There are also NGOs that are contributing significantly to the generation of ideas and insights for improved practice in adult education. Examples of these are Literacy and Adult Basic Education (LABE) and ActionAid's REFLECT Co-ordination Unit.

Apart from strengthening themselves internally, these various institutions would make themselves more effective through greater networking and collaboration. A regular forum for sharing of ideas and experiences, such as an annual adult education conference, is highly desirable in this connection. In addition, adult education practitioners in Uganda would do well to think of reviving the *Uganda Adult Education Journal,* which published only a couple of issues and then stopped, a few years ago. Increased joint effort in lobbying and advocacy for adult education with the government is another area of contribution that offers significant prospects.

Poverty reduction and redressing imbalances
Poverty eradication is undoubtedly the biggest challenge facing Uganda today. Over 66 per cent of the population live in absolute poverty while 86.2 per cent suffer from relative poverty (PEAP, June 1997).

Over 80 per cent of the country's total population live and earn their livelihood in rural areas, which are largely deprived of development services and infrastructure.

One of the ways to reduce poverty and eventually achieve sustainable development in Uganda is through an improved education system that lays greater emphasis on education for life than the current one. The burning questions of equitable access to education by the less privileged, their profitable employment and participation in development, demands that a non-formal education (NFE) system be put in place to address the issues of: adult functional literacy, vocational training, second chance education for early school leavers, alternative formal schooling and accreditation for non-formal education.

Some government plans have recognised the role literacy can play in poverty reduction. While basic literacy enables a person to 'read and write a short statement on his/her everyday life' with understanding, functional literacy moves a step further so that the individual can, in addition to reading, writing and calculation, analyse and take considered decisions relating to his/her community development (National Plan for Functional literacy, 1996). The National Adult Literacy Strategic Investment Plan 2002-2007 is based on the recognition that the promotion of adult literacy has the potential to contribute to the four pillars of the government's Poverty Eradication Action Plan. On this basis adult literacy was included among the programmes to have access to the Poverty Action Fund.

The 1999 evaluation of adult literacy programmes in Uganda (Okech et al 2001) showed that adult literacy programmes did effectively target the poor and the marginalised. They do this in the first place by focusing on the rural population, who are generally poorer than the urban population. Moreover, the majority of the learners in both government and NGO programmes were women, who not only constitute the majority of the illiterate community but are also marginalised in many other ways. The evaluation specifically looked at the link between literacy programmes and income generation and many of the participants were enthusiastic in reporting that the programme had enabled them to improve economically as well as in other ways. Adult literacy programmes thus seem to offer good prospects for poverty reduction but, as the evaluation concluded, there is still much to be done to make the results significant.

Adult literacy programmes in Uganda include the youth above primary school age (about 15 years upwards) and so offer some form of alternative mode of education for youth. The Ministry of Education and Sports is trying out the COPE initiative with support from UNICEF, targeting the youth of primary school age who are for various reasons unable to go to school. Adult education programmes are also making a special effort to address the needs of people with various disabilities. Adult and non-formal education beyond adult literacy programmes therefore seems well poised to make a significant contribution to addressing the situation of the poor and marginalised.

Decentralisation and rural development
During the last one-and-a-half decades, there has been a dramatic transformation within the wider context of Uganda, stimulated by government policies of privatisation, deregulation, democratisation and decentralisation. These policies have ushered in a new era of great concern for rural development. The process of decentralisation, which began in 1993 as a new approach to local governance, led to the expansion of the private and non-governmental organisations sectors in the districts and encouraged local communities to become active participants in their own development. These developments have increased demand at district level for appropriately trained and educated personnel within the public, private and non-governmental sectors as well as among community groups, in the areas of development management, business entrepreneurship, governance and service delivery.

The Government of Uganda has called upon the universities to play a more proactive role in the wider transformation of the country while helping to fill the human resource needs created by liberalisation. Makerere University particularly has been called upon to design programmes which will enhance the human capital currently managing the decentralised government units, promote community-based learning, and expand research and capacity development focused on decentralisation. University adult education has a strong role to play in this.

The university has responded to the government call by initiating a Capacity Building Programme for Decentralisation with support from the Rockefeller Foundation. The programme undertook a comprehensive human resource needs assessment for the decentralised district service delivery and recommended that 'short-term tailor-made courses of raising skills levels of staff in-post at district level' be conducted. Education development in the form of outreach programmes has also been recommended.

The Institute of Adult and Continuing Education, through its outreach centres, is well placed to implement these recommendations. It has carried out a feasibility study for training district officials and rural development practitioners in the various areas of rural development management and launched a number of programmes to respond to the needs.

Civil society and community participation
As the local community increasingly becomes the focal point for basic and non-formal education, and as decentralisation allows a larger measure of community-based decision- making in development, mobilisation, participation and participatory management will stand out as key issues. Because basic and non-formal learning needs are complex and diverse, meeting them requires multi-sectoral strategies and action, which are integral to overall development efforts. Many partners must join with the education authorities, teachers, and other educational personnel in developing basic and non-formal education if these are to be seen as the responsibility of the entire community. This implies the active involvement of a wide range of stakeholders – families, teachers, communities, private enterprises, government and non-governmental organisations and institutions – in planning, managing, and evaluating the many forms of basic and non-formal education.

One avenue for community participation is through the civil society organisations. The rapid increase in the number of NGOs and CBOs therefore offers many prospects for community participation. The prospects will be even brighter if the growing collaboration between the government and civil society organisations in adult and non-formal education can be enhanced and systemised as has, for example, been done in the health sector.

The future

This book undertook a critical review of adult education in Uganda, combining a historical assessment with an analysis of the current situation. It has shown that although adult education has been practised in Uganda for a long time, there has never been a coherent public policy to guide it. The practice has, as a result, not been supported by legislation and has benefited from rather little national commitment. Lack of a coherent policy has led to inadequate government planning so that government financing for adult and non-formal education has fallen far short of the need and even the possible. Many government programmes have had activities that included adult and non-formal education so that government funding has gone into adult education in a variety of ways; but in practically all cases adult educational activities made up only a small fraction of the total programmes.

The review has revealed that, in spite of these weaknesses, adult education has not only survived even during the most difficult times but has in some cases also positively thrived. There is thus already a rich history of adult education on which the future can build. There are a number of appropriate structures in place; the human resource of adult education professionals is gradually being strengthened; and a rich experience is being gained as a result of a number of interesting innovative initiatives. The beneficial results of adult and non-formal education in Uganda are increasingly acknowledged within and outside the country and as a result there is growing public recognition of its importance.

Current trends in the field seem, therefore, to indicate that, if the same impetus continues, adult and non-formal education in Uganda will in the near future benefit from: comprehensive policy and legislation leading to greater national commitment; enhanced professional practice resulting in better planning, designing and implementation; and increased participation by civil society organisations and the local communities. Its beneficial results will contribute significantly to poverty eradication, development and prosperity in all aspects of life. The pre-condition is, however, that government, various agencies and the civil society all work together to address the gaps and weaknesses that have been brought out in this review.

15
Epilogue: Why Andragogy?

Charles Kabuga

It can be illustrated that education in any society which employs the techniques of pedagogy – whether African, European or any other – is oppressive, silencing and domesticating, among many other ills. For example, there is no doubt in my own mind that because traditional African education was one-way traffic, glorifying the teacher whose wisdom could not be questioned, it oppressed, silenced and domesticated the learner. Such an education might have produced men with great memories, but not so many men with developed thinking faculties. It appears to me that people who remember most may not necessarily be the ones who think more. While remembering is a backward-looking activity, thinking is a future-looking one, and it is my conviction that any dynamic society needs more of such future-looking citizens. It is because pedagogy does nothing other than develop the memory of the learner that it is outmoded, as a tool for the education of both children and adults.

There is no doubt in my mind, too, that western education is oppressive, domesticating and silencing simply because it employs the techniques of pedagogy. It is no wonder, therefore, that white educators themselves have expressed their distrust of this education. Ivan Illich's *Deschooling Society* (New York 1971) is a typical example of a violent attack on western education which we are anxious to modify rather than throw overboard. In his book the author advocates that there should be no schools in society; that whoever has a skill to sell should advertise it and those who wish to learn it should apply.

Whether pedagogically-conceived education is locally consumed or is exported to other countries as it was to Africa, it still retains its oppressive characteristics. However, it is worse when it is exported than when it stays in its natural habitat.

Oppression at the level of content and techniques
It is worse abroad because it oppresses at two levels:
- The level of content and, like all pedagogically-conceived education, at
- The level of techniques.

Consider the white man's content of education in Africa, for example. The white man stressed the empire where the sun never set but never the great Sudanic kingdoms. The white man taught the greatness of the Duke of Wellington but the barbarism of Shaka the Zulu. Such irrelevant, ethnocentric information devalued and demoralised the knowledge of the old men with their accumulated relevant experiences. The white man's irrelevant and alien information violated a basic educational principle – that of learning from the known to the unknown. We started with the unknown and we have remained in the unknown. The violation of this principle therefore meant that we were turned into human tape recorders of meaningless and static pieces of knowledge.

Meaningless as it was, the converted young African teachers reaped large economic and social benefits from teaching the content of the white man's education. To learn, or rather to cram, the white man's content of education became such a profitable industry that all the Africans hankered after it. In turn, this devalued the content of traditional African education. Even today, many of us seem to be happy that our children speak English better than they speak the mother tongue.

In Africa, therefore, we should be unhappy about this education not only at the level of content but also at the level of techniques. Unfortunately, because the content of our education is alien, we seem to have concentrated more on content modification than on the modification of techniques. For example, we have been very anxious to include in our curriculum subjects like agriculture, as though it is possible to turn out farmers from school gardens. If we wish to rid our education of its crippling characteristics, we must show equal concern for both the content and the techniques. As far as I am concerned, Africanising the syllabus does not liberate the learner as long as the techniques used carry with them oppressive, domesticating and silencing characteristics. Thus, any content transmitted pedagogically is incapable of being useful or of functioning or of liberating. It is incapable because such content of education merely gets stored in the heads of learners and awaits recollection at an appropriate moment. Such content may be likened to undigested food. Just as food builds our bodies when we have digested it and made it part of us, the educational content we acquire becomes useful when it helps us solve the problems we meet through our processes of growth and development. Pedagogy, with its techniques of narrating, receiving, memorising and repeating, prevents the digestion of the content, particularly the alien content, so that it is not used. We need new techniques.

Before thinking about such new techniques, we have to be absolutely clear about what we want out of education. It will be only then that we shall look for techniques that will give us what we want. We can, however, straightaway say that unlike the case of pedagogy, the new techniques have to be premised both on the dynamic nature of society and on that of the students and teachers, all of whom are in a constant process of maturation. These techniques must lead the learner to the realisation of the most important thing education can give.

In my view, the most important thing education can give to anyone is: *'How to learn'*. This concept is beautifully illustrated by the words of the great Chinese poet by the name of Kuan Tzu who once said: 'If you give a man a fish, he will have a single meal. If you teach him how to fish, he will eat all his life'.

Life is such an endless research problem that no student can ever come out of any educational institution with ready-made solutions to it. The best that a student can hope to come out with are the techniques of learning and thinking about any problem life might present. With such techniques the student will have been prepared to manage life on his own, and to discover new knowledge for himself. Then, it will be easy for him with such techniques to see the relationship of things and facts that were otherwise isolated and meaningless. These techniques will be his master key both to the doors of life and to the rooms of ignorance wherever the light of knowledge must shine.

Why andragogy?

Andragogy is defined as the art and science of helping adults learn (Knowles 1980. Unlike pedagogy, which is premised on a static culture, andragogy is premised on a dynamic culture. This is so because of the dynamic learner characteristics on which andragogy is built. Of the adult learner characteristics I wish to address myself to only three, the instructional implications of which appear more difficult to apply to the education of children: self-concept, experience and time perspective.

Self-concept

Simply put, self-concept is the image each of us has of himself or herself. As each person grows, this self-concept moves from being a dependent personality to a self-directing one. Increasingly, we become autonomous individuals capable of taking decisions and facing their consequences. We resent being treated as if we were children. Because of such self-concepts, Knowles observes that no adult learner will ever learn under conditions incongruent with his self-concept.

It might be argued that andragogy techniques cannot be employed in the education of children who, after all, are dependent personalities – at least physically and emotionally. These techniques may further be considered unsuitable on the grounds that children cannot be involved in the diagnosis of their needs and the planning of their educational experiences because they are too young to know their needs and their experiences are limited.

In my view, the school strikes, riots, rebellions and all the abundant discipline problems in classrooms, together with the cry for involvement in the university decision-making processes by students, largely stem from lack of recognition of the self-concept of students. It is my submission that because it recognises this learner characteristic, andragogy becomes a relevant and meaningful tool in education at all levels.

Unfortunately, we have shied away from it with regard to youth education and as a consequence done irreparable harm to the creativity of our children, since creativity comes with the development of the self-concept. In spite of their rebellions and strikes, children have failed to liberate themselves from the horrors of pedagogy simply because we have tamed them with either the stick or the carrot of a desired career. Because self-concept is so closely linked with intrinsic motivation, techniques which do not exploit it, at any level, are ineffective educational tools. As I see it, it is the techniques of andragogy that are capable of adequately exploiting the learner's self-concept. This being so, these techniques should be employed at all levels of education because children see themselves as self-directing fairly early in life.

Experience

Experience is the second characteristic of the adult learner that I propose to discuss. It is argued that because the adult has lived longer than the child he has a variety of experiences which make him a rich resource in the class. In order to exploit this educational resource, andragogy would require techniques like work conferences, group discussions, seminars, field projects and consultative supervision to be used. In this way, the learners and the teachers would share experience to the advantage of them all.

Such techniques may appear inapplicable to the education of children because it is difficult to imagine seminars and conferences for children. However, let it be said that children, like adults, have experiences and that each child is definitely a rich resource. Where pedagogy went wrong was to require children to learn adult experiences which children never appreciated because they did not understand them. What needs to be pointed out is that just as adults benefit from one anothers' experiences, so children may benefit from the experiences of their fellow children. As a matter of fact, children learn more (at least horizontally) from their peers than they learn from adults. By using the techniques of andragogy, peer learning would be greatly enhanced and made more meaningful and rewarding. And these techniques can be used in the education of children because andragogy does not overemphasise the student contributions. Rather it invites a dialogue between the teacher and the learner and between learner and learner, with the teacher serving as a guide, a resource person and a manipulator of the environment in order for the learner to be afforded experiences appropriate to his needs and potentialities.

Epilogue: Why Andragogy?

In youth education, just as in the education of adults, the teacher has to discover the language of the learner in order to pitch what he wants to teach at the level of the experiences of the learner. Without first discovering the language of their experiences, the teacher would merely be turning the learner – child or adult – into a receptacle of the meaningless words of the teacher. Learners would inevitably be tongue-tied, for the words in the experience of the teacher would be alien to them. By way of an illustration it was only after Paolo Freire had discovered that he should go to the people in order to discover the words in their universe, which he used to write ABC primers for them, that he was able to teach them how to read and write in 45 days. The primers written in words from Friere's universe were meaningless to the learners. If our teaching it to be liberating, discovering the universe of adults, therefore, is just as important, necessary and possible as discovering the universe of children.

Time perspective

This is the third learner characteristic to be discussed. Because most adults learn in order to be equipped to overcome problems which their life-situations present, they wish to put to immediate use what they learn. They are mostly motivated to learn because they are seeking solutions to the problems they encounter in their roles as parents, workers, citizens and so on.

In this regard, andragogy recommends that teachers of adults be people-centred rather than being subject matter-centred. As such, the subject matter concept of curricula should give way to one which is problem-centred. Andragogy further recommends that the starting point for every learning situation should be the problems which the learners have on their minds.

It might be argued that since the problems of children are taken care of by their parents, children are not so much motivated to learn in order to overcome problems of their life situation. As such, children are considered to have a perspective of postponed application of what they learn. Consequently, it may be argued that in their case we can afford a curriculum of seven or eight subjects rather than a curriculum of problem areas.

Further, it might be argued that since their problems are taken care of by the adult world, children have no problems with which teachers can start as in the education of adults.

Let it be emphasised that if this learner characteristic holds true for adults, it also holds true for children. One may ask: Are we sure that the children do not wish to apply immediately what they learn? Are we adults not the ones who have decided that children should be stores of information in the hope that it will be useful to them at some future date? And what is wrong with children applying what they have learnt immediately? What is wrong with using problem-centred ways in teaching children? If the aim of education is to develop the children's ability to think, must we not systematically and consciously teach through formulating trial problems for children to solve? Are we not aware that such problem-solving activities for young children lead to new learning?

Conclusions

In my estimation, the few inventors Africa has had are not necessarily a creation of the white man's education. They have hardly existed because education has not used the techniques of andragogy. The pedagogical methods of postponed application killed our instincts to be creative. That is why we must go barefoot when we export our hides and skins. That is why we must either wear nylon or shoddy because we export our excellent cotton. That is why we must import glue because we throw away hoofs of the animals we butcher. That is why we must import buttons because we do not see the use of horns we throw away. That is why we must import barley for beer brewing because we do not see the value of sorghum. That is why we must import plastic toys because we cannot see how rich our environment is. That is why we must borrow colours to name our things as though our vegetation does not have all these colours. That is why we must be poor because the products of our education have no respect for local things. They are consumers rather than producers. They are parrots rather than thinkers.

It is a fact that all of us have been disillusioned about this western type of education. We have attempted to modify it to serve our needs. Unfortunately, by trying to adapt it to our habits, we have made it impossible for ourselves to think afresh about an education that will save and serve us.

As I see it, liberating education may be found in andragogy. Accordingly, I invite all serious-minded educators to examine it and to give it the appraisal it deserves. For me, the advantages of andragogy are many. First, it has tremendous potentialities for liberating both the youths and adults to believe in themselves, to think and to create.

Secondly, by inviting a dialogue between the teacher and the taught it puts an end to the long-standing problem of teacher-student contradiction where, in the words of Freire, 'the teacher teaches and the students are taught; the teacher knows everything and the students know nothing; the teacher thinks and the students are thought about...' (*Pedagogy of the Oppressed*, New York 1968, p. 59) Andragogy, therefore, shatters the myth that knowledge is the private property of teachers. Because it rightly assumes that no teacher can really teach in the sense of making a person learn, andragogy believes that one person merely helps another person learn.

The third advantage of andragogy is that it does not divide education into compartments of adults and youth education. It means helping human beings learn. With it, education is a meaningful whole, seeking to exploit the best in a human being at whatever age he is. It seeks to utilise all sources of information and rejects the myth that the written word is the only source of information. With andragogy, therefore, it is possible to educate without necessarily making literate for immediate social and economic development. It is after we have weaned ourselves from falsely equating knowledge and learning with schools and have acquired skills of how to learn that we shall become self-directed learners, making use of any resources available to turn ourselves into fully functioning liberated human beings.

> *This article was first published in the Journal Adult Education and Development (No. 19, 1982: 53-60) which invites its readers to reproduce and reprint the articles provided acknowledgement is given and a copy is sent to the publishers of the journal (German Adult Education Association – IIZ/DVV).*

Bibliography

ACFODE (1995). 'Visible at Last: NGO Contribution to Women's Recognition in Uganda'. Kampala

Afrik, Tai (2000). 'Significant Post Independence Developments'. in Indabawa Sabo A. et al (eds), *The State of Adult Education in Africa*, Windhoek: University of Namibia Dept of Adult and Nonformal Education in association with IIZ/DVV.

Aguti J.N.(1996). *Makerere University External Degree Programme: The Dual Mode Approach,* dissertation for MA Education and Development: Distance Education, Institute of Education, University of London.

Aguti J.N., (2000). 'Makerere University, Uganda' in Reddy V. & Majulika S. *The World of Open and Distance Learning,* pp 255-280, New Delhi: Viva Books Private Limited.

Akite, Judith Monica (2002). 'A Mid-term Review of the Reintegration of Children Affected by War Project of CPAR in Uganda in Otwal and Ngai Sub-counties in Apac District', unpublished research report submitted for Bachelor of Adult and Community Education at Makerere University.

Alan, R. (1992). *Adult Learning for Development*, London and New York: Cassell Education Ltd.

Althusser (1971). *Lenin and Philosophy,* New York: Monthly Review Press.

Amundsen C.,(1996).'The Evolution of Theory in Distance Education', in D. Keegan (ed), *Theoretical Principles of Distance Education*, pp. 61-79, London: Routledge.

Archer, D and Cottingham S.(1996) *The REFLECT Mother Manual*, London: ActionAid

Atim, D.K. (1982). 'Developing Makerere Centre for Continuing Education in the Context of Uganda's National Development', unpublished M.Ed. Admin. thesis.

Awori, Achoka (1996). *Uhai, a Model for Sustainable Livelihood and Natural Resources Management in Afrika.* Nairobi: KENGO.

Babikwa Daniel (2003), 'Environmental Policy to Community Action: Methodologies and approaches in Community Based Programmes in Uganda', thesis submitted for the award of Doctor of Philosophy at Rhodes University.

Bakka P. (2000). 'Back to Books: Functional Literacy', in K. Parry (ed) *Language and Literacy in Uganda*, Kampala: Fountain Publishers.

Barton, D. (1994). *Literacy: An introduction to the ecology of written language*, Oxford, UK and Cambridge, Mass.: Blackwell.

Bates A. W. (1994). 'Distance Education, Educational Technology', in Husen, T. and Postlethwaite T.N. (eds), *The International Encyclopedia of Education*, pp.1573-1579, Vol. 3, second Edition. Oxford: Pergamon Press.

Bernardo, A. B. I. (1998). *Literacy and the Mind. The contexts and cognitive consequences of literacy practice*, Hamburg and London: UNESCO Institute for Education and Luzac Oriental.

Bhola, H.S. (1994). *A Sourcebook of Literacy Work: Perspectives from the Grassroots*, London: Jessica Kingsley Publishers and UNESCO.

Bloch, M., Beoku-Betts, Tabachnick (eds) (1998). *Women and Education in Sub-Saharan Africa: Power, Opportunities, and Constraint*, London: Rienner Publishers.

Boshier R. (1985). *A Conceptual Framework For Analysing the Training of Trainers and Adult Educators*. London: Routledge Series.

Bown L. and Okedara, J.J. (1981). *An Introduction to the Study of Adult Education*, Ibadan: Ibadan University Press Limited.

Bown, L. & Mayatsa (1998). 'Training for literacy choices: A midterm review and evaluation of the work of LABE (Uganda) in training of literacy trainers, women's literacy and continuing literacy support'. WUS (UK) & LABE (Uganda)

Brookfield S., ed. (1988). *Training of Educators of Adults: Theory and Practice of Adult Education In North America*, Routledge Series.

Carr M. & Kemmis S. (1986). *Becoming critical: Education, Knowledge and Research*, Basingstoke: Falmer Press: Deakin

University.
CDRN, (2001) Annual Report 2001, Kampala: CDRN.
Centre for Adult Education (2001). *Glossary of Adult Education Terms*, Pietermaritzburg: Natal University.
Centre for Continuing Education, (1990). A Proposal to Start the External Degree Programme, Kampala: Makerere University Centre for Continuing Education (unpublished).
Chale E. M.,(1993). 'Tanzania's Distance Teaching Programme', in H. Perraton (ed.) *Distance Education for Teacher Training*, pp.21-41, London: Routledge.
Champion, A. (1975) 'Marginal or Peripheral: The Place of Adult Education' in *Studies in Adult Education*.
Chick J. (1990). *Building for the Future: The Development of Distance Education Programmes at Makerere University Uganda*. Vancouver: Commonwealth of Learning.
Chivore B. R. S. (1993). 'The Zimbabwe Integrated Teacher Education Course', in H. Perraton (ed.), *Distance Education for Teacher Training*, pp.42-66, London: Routledge.
Clark R. F. (1967). 'Adult Education,' Pamphlet No.1, Kampala: Makerere Adult Studies Centre.
Clarke A. (July 2001). 'The Recent Landscape of Teacher Education: Critical Points and Possible Conjectures', in *Teaching and Teacher Education*, Vol. 17, No. 5, pp. 599 - 611.
Clarke, Ronald (1970), 'Cultivating a Delicate Hybrid' in *Adult Education*, Vol. 43, May 1970.
Commonwealth of Learning (2000a). *Glossary of Open and Distance Learning Terms*, Commonwealth of Learning, http://www.col.org - 14th August 2001.
Commonwealth Secretariat (1998). *Policy, Planning and Implementation*. London.
Commonwealth Youth Programme (1996). *A handbook on the formulation and implementation of a National Youth Policy*, London: Commonwealth Secretariat.
Coombs, P.H. (1985). *The World Crisis in Education: The View from the Eighties*, New York: Oxford University Press.

Coombs, P.H. (1989). 'Formal and nonformal education: Future strategies', in C.J. Titmus (ed), *Lifelong Education for Adults: An International Handbook*, pp.57-60, New York: Pergamon Press.

Coombs, P.H., R.C. Prosser and M. Ahmad, (1973). *New Paths to Learning for Children and Youth*, New York: International Council for Educational Development.

Cottingham, S. et al. (1995). 'A Process Review of Functional Literacy Project in Uganda', Kampala: Ministry of Gender and Community Development.

Darkenwald, G.G, and Merriam, S.B. (1982). *Adult Education: Foundations of Practice*, New York: Harper and Row Publishers.

Dei, George & Hall, Budd (2000). *Indigenous Knowledges in Global Contexts*, Toronto: University of Toronto Press.

Doronila, M.L.C. (1996) *Landscapes of Literacy: an ethnographic study of functional literacy in marginal Philippine communities*. Hamburg and London: UNESCO Institute for Education and Luzac Oriental.

Drah, K. (1995). 'Civil society: Lessons and comparison from elsewhere in Africa', in Humphries, R. and Reitz, M. (eds), *Civil society after apartheid*, Johannesburg: Freidrich Ebert Stiftung.

Durand, D.N., Principal Assistant Secretary, Finance, Ministry of Education, Memorandum Concerning the Administration of the Centre for Continuing Education at Kampala, Makerere University, 21st March, 1972.

Eisenstein, E. (1979). *The Printing Press as an Agent of Social Change*, Cambridge, Mass.: Harvard University Press.

Elias, J. L., and Merriam, S., (1980). *Philosophical foundation of Adult Education*. Malabar: Robert E Krieger Publishing Company.

Federal Republic of Nigeria (1985). *National Policy on Education* (revised), Lagos: Federal Government Press.

Fleming Jean Anderson (1997), 'Pertinent Perceptions of Residential Learning', AERC.

Fordham, Paul (1970). 'Adapting a Tradition: Extra-Mural Policy in Africa', *Universities Quarterly*, Vol. 25, No. 1, Winter 1970.

Fowler, A. (1996). Strengthening civil society in Transition economic-from concept to strategy: Mapping an exit in a maze of mirrors, in Clayton, A. *(ed.), NGOs, civil society, and the state: building democracy in transitional societies*.pp12-29, Great Britain: INTRAC publication.

Freire P. (1970). *Pedagogy of the oppressed*, New York:The Seabury Press.

Freire, P. (1974). *Education for critical continuousness*, p.41. New York: The Seabury Press

Freire, P., Ana Maria Araujo and Donald Macede (eds.) (2000), *The Paulo Freire Reader*, New York: The Seabury Press.

Garrison D. R.(1996). 'Quality Access in Distance Education: Theoretical Considerations', in D. Keegan (ed.), *Theoretical Principles of Distance Education*, pp.9-21, London: Routledge.

Gee, J.P. (1990). *Social Linguistics and Literacies: Ideologies in Discourses*, Basingstoke: The Falmer Press.

Giroux H. (1983). *Theory and Resistance in Education: A Pedagogy of Opposition*, New York: Bergin and Garvey Publishers Inc.

Goody, J. (1968). *Literacy in Traditional Society*, Cambridge: Cambridge University Press.

Goody, J. (1986). *The Logic of Writing and Organisation of Society*, Cambridge: Cambridge University Press.

Gordon, Hopeton L.A. (1979). 'The Orientation of University Adult Education Work in the Caribbean', in *Journal of African Adult Education Association*, Vol. 1, No. 1 p.49, Nairobi: Kenya Literature Bureau.

Government of Uganda (1995a). *The National Constitution of the Republic of Uganda*, Kampala

Grundy S. (1987). *Curriculum: Product or Praxis, London:* Falmer Press.

Gumede, Ellen (1997). 'On the periphery: The Needs of Rural Women', in Walters, S. (ed.), *Globalization, Adult Education and Training. Impact and Issues*, London and New York: Zed Books.

Habermas J. (1972). *Knowledge and human interests*, (translated by Jeremy Shapiro), London: Heinemann Educational.

Halford and Jarvis (eds.) (1998). *International Perspective on*

Lifelong Learning, London: Kogan Page.
Hallenbeck W. C. (1948). *Training Adult Educators,* London: Routledge Series.
Hansard (1950), *Parliamentary Debates: House of Commons Official Report: Session 1950 - 3rd to 21st July 1950.* London: HMSO.
Harries, Jenkins Gwyn (1982). *The Demise of Liberal Studies,* Kingston upon Hull: The University of Hull.
Harris, J.W. (1954). *Annual Report for the Period November 1953,* Kampala: Extra-Mural Department, Makerere University.
Havelock, E. (1982). *The Literate Revolution in Greece and its Cultural Consequences,* Princeton: Princeton University Press.
Hawk W. B. (2000). 'Online Professional Development for Adult ESL Educators,' Education Resources Information Center (ERIC), Web: http://edrs.com/
Heath, S.B. (1983). *Ways with Words: Language, life and work in communities and classrooms,* Cambridge: Cambridge University Press.
Higgs P. (ed) (1998). *Meta-theories in Education theory and Practice,* Sandton, Johannesburg: Heinemann.
Hillbur P. (1997). *The Knowledge Arena: Approaching agro-forestry and competing knowledge systems – a challenge for agricultural extension, Lund:* Lund University Press.
Holmberg B. (1986). *Growth and Structure of Distance Education,* London: Croom Helm Ltd.
Holmberg B. (June 1995). 'The Evolution of the Character and Practice of Distance Education', in *Open Learning* pp. 47-53.
Horton, M. (1990). *Long haul,.* New York: Doubleday.
Illich, Ivan (1971). *Deschooling Society,* New York
Inspectorate of government and Freidrich Ebert Stiftung. (1997). Speech made at the opening of a workshop on public awareness against corruption in Uganda 24th to 26th February 1997, in *The crusade against corruption in Uganda: a collection of papers,* pp11-19. Kampala: Freidrich Ebert Stiftung.
Jackson, Keith (1997). 'The State Civil Society and Economy', in Shirley Walters (ed.), *Globalization, Adult Education and Training - Impacts and Issues,* London: Zed Publications.

Jitta, Jesca & A. Ndidde (1998). 'A Research Report on the Assessment of Poor People's Access to Health and Education', Kampala: (CHDC/OXFAM)

Jorgensen, L. (1996). 'What are NGOs doing in civil society?' in Clayton, A. (ed.), *NGOs, civil society and the state: building democracy in transitional societies*.pp36-53, UK: INTRAC publication.

Karugire S. (1981). *A Political History of Uganda,* Exeter, New Hampshire: Heinemann Educational Books.

Katahoire, A.R (2002). Annex '5 cases from Uganda', in Oxenham et al (eds.), *Skills and Literacy Training for better Livelihoods: a review of approaches and experiences,* pp. 105-117 Washington: The World Bank.

Kaye A. R.(1989). 'Distance Learning Systems', in Eraut, M. (ed.), *The International Encyclopaedia of Educational Technology,* pp.286-291, Oxford: Pergamon Press.

Khayinza. I. & Rugadya M. (1997). NAWOU Directory – A Directory of Women Organizations Affiliated to NAWOU, Kampala: National Association of Women Organizations in Uganda.

Kirkwood, G. & Kirkwood, C. (1989). *Living adult education: Frieire in Scotland,* pp.1-14. UK: Open University Press.

Kisira, S. & Mwesigwa J. et al (1999). 'Mid-term Review Report of Female Adult Literacy Project: Arua District'.,Arua, Uganda: Save the Children, UK.

Kiwanuka S M. (1972). *History of Buganda: From Foundation of the Kingdom to 1900,* New York: African Publishing Corporation.

Knowles, M. S. (1980). *The modern practice of adult education: From pedagogy to andragogy,* (revised and updated), pp. 275-300, Cambridge: The Adult Education Company.

Knowles, M.S. (1964). 'The Field of Operations in Adult Education', in Jensen, G., Liveright, A.A. and Hallenbeck, W (eds.), *Adult Education: Outlines of an Emerging Field of University Study,* Washington D.C.: Adult Education Association of the U.S.A.

Korsgaard, O. (1997). 'The impact of globalisation on adult education', in Walter, S. (ed), *Globalisation, Adult education & Training.* pp. 15-25, Cape Town: CACE Publication.

Kwesiga and Katahoire (1995). 'The Changing Nature of University Adult Education in Uganda', in *Uganda Adult Education Journal*, Vol. 1 No. 1 1995.

Kwesiga, C. Joy (1995), 'The Women's Movement in Uganda: An Analysis of Present and Future Prospects', in *The Uganda Journal*, Vol. 42. Kampala: Uganda Society.

Kwesiga C. Joy (1995), 'Women, Education and Empowerment in Sub-Saharan Africa', paper presented at the International Conference on Education and Women's Empowerment, New Delhi, India.

Kyambogo University (2002). 'Diploma in Primary Education Records', Kampala: Kyambogo University.

LABE (2001) LABE Newsletter, Kampala.

Legge, D., (1982) *The Education of Adults in Britain*, Milton Keynes: Open University Press.

Ling and Hewett (1992), 'Social Mobilization' in Background Paper for a Panel Discussion, Education for all Summit, New Delhi 12-16 December, 1993.

Liveright A. A. (1964). 'The Nature and Aims of Adult Education as a Field of Graduate Education,' In Brookfield, op.cit., 1988, p. 50

Lotz H. B. and Ward M. (2000). 'Environmental Education Processes and changing theories within education: trends and patterns.' Rhodes University/SADC course in Environmental Education, core text. Grahamstown: Rhodes University.

Lowe, J. (1975), *The Education of Adults: A World Perspective*, Paris: UNESCO.

Lubwama S (1999). 'British not parties to blame for ruining Uganda', in *The Monitor*, Sat. 9 October 1999, Kampala: Monitor Publications.

Makau B. M. (April 2001). *Report on the Teacher Development and Management System (TDMS) Component*, Kampala: Teacher Development and Management System.

Makau B.M. (2001). A Three-Year Primary Teacher Development and Management Plan: A Review. Kampala: Ministry of Education and Sports.

Mason R. (2001). 'Institutional Models for Virtual Universities', in Tschang, F.T. & Senta,T.D. (eds). *Access to Knolwedge: New Information Technologies and The Emergence of the Virtual University,* pp. 267-287, Tokyo: United Nations University, Institute of Advanced Studies

Mayo P. (1999). *Gramsci, Freire and Adult Education: Possibilities of Transformative Action,.* New York: Zed Books.

Mazima, Eliphaz (1994). 'Sustainable Development and persons with disabilities', keynote address to ADF/ILO Persons with Disabilities Workshop at Lake Victoria Hotel, Entebbe, Uganda

Mbilinyi J M (1977). 'Basic Education a tool of exploitation or liberation?' Research Report No. 21, Bureau of Resource Assessment and Land use Planning, Tanzania: University of Dar-es-Salaam

Mbilinyi Marjorie (1993). 'Transformative Adult Education in the Age of Structural Adjustment: A Southern African Perspective', keynote address during a conference: Adult Education: Issues for the Future held at the Centre for Adult and Continuing Education, University of Western Cape

Merriam S. (1985). 'Training Adult Educators in North America', in Brookfield op. cit., p.30.

Merriam, Sharan and Mazanah Muhamad (2001). 'A Map of the Field', in Mazanah Muhamad & Associates, *Adult and Continuing Education in Malaysia,* Serdang, Malaysia: Universiti Putra Press and Hamburg: UNESCO Institute for Education.

Mezirow, J. (1996). 'Contemporary Paradigms of Learning' in *Adult Education Quarterly* Vol..46 No.. 3, pp. 158-172.

Michelson, Elana(1997). 'The Recognition of Experiential Learning' in Shirley Walters (ed), *Globalization, Adult Education and Training: Impacts and Issues,* p.144, London and New York: Zed Books.

Ministry of Agriculture, Uganda (2000). *Plan for Modernization of Agriculture,* Kampala.

Ministry of Agricultural, Animal Industry and Fisheries and Ministry of Finance, Planning and Economic Development (2000). *Plan for Modernisation of Agriculture.* Kampala: Government of Uganda.

Ministry of Education and Sports (1992). *Education for National Integration and Development,*. Government White Paper, Kampala.

Ministry of Education and Sports, (n/d). *Primary Education and Teacher Development Project: Final Supervision Report'* Kampala.

Ministry of Education and Sports, Uganda (1998). *Education Sector Investment Plan,* Kampala.

Ministry of Finance, Planning and Economic Development (1998). *Poverty Eradication Action Plan,* Kampala.

Ministry of Finance, Planning and Economic Development (1998). *Vision 2025: A Strategic Framework for National Development,* Kampala.

Ministry of Finance, Planning and Economic Development (MFPED) (1991). *Public Enterprises Reform and Divestiture,* Kampala.

Ministry of Finance, Planning and Economic Development (MFPED) (2002). Budget Speech for 2002/2003, Kampala.

Ministry of Finance, Planning and Economic Development (MFPED) (2002). *Background to the Budget: Financial Year 2002-2003.* Kampala.

Ministry of Finance, Planning and Economic Development (MFPED) (2001). *Poverty Eradication Action Plan 2001-2003,* Kampala.

Ministry of Finance, Planning and Economic Development (MFPED) (2003). *Draft Estimates of Revenue and Expenditure 2003/2004.* Kampala.

Ministry of Gender and Community Development (1995). *Report of the International Conference on Women's Education and Empowerment.* Kampala.

Ministry of Gender and Community Development (1996), *National Plan for Functional Literacy.* Kampala.

Ministry of Gender and Community Development (1998). *National Gender Policy.* Kampala.

Ministry of Gender and Community Development (1999). *Report on the 1997 Annual Review of the Functional Adult Literacy Programme.* Kampala.

Ministry of Gender and Community Development (1999). *Balancing*

Scales: Addressing Gender Concerns in National Development Programmes, Participants' Manual. Kampala.

Ministry of Gender, Labour and Social Development (MGLSD) (1998). *The National Strategy for Girls' Education.* Kampala.

Ministry of Gender, Labour and Social Development (MGLSD) (1999). *The National Gender Policy.* Kampala.

Ministry of Gender, Labour and Social Development (MGLSD) (2002). *The National Adult Literacy Strategic Investment Plan.* Kampala.

Ministry of Gender, Labour and Social Development (MGLSD) (2001). *The National Youth Policy.* Kampala.

Ministry of Health (MOH) (2001). *National Health Policy and Action Plan.* Kampala.

Ministry of Local Government (1997). *The Local Government Act.* Kampala.

Ministry of Water, Lands and Environment (2000). *National Policy for Water and Wetlands.* Kampala.

Moore M. G. (1993). 'Three Types of Interaction', in Harry, K., John, M and Keegan, D. (eds.), *Distance Education: New Perspectives,* pp.19-24, London: Routledge.

Moser, Caroline (1993). *Gender Planning and Development: Theory, Practice and Training.* London: Routledge.

Mutibwa, P.M., (1981) *A Note on the Recent History of Uganda,* Kampala: Makerere University Department of History.

NABCE Interim Report, 'Non Award Bearing Continuing Education of the Higher Education Funding Council for England'.

Nakayenga, Regina (2000). 'A research report on the study to establish Education Needs of the Internally Displaced Persons in Banda parish, Kampala District', unpublished research report submitted for Bachelor of Adult and Community Education at Makerere University, Kampala..

Nandago (1998). 'Challenges in Facilitator Recruitment and Training', in *PLA NOTES: Participation, literacy and empowerment. I*ssue 32 June, 1998, IIED.

National Environment Management Authority (1997). *National Non-formal Environmental Education and Community Training*

Strategy. Kampala (also at www.nemaug.org).

National Environment Management Authority (1999). *Non-Governmental Organisations and Community Based Organisations Operating in the Field of Environment in Uganda.* Kampala (also at www.nemaug.org).

Newman, M. (2001). 'Learning in a brittle society' paper given at a conference held at SCUTREA.London. UK.

Nielsen H. D., Tatto M. T. (1993). 'Teacher Training in Sri Lanka and Indonesia', in Perraton, H. (ed.) *Distance Education for Teacher Training,* pp.95-135, London: Routledge.

Nikitin P I. (1985). *The fundamentals of political economy,* Moscow: Progress Publishers.

Nyang'oro, J. E. (1993). 'NGOs, civil society and the state in Africa: in search of relevance (introducing phase I and II of the study)' in *Civil society, the state & African development in the 1990s,* pp.54-75, Arusha , Report of study by WENGO and All African Conference of Churches.

Nzimande, B. & Sikhosana, M. (1998). 'Civic society': A theoretical Survey and Critique of some South African Conceptions', in SachiKonye, L.M (ed.), *Democracy. Civil Society and the State: social movement in southern Africa,* pp. 20-45, Harare: Sapes Books.

Obanya Pai (1996) *Functional Literacy as a path to empowerment*

Ocitti, Jakayo P. (1994). *An Introduction to Indigenous Education in East Africa,* Bonn: German Adult Education Association (IIZ/ DVV).

Odaet C. F., Higwira F. M. N. (1994). Design of Outreach Tutor Training Plan for Residential Induction and Training of Outreach Tutors. Submitted to SUPER, Ministry of Education and Sports, Kampala.

Oduaran, Akpovire, 'Research and Scholarship in Adult and Continuing Education in Africa', in Indabawa Sabo, A. et al (eds), *The State of Adult and Continuing Education in Africa,* Windhoek: University of Namibia Dept of Adult and Nonformal Education in association with German Adult Education Association (IIZ/DVV).

Odurkene, J.N. and Okello (1985). *The Development of Adult*

Education in Uganda, 1900-1985. Kampala: The Uganda National Commission for UNESCO.

Ojok Isaac and Onyango (1969). 'Report on the Present System of Organiser'. Kampala: Makerere University.

Okech, A.(1994). 'Innovative Approaches to Adult Literacy/Education currently used in Uganda', Kampala: SNV.

Okech, A. (1984). *Directory of Adult Education Agencies in Uganda: Basic information on the organisation Personnel facilities and courses available for community education in Uganda in 1984.* Kampala: Makerere University Centre for Continuing Education in collaboration with UNESCO.

Okech, A. (1991). A Review of Current Adult Literacy Activities and a Proposal for a Post-Literacy Programme. Kampala: ActionAid Uganda

Okech, A. (1999). Baseline Study for Community Education Programme in Karamoja,. Kotido: Church of Uganda, Diocese of Karamoja.

Okech, A. (2000). *Needs Assessment Survey for Functional Adult Literacy in Karamoja Uganda 2000.* Kampala, Ministry of Gender, Labour and Social Development and World Food Programme

Okech, A. (2002a). 'Participation in the ICAE World Assembly: Thematic workshop on documentation and on Training of Adult Educators', in *Adult Education and Development*, 58, pp.177-181.

Okech, A. (2002b). 'Multilingual Literacies as a Resource', in *Adult Education and Development*, 59, pp. 117-125.

Okech, A. and Majanja-Zaaly'Embikke I.M. (2002). 'Report of Needs Assessment Survey and Baseline Study for Functional Adult Literacy in Kalangala District'. Kampala: Icelandic International Development Agency

Okech, A. et al (2001). *Adult Literacy Programs in Uganda.* Washington: The World Bank.

Okech, A. et al. (1992). 'Needs Assessment for Integrated Non-Formal Basic Education in Uganda', Kampala: Ministry of Local Government.

Okech, A., Carr-Hill, R. A., Katahoire A. R., Kakooza T. and Ndidde A. N. (2001), *Adult Literacy Programs in Uganda.* Washington: The World Bank

Okech, A., Carr-Hill, R. A., Katahoire A. R., Kakooza T. and Ndidde A. N. (1999). *Report of Evaluation of the Functional Adult Literacy Programme in Uganda 1999.* Kampala: Ministry of Gender Labour and Social Development with World Bank Mission in Uganda.

Okunga, D.N (1980). 'The University Extension Tortoise in Uganda is in a Deep Coma: a Reflection', in *Adult Education and Development,* No. 15, September 1980, pp 19-26. Bonn: German Adult Education Association (IIZ/DVV).

Okunga, D.N. (1974). 'The Repercussions of the Financial Position on the Activities of the Centre', paper BC/2/3/74 of 26th July 1974. Kampala: Makerere University: Centre for Continuing Education

Oliveira J. B., Orivel F. (1993). 'Logos II in Brazil', in Perraton H, (ed.), *Distance Education for Teacher Training,* pp.69-94. London: Routledge.

Olson, D.R. (1994). *The World on Paper: The conceptual and cognitive implications of writing and reading,* Cambridge: Cambridge University Press.

Olson, D.R. and Torrance N. ed. (2001). *The Making of Literate Societies,.* Oxford, UK and Malden, Mass.: Blackwell.

Orivel F. (1994). 'Distance Education: Economic Evaluation', in Husen T. and Postlethwaite T.N. (eds), *The International Encyclopedia of Education,* pp. 1567-1573 (second edition), Oxford: Pergamon Press.

Oxenham J., Diallo A.H., Katahoire A.R., Petkova-Mwangi A. and Sall O. (2002). *Skills and Literacy Training for Better Livelihoods: A review of approaches and experiences,* Washington: The World Bank.

Pandak C. A. (2000) 'Voluntary Organisations and Non-formal Education in Hungary: Professionalisation and the Discourse of Deficiency', Northern Illinois University.

Parry, K. ed. (2000). *Language and Literacy in Uganda,* Kampala: Fountain Publishers.

Paul R. S. (1990). *Open Learning and Open Management: Leadership and Integrity in Distance Education,* London: Kogan Page.

Pemah Asheri Sams (2000). 'Women's Empowerment: Processes, Benefits and Constraints: A case study of rural women in Upper Madi – Arua District', unpublished research report submitted for Bachelor of Adult and Community Education at Makerere University.

Perraton H. (1993). 'The Context', in Perraton, H. (ed.). *Distance Education for Teacher Training,* pp.1-17, London: Routledge.

Perraton H. (2000). *Open and Distance Learning in the Developing World,* London: Routledge.

Peters O. (1996). 'Distance Education in Post Industrial Society', in D. Keegan (ed.), *Theoretical Principles of Distance Education,* pp.39-58. London: Routledge.

Plucknett, D. L., Matsumoto, T. and Asanuma, S. (2002). *A Review of the Sasakawa Global 2000 in Uganda,* Tokyo: The Nippon Foundation.

Popkewitz, T. S. (1984). *Paradigm and ideology in educational Research: The social functions of the intellectual,* London: Falmer Press

Popov Y (1984*). Essays in Political Economy: Imperialism and the Developing Countries – A guide to Social Sciences,* Moscow: Progress Publishers.

Posthumus, B. Huggins, G. Cisse, Y. Eds. (1999). *Civil society participation in a new EU-ACP partnership,* pp.32-44, Amsterdam: INZET Association.

Prah, K.K. (1995). *Afrikan Languages for the Mass Education of Afrikans,* Bonn: DSE.

Prah, K.K. (1995). *Mother Tongue for Scientific and Technological Development in Afrika.* Bonn: DSE.

Prah, K.K. (2002) *Language, the Afrikan Development Challenge,* Cuba, Havana: Tricontinental, No.150.

Pretty, J. (1995). *Regenerating Agriculture: policies and practices*

for Sustainability and Self-Reliance, London: Earth Scan Publications.
Prinsloo, M. and Breier, M. ed. (1996). *The Social Uses of Literacy*, Cape Town· Sached Books and John Benjamins Publishing Co.
Rees, Ben (1981). *Preparation for a Crisis; Adult education 1945-1980.* California: G.W & A. Hesketh.
Republic of Uganda (1992). *Education for National Integration and Development,* Government White Paper on the Education Policy Review Commission:. Kampala.
Riguera, Florencio (1996) 'Civil equality of religions in society', in McLean, G.F. (ed), *Civil society and social reconstruction,* p. 212, http://www.crvp.org/book/series01/1-16.htm 17th/ 7/2002.
Robinson B. (1996). *Distance Education for Primary Teacher Training in Developing Countries,* The World Bank. http://wbln0018.worldbank.org/hdnet/hddocs.nsf/49f1232ecebf88148525667100585ddf/4497108d81e059d08525668d00662afb - 26th July 2001.
Robinson B., and Murphy P. (October 1996). 'Upgrading the Qualifications of Serving Primary Teachers Using Distance Education in Uganda: A Comparative Study of Costs and Effectiveness'. Penultimate Draft (unpublished).
Rogers, A. (2001). 'Some Contemporary Trends in Adult Literacy from an International Perspective' in *Adult Education and Development (56:2001).* Bonn: Institute for International Development of the German Adult Education Association (IIZ/DVV).
Rogers, A. (2001). *Re-thinking Adult Literacy and Post-Literacy – from an international perspective,* Uppingham, UK: Uppingham Press.
Rukare, H., (1977). The Final Report on the Namutamba Pilot Project. Kampala: The Uganda National Commission for UNESCO.
Rumble G. (1992). *The Management of Distance Learning Systems,* UNESCO: International Institute of Educational Planning, Paris.
Rumble G. (2000). 'Student Support in the 21st Century', Paper presented at The Workshop on Student Support for Distance

Education Students, 8 - 15 October 2000, Kampala, Uganda.

Rumble G. (2001). 'The Costs of Providing Online Student Support Services', *Student Services at the UK Open University. Papers presented at the 20th World Conference of the International Council of Open and Distance Education, 1-5th April 2001, Dusseldorf, Germany*, 73-82. Milton Keynes: Open University.

Rutangye, M.G.B.N. (1995). 'A Study to Determine the Training Needs of Adult Learners in Uganda'. Kampala: Makerere University Institute of Adult and Continuing Education

Sachikonye, L.M. (1998). 'Democracy, civil society, and social movement: an analytical framwork', in SachiKonye, L.M. (ed.), *Democracy. Civil society and the state: social movement in southern Africa*, pp. 1-19 Harare: Sapes Books.

Saint W. S. (1992). *Universities in Africa: Strategies for Stabilization and Revitalization*, Washington, DC: The World Bank.

Sauve L. (1996). 'What's Behind the Development of a Course on the Concept of Distance Education', in D. Keegan (ed.), *Theoretical Principles of Distance Education*, pp.93-109, London: Routledge.

Scribner, S. and Cole M. (1981). *The Psychology of Literacy*. Cambridge, Mass.: Harvard University Press.

Sebahara, P. (1998). 'Reflection on civil society', in *Courier ACP-EU No 170*.

Steytler, N. et al ,(1998).' State-civil society relations in South Africa: toward a model of good governance', in *Winds of small change: civil society interaction with African state*, pp. 119-132. Australia: Australia Development Co-operation.

Street, B. V. (1984). *Literacy in Theory and Practice*, Cambridge: Cambridge University Press.

Street, B. V. (1993). *Cross-Cultural Approaches to Literacy*, Cambridge: Cambridge University Press.

Street, B. V. (1995) *Social Literacies: Critical Approaches to Literacy in Development, Ethnography and Education*, London: Longman

The Government of Uganda (1996). National Plan for Functional Literacy
The Government of Uganda (1996). The Uganda Report of ILO and UNDP's Employment and Advisory Mission 1995.
The Government of Uganda (1997). *Poverty Eradication Action Plan.*
The Government of Uganda, (1995). *Constitution of the Republic of Uganda.*
Townsend Coles, E.K. (1977). *Adult Education in Developing Countries*, (2nd ed.) Oxford: Pergamon Press.
Triebel, A. (2001). 'The Roles of Literacy Practices in the Activities and Institutions of Developed and Developing Countries', in Olson, D.R. and Torrance, N (eds.), *The Making of Literate Societies*, Oxford, UK and Malden, Mass.: Blackwell
Twimukye, Macline (2000). 'Inclusion and exclusion in the education sector with specific reference to people with disabilities in Uganda', paper presented at a panel discussion held at the International Conference Centre, Kampala.
Uganda (1920). *Report of the Uganda Development Commission*, Entebbe: Government Printer.
Uganda Management Institute, http:/allafrica.com/stories/200204040269.
UNESCO (1972). 'Third Conference on Adult Education', in *Adult Education and Development,* 43, 1994 pp. 360-365.
UNESCO (1976). 'Recommendation about the Development of continuing Education', in *Adult Education and Development,* 43, 1994 pp. 372-373.
UNESCO (2000), *Education For All (EFA): Meeting our Collective Commitments.* Paris.
UNESCO (2000). World Education Forum: The Dakar Framework for Action. Paris
UNESCO Institute for Education (1997a). *Reference Points. The four first international conferences on adult education and their political, social, cultural and educational context,.* Hamburg.
UNESCO Institute for Education (1997b). *The Hamburg Declaration on Adult Learning,* Hamburg.

United Nations (1994). *AIDS and the Demography of Africa*, New York: United Nations.

United Nations (1999). *World Population Prospects: The 1998 Revision Volume I Comprehensive Tables*, New York: United Nations.

Usher R. Bryant I and Johnston R (1997). *Adult Education and the post-modern Challenge: Learning Beyond Limits*, London: Routledge.

Van Spanckeren, Kathryn (1994). *An Outline of American Literature*, US Information Agency.

Volkov M I (1985*). A Dictionary of Political Economy*, Moscow: Progress Publishers,

Waliggo, John Mary, (1999), 'The Socially Marginalised: Which Way to Liberation?', DENIVA Occasional Papers No. 1.

Wandira, A. (1972) 'Early Missionary Education in Uganda: A Study of Purpose', in *Missionary Education*, Kampala: Department of Education, Makerere University.

Wandira, A. (1980) Address by A. Wandira, Vice-Chancellor, Makerere University during the International Donors' Conference at Como, Italy 1980, quoted in Dudley, S., *Academic Quality Research and Scholastic Materials*.

Wangoola, P. (1995). *Mpambo, The Afrikan Multiversity: a Philosophical Sourcebook*, Mpambo.

Wangoola, P. (1995). *The Afrikan Multiversity: a Handbook to a Philosophy to Rekindle the Afrikan Spirit*, Mpambo.

Wangoola, P. (2002). *Development Outside a People's Mother Tongue and Culture is like Borrowing Another Person's Consciousness and Memory*, Mpambo.

Williams, W.T. (1968) 'Liberal Education in a Developing Country', in *Adult Education*, UN, 42 No. 5, January 1968.

Women Empowerment Programme (WEP) West Nile: Annual Reports 1997, 1998 & 1999. Arua, Uganda.

Wrightson T. (1998). *Distance Education in Action: The Northern Integrated Teacher Education Project in Uganda*, Cambridge: International Extension College.

Youngman F. (1986). *Adult Education and Socialist Pedagogy: Radical Forum on Adult Education.* London: Croom Helm Ltd

Youngman, F. (2000). *The Political Economy of Adult Education and Development,* Leicester and London: NIACE and Zed Books.

Index

A

AALAE 82, 240, 251, 254, 263-5, 282
ActionAid Uganda 75-6, 131, 252, 258, 261
Adult basic education 2, 81, 83, 119, 126, 128, 145, 187, 252, 277, 284
Adult education, development of 15-34; political economy of 35-50; economics and financing of 124-145; government policies for 51-66; international involvement in 247-66; challenges and prospects of 267-89
Adult Education and Development 111, 128, 119, 251, 262
Adult Education Centre 26, 28, 251
Adult literacy and Basic Education Centre 81
Adult literacy education 2, 56, 69-70, 75, 78, 82-3, 140, 182, 187-8, 190-1, 198, 206, 275
Adult Studies Centre 113
Adventist Development and Relief Agency 74, 78, 188
African Association for Literacy and Adult Education 251, 254
African (Afrikan) Virtual University 152, 162, 225-246
Afrikan Association for Literacy and Adult Education 241
AFROLIT 256, 282
Aguti, J.N. 12, 146, 152, 163-4, 177
Alan, R. 15, 179-80, 197
Ampene, K. 253
Andragogy 14, 290, 290-7
APAL 262
Atim 10, 13, 15, 24, 267-8, 274, 276

B

Babikwa, D. 10, 36, 45-7, 49, 220-1, 223
Behavioural 36, 45-6
Bhola, H.S. 5
Bown, L. 111, 115, 215, 253
BREDA 130, 262
British Council 94, 253, 282
Brookfield, S.D. 15, 110, 115

C

Christian churches 72, 74
Christian missionaries 21, 70-1
Church, the 21-2, 28, 30, 55, 71-4, 86, 99-100, 132, 182, 189, 245, 261
Churches 21-2, 24, 28, 30, 72-4, 99, 182, 189, 204
Civic education 3, 6, 23, 119, 193
Civil society organisations (CSOs) 10-11, 19, 65, 67-70, 75-6, 81-2, 84-5, 86, 126, 130, 252-3, 274-6, 288-9
Clarke, R. 17, 18, 26, 107
CMS 21, 182
Co-operation 13, 22, 75, 91, 130, 183, 235, 247-66
Co-operative education 3, 4, 7, 132, 135-6
Co-operative Movement 24, 200
Commercial institutions 138, 271
Community Development Department 24, 113-4
Community Education Programme 132, 261
Computer mediated communication 147
CONFINTEA V 1 6, 124, 200, 248, 251
Constitution of the Republic of Uganda 212

Index

Continuing and further education
3, 8, 126, 137, 139, 145
Coombs, P.H. 2, 9
Correspondence courses
90, 96, 98, 163, 168-9
Correspondence education 107, 148

D

Dakar Framework for Action 57, 212
DANIDA 95, 254, 282
Darkenwald, G.G. 2, 15, 16
Definition of adult education 1, 78
Demand for adult education 13, 86, 268, 270
Department of Adult Education and Communication Studies 130, 280
Department of Extra-Mural Studies 23-4, 26-7, 96, 98, 103-4, 113, 260
Diploma in adult education 84, 119, 120, 280
Directory of Adult Education Agencies in Uganda 121
Distance education 8, 9, 12, 54, 82, 107, 119, 139, 146-65, 168-77, 187, 257, 260, 262, 284
Distance education and open learning 9, 12, 146, 152-8, 168-77
Distributed learning 149-51
District Farm Institutes 23, 26
Drop out 78, 166 174-76, 216, 270
Dual mode institutions 169-70

E

Education Strategic Investment Plan 63
Environmental education 3, 4, 6-7, 76, 79, 82, 134-5, 193
Extension education 3, 5-7, 59, 126, 128, 133-4, 140, 215, 277
External Degree Programme 155, 163-5, 171-5, 177, 271

F

Faith-based organisations 67, 70, 74, 132
Fees 72, 74, 127-8, 175-6
Flexible learning 148-9,, 157
FM radio 59
Formal adult education 8, 9, 34, 128, 278-9
Freire, P. 19, 36, 39 49, 77-8, 89-90, 141, 186, 198, 207
Functional adult literacy 2-5, 7, 9, 33, 43, 47-8, 56, 64, 78, 128, 131-2, 144, 188, 206, 215, 217, 221, 223, 257, 270, 277-8
Functional adult literacy programmes 4, 5, 7, 9, 33, 43, 64, 78, 128, 131, 144, 207, 215, 217, 221, 223, 257, 261

G

Gender 4, 44-5, 47, 58-63, 116, 212-5, 218-23, 276
German Adult Education Association (IZZ/DVV) 118, 128, 130, 132, 187-8, 197, 250-65, 282-3, 297
Giroux 36, 39, 50
Government of Uganda 55, 101, 104, 128, 175, 186, 213, 274, 187

H

Habermas, J. 36
Hamburg Declaration 69, 125, 201
Harris, J.W. 91-5, 99, 104
Health education 3, 6, 24, 59, 76, 133, 136-7, 140, 215, 220, 256, 261
Health Manpower Development Centre 160
HIV/AIDS 6, 9, 59, 136, 142, 211, 264

I

Icelandic International Development

Agency (ICEIDA) 257
Illich, Ivan 292
Illiteracy 18, 29, 30, 33, 46, 53-4,
    57, 85, 128, 130, 179, 186,
    190, 194, 221, 248, 262, 270
Indigenous education 8, 15
Informal adult education 9
Information Supports for Adult
    Education 252, 256
Institute of Adult and Continuing
    Education 1, 33, 83, 251,
    271, 279-80, 284, 287
Institute of Public Administration 27,
    97, 113
Instrumentalism 44
Internally displaced persons 210-2,
    216-7, 219, 222
International co-operation 13, 247-53,
    263-6
International Council for Adult
    Education 251, 254

K

Karamoja 74, 81, 132, 216-7,
    257, 261
Katahoire, A.R. 11, 86, 110, 262, 281
Kemmis, S. 37, 48, 50
Kiira Adult Education Association
    30, 33, 81-2, 129-30, 187, 257
Kironde Report 27, 96
knowledge-constitutive interests 36,
    38
Knowles, M.S. 2, 14, 111
Kwesiga, J.B. 70, 102, 113-4,
    122, 219
Kyambogo 23, 97, 162-3, 168-71,
    256

L

LABE 81, 83-4, 116, 119, 121, 132,
    187, 222, 252-3, 264, 275, 284
Language 13, 14, 96, 100, 117,
    122, 179, 181, 184, 204, 206-
    7, 223, 225-6, 230, 234-46,
    268, 279-80
Language policy 239, 246
Lifelong learning 20, 69, 90, 269
Literacy and Adult Basic Education
    81, 83, 119, 128, 187, 252, 277,
    284
Literacy Network for Uganda 34, 83,
    275
Literacy practices 12, 178, 205-6
Lowe, J. 25

M

Makerere University Business School
    105, 171
Makerere University Extra-Mural
    Department 93
Management Training and Advisory
    Centre 27, 31
Marginalised groups 12, 13, 210-24
Marxist social theory 37
Mass Literacy Campaign 28, 128, 185,
    190, 209
Mass media 9, 53, 96, 113, 136
Mature Age Entrance 155
Merriam, S.
    2, 9, 15, 16, 71, 116, 117
Micro-finance 220
Ministry of Health 6, 24, 31, 59,
    112, 136, 161, 261
Multimedia distance education 147
Museveni, Yoweri 244

N

NALSIP 53-7, 65, 132-3, 188-9,
    213-4, 216, 272, 275-6
National Adult Education Association
    18, 31, 33, 81-2, 117, 119,
    129-30, 187, 251, 257
National Adult Literacy Strategic
    Investment Plan 53, 55, 132,
    188, 191, 216, 272, 274, 285
National Agricultural Advisory
    Services 133, 140
National Book Trust of Uganda 208

National Curriculum Development
  Centre 31, 54
National Environment Management
  Authority 6, 135, 261
National Organisation of Trade Unions
  86
National Resistance Movement
  (NRM) 33-4, 50, 130, 239
Ndidde, A.N. 12, 210, 220
Needs Assessment Survey
  118, 186, 190, 194, 261
Netherlands Development Organisation
  75, 131, 182, 252
Newspapers 21, 25, 28, 53, 113,
  206-7
Ngaka, W. 10, 15
Non-formal adult education 8, 9, 128,
  278-9
Non-governmental organisations
  (NGOs) 6, 34, 35, 64, 67,
  70, 75, 83, 99, 118, 127,
  135, 145, 159, 213, 255, 286, 288
Nsamba, Y.N. 11, 88
Nsamizi Training Institute 97, 284
Nyerere, Julius 18, 19, 228

O

Obbo, D.K. 10, 51
Ocitti, J.P. 8
Odurkene, J.N. 10, 15, 22, 26, 29,
  31, 160, 259
Ojok, Isaac 98
Okech, Anthony 1, 8, 11, 12-13, 33,
  70-2, 83, 85-6, 112, 114, 122,
  124, 126-7, 131, 133, 135-6,
  141, 143-4, 178, 182, 186-7,
  189, 201, 204, 214-8,
  223, 247, 259, 262, 266-7,
  270, 277, 280-1, 285
Okello, M. 10, 15, 22, 26, 29, 31-
  2, 259
Okunga, D.N. 29, 95, 96, 98-9,
  102, 104
Open learning 8, 9, 12, 107, 146,
  148-9, 152-8, 168-78
Open University 148-9, 159-60
Openjuru, G.L. 10, 67
Oxenham, J. 188, 197, 253, 262, 281

P

PAF 140, 275
Partnership 13, 31, 61, 65, 83,
  108, 136-7, 226, 246, 247,
  257, 265, 273, 283
PEAP 52, 57, 132, 140, 213, 285
Pedagogy 192
People with disabilities 210, 212, 214-
  5, 218
Plan for Modernisation of Agriculture
  (PMA) 58-9, 140, 213
Poverty Action Fund 57, 65, 131-2,
  140, 145, 188, 275, 285
Poverty Eradication Action Plan
  52, 55, 57, 132-3, 140, 188,
  278, 285
Private sector 3, 62, 170, 273, 277-8
Professionalisation of adult education
  110-123
Purpose of adult education 10, 15, 16

R

Radio Uganda 23-4, 104
Reading Association of Uganda 218
REFLECT 5, 76-7, 131, 197-201,
  214, 222, 258, 264, 284
Refugees 84, 210-11, 215-7, 219
Research and publication 250, 259,
  261
Rural Training Centres 23

S

SOCADIDO 74, 132, 187, 189
Socio-economic formation 39-45

T

Tororo Community Initiated Development Association 33, 255, 258
Townsend Coles 16

Training of adult educators 110-123

U

Uganda Joint Action for Adult Education 33, 81, 83, 132, 275
Uganda National Commission for UNESCO 256
Uganda Rural Development Training Programme 32, 251
UJAFAE 33, 81, 83, 132, 275
UNESCO 1, 2, 16, 19, 57, 69, 83, 97, 124, 126, 130, 186-7, 191-2, 201, 205, 209, 247-9, 251-3, 255-6, 259, 262-3, 269, 282
UNESCO Institute for Education 124, 248, 252, 262
UNICEF 31, 130, 136, 152, 187, 257, 282, 286
University Adult Education 88-109
University adult educators 13, 118, 225-6, 228, 234, 245, 246, 297

V

Virtual learning 151-2
Vocational education 4, 7, 89, 114, 214
Volunteers/voluntary work 22, 24, 28, 30, 34, 67-8, 128-9, 132, 145, 161, 187, 193, 201, 240, 260, 276

W

Wandira, A. 21
Wangoola, P. 13, 225
White Fathers 21, 22, 182
World Food Programme 75, 217, 257

Y

YMCA 30, 85, 114, 132
Youngman, F. 19, 36, 37, 50
YWCA 30, 31, 85, 114, 132

www.ingramcontent.com/pod-product-compliance
Lightning Source LLC
Chambersburg PA
CBHW021353290426
44108CB00010B/220